Second Edition

MANAGING AND COORDINATING MAJOR CRIMINAL INVESTIGATIONS

Second Edition

MANAGING AND COORDINATING MAJOR CRIMINAL INVESTIGATIONS

Robert F. Kilfeather

CRC Press
Taylor & Francis Group
Boca Raton   London   New York

CRC Press is an imprint of the
Taylor & Francis Group, an **informa** business

CRC Press
Taylor & Francis Group
6000 Broken Sound Parkway NW, Suite 300
Boca Raton, FL 33487-2742

© 2011 by Taylor and Francis Group, LLC
CRC Press is an imprint of Taylor & Francis Group, an Informa business

No claim to original U.S. Government works

Printed in the United States of America on acid-free paper
10 9 8 7 6 5 4 3 2 1

International Standard Book Number: 978-1-4398-4922-4 (Paperback)

Visit the Taylor & Francis Web site at
http://www.taylorandfrancis.com

and the CRC Press Web site at
http://www.crcpress.com

Table of Contents

Preface   xi
Acknowledgments   xiii
Introduction   xv

Part I

REACTIVE CASES

1   Definitions   3

Principal Entities   5

2   Investigative Phases   7

Reactive Cases   7
Proactive Cases   8

3   The Preparatory Phase   11

Organization Responsibilities   11
Functional Unit Duties   24
    Dispatcher   24
    Uniform Patrols   27
    Other Agencies   30
    Detective Command   33
    Investigators   38
    Crime Scene Unit   41
    Laboratory   43
    Medical Examiner's Office (ME)   45
    Prosecutor's Office   47
    Press Officer (Public Information Officer)   48
Summary   51

4   The Response   55

Duties of Responding Units   56
    The Dispatcher   56
    Uniform Patrols   58

IACP—Patrol Operations   62
Other Agencies   62
Detective Command and Supervisor   63
Investigators   65
Public Information Officer (PIO)   65

5   The Crime Scene   69

Department Command   69
Dispatcher   70
Uniform Patrols   73
Other Agencies   73
Detective Command   74
Crime Scene Unit   75
Laboratory   78
Medical Examiner (When Needed)   79
Prosecutor   80
Public Information Officer (PIO)   81

6   The Investigation   85

Department Command   86
Dispatcher   86
Uniform Patrols   87
Investigators   89
      The Scene Team   89
Detective Command   96
Detective Supervisor   98
The Coordinator   98
Crime Scene Unit   115
Crime Laboratory   119
Medical Examiner   119
Prosecutor   120
Public Information Officer   121
Support Services   121

7   The Arrest, Trial, and Appeal   125

The Public Information Officer   127
Supervisors and Investigators   128
Laboratory   130
Press Officer   130
Prosecutor   130
Defense Counsel   132

8   Management of Resources   135

Department Command   135
Principal Entities   137
    Resource Management   137

Part II

PROACTIVE CASES

9   The Preparatory Phase   143

Department Command   144
Detective Command   154
Supervisors/Investigators   158
Analysts   159
Other Agencies   160
Prosecutor's Office Investigator/Prosecutor Teams   162

10   Intelligence Phase   165

Department Command   165
Detective Command Review   166
Investigator/Analysts/Surveillance   171
First-Line Supervisors   173
Prosecutor   174
Department Intelligence Section Flag System   174

11   The Investigation   177

Department Command   177
Detective Command—Monitor Progress   177
Supervisor/Coordinator (One, Two, Three ... People)   181
Investigators/Analysts   186
Prosecutor   188

12   Arrest and Trial   193

Department Command   193
Detective Command   193
Supervisor   196
Investigators   197
    Arrest   197
Prosecutors Prepare for Court   198

13   Intelligence/Critique   **201**

14   Resource Management   **205**

Resource Control   205
People Wasters   207
Some General Comments   210

15   The Index   **211**

Public Records Law Issues   218
Police Sources of Information   224
    Citizens   224
    Officer Observations and Probes   224
    Investigations   225
    Intelligence Operations   226
    Other Agencies   226
    Electronic Measures   227
Case Index   228
    Closing Procedures   235
Flag Systems   235

16   The Wind-Up Chatter   **241**

More Chatter   242
More Chatter   243

Exercises   **249**

Part III
APPENDICES

Appendix A: Dispatcher's Guidelines   **257**

Appendix B: General Post Orders   **259**

Appendix C: Press Guidelines   **263**

Appendix D: Crime Scene Contamination Card   **267**

Appendix E: Duties of Neighborhood Interview Team(s)   **269**

Appendix F: Case Coordinator Duties   **271**

Appendix G: Case Assignment Sheets   **275**

Appendix H: Authority   279

**Appendix I: Patrol Post Report (or Field Interview
         Report)**   287

**Appendix J: A Think Tank Method That Works for Law
         Enforcement Organizations**   289

Appendix K: Follow-Up Think Tank   295

Appendix L: Twenty-Year Plans   297

Index   303

Preface

The first edition of this book (1981) was the result of a perceived need identified while I was the Director of the FDLE, Division of Criminal Investigation. Florida found itself literally inundated with large, well-organized drug-smuggling rings. That, plus the ever-increasing major-crime workloads, strained law enforcement resources beyond their capabilities for an effective response. (Florida averaged a population growth of 1,000 people per day, steady for the past twenty-five years; that is 7 to 8 million.) The complexity, nature, and size of individual major cases had outstripped administrative ability to handle them.

Major drug rings routinely numbered in a range of 750 to 1,000 plus members, each. An effective system of managing and coordinating major cases needed to be developed and then implemented. The answer is to develop criminal investigators, agency supervisors, and administrators into competent case managers. All well and good, but they must have case information and a control system at their fingertips.

In 1981, a training seminar was developed and then presented at regular intervals in Florida. The enthusiastic response to this training program by attending law officers from numerous state, county, and city police and prosecutors' agencies, from many regions across the United States, prompted that first edition. The first edition of this book was used as a lecture guide and handout reference material. The audience consisted of highly experienced case investigators and managers looking for improved control and efficiency of systems. Each meeting was a quiet, slow, and detailed discussion of our problems, with resulting solutions.

This second edition is presented due to several well-informed prosecutors and police officials suggesting a need for an "update." The outline format of the first edition needed expansion; more detail was required, and case systems needed updating. The update and expansion will broaden the audience for this book. Detective trainees and uniform supervisors will benefit. In addition, technology has radically improved over the past twenty-five years; but in many places, management has not been able to develop the advanced system capabilities now available. The reasons are numerous and include political failure to fund improvements, inertia in some organizations, and, in a few places, a lack of management initiative. There is no excuse in the current operating theater of law enforcement that a single agency that is legislatively charged with major criminal case investigation not be equipped with the tools to succeed. If they are not, they *must* defer and coordinate such cases with a higher state authority.

The aim of this book is to help the reader coordinate and manage a major-case investigation successfully. I have tied together some of the best ideas and successful methods of case control, learned by supervising major cases and with the assistance of many competent police officers and agencies. The book's approach is broad enough to apply the controls to fit any agency, whether large or small. The approach is specific enough to see the practical values and not leave you with a book full of theory and little substance. Departments will provide the in-house details to fit the requirements of agency case management.

Please take a moment to reflect on some of the 1980s material I did not edit out where it now seems inapplicable; I left it for background reasons. Actually, some of it is fun to read; it will make you smile, thinking "Was that still a problem in the 1980s?" Yes, it was, and guess what? Much of it is still a problem. **Technology increases efficiency; case control still requires the fundamentals of good organized police work.**

Acknowledgments

The ideas in this book were gathered during my thirty-eight years of experience in law enforcement as a police officer, prosecutor, and judicial hearing officer. Experienced major-case managers and administrators of many different agencies made helpful contributions. It would be impossible to mention and thank everyone who helped my life's learning process. However, there are several whose expertise and assistance was of extraordinary value:

First, Colonel Warren B. Surdam, Deputy Superintendent, New York State Police, who more than any other man taught me the value of programs and systems. Commissioner William Troelstrup and Director Fred Johns, Florida Department of Law Enforcement, who assisted in putting together Florida's first "homicide seminar," bringing together investigators, prosecutors, forensic scientists, and medical examiners for case discussions, and Dick Scully, Chief of Intelligence at FDLE. I appreciate their loyalty. Fred Scullin, the former head of the Florida Statewide Organized Crime Task Force and now Chief Federal Judge of the Northern District of New York. We shared the office space and the creation struggles of what is now Florida's Office of Statewide Prosecution. (It took a Florida constitutional amendment in 1986 to settle the issue.) I extend my deep gratitude to Captain Henry Williams and Lieutenant Sam Slade of the New York State Police; they are the type of men who make the system work with good solid police work and many major-case successes. Finally, thanks to David Ege, a good friend and worthy adversary. Dave, a notable central Florida defense attorney, contributed his always accurate and sometimes vexing legal details to a justice system in need of more such dedication. It was a pleasure working with them all.

MGT of America, Inc., a management-consulting firm in Tallahassee, Florida, deserves mention. MGT is an excellent management company with an outstanding reputation and a solid performance record. The original major-case seminar training program was promoted through their assistance and good grace. Their managing partners have worked over the years to promote professional law enforcement. MGT adopted a quiet public service policy, a mission to improve and develop good management in law enforcement because it is the right thing to do. I know they did not profit by that program, and at times, I wondered if they broke even.

Thank you all.

Introduction

This book attempts to place in perspective the problems of managing and coordinating the investigation of major crimes. It provides police supervisors with tools to improve or develop a systemic approach to the control of major investigations. More importantly, it creates the necessary mind-set in supervisors to manage any major crime effectively: how to plan for the event, make resource agreements with all other participants in the investigation, and implement a coordinating system within the investigating agency. That is what this book is all about.

There is a need in law enforcement for this treatment. Numerous "how to" books have been written about the investigation of major cases. Those books are concerned with detailed steps in the actual investigation of crimes, or a critique and analysis of a specific case. Several books are available on the managing of criminal investigative divisions. They deal with the overall responsibility, decision making, and distribution of resources for an entire detective command. In these pages, the subject dealt with is the managing and coordinating of major events (single or multiple). It will stay as far away as possible from the management of detective commands; it will not delve into actual detailed methods of case investigation. This is not a "how we used to do it" book; it is for you to determine your own requirements to meet your own needs, not someone else's. This book will aid you in **your thinking** of how to do just that: to think for yourself using your experience and the situation existing within your department, and then decide your own applications and uses.

An example of what I am saying can be explained this way: the current terrorist, and the terrorism threat used as a political tool, is now the first priority of the nation; our survival depends on how we deal with those issues. Management of the terrorist problem is a concern of department managers in coordination with federal, state, local, and international enforcement agencies, and now we must include the military. The managing of a specific case or cases of terrorist cells and associated organizations, and defeating their intent, is the problem of individual agencies, or multiagency task forces, focused on a particular person, group, or suspects. Mostly, the terrorist issue is a federal responsibility in cooperation with state and local law enforcement. **The state and local police are still required to handle and are responsible for the investigations of *all* criminal acts committed within**

their jurisdictions. The challenge is to be able to coordinate *all informa-* **tion collected with compatible systems, including the "regular" or "nor-** **mal" cases that are the routine business of police investigations and not** **directly related to terrorist activity,** then ensure that it is sorted, stored in a master file, searched against other records, and fed to units for analysis, action, or retention. Along with all this there must be a retrieval capability regardless of what level or sublevel at which the information is filed. This is an integration of systems. If you look at the new terrorist threat, it is just another major-case control system, magnified in importance.

Included within that challenge is the development of more street aware-ness of officers and investigators in the value of simple **"street information."** That **information** can be captured, then analyzed and turned into *intelli-* *gence,* then classed, assigned, and looked into by the appropriate people or agencies. That is integration of systems at work.

This book will assist police administrators, command and staff personnel, operational unit commanders of uniform and nonuniform services, supervi-sors, and the actual case investigators and patrol officers. It is written in a comfortable tone. Prosecutors and their investigative staff will also find much to interest them. Further, city managers, mayors, county commissioners, and state legislature staff people might gain an insight into matters that they are responsible for funding. They need to understand the complexity of the work to identify the capabilities and shortfalls of agencies they politically control.

The major investigations we will discuss are divided into two categories, reactive and proactive, and then dealt with separately. Although many of the same principles apply to both types of investigation, proactive and reactive cases clearly create two different sets of managing and coordinating prob-lems. Each type of investigation is separated into phases and identified by milestones of progress as a case moves from one phase to the next. The man-aging and coordinating problems of the many major investigative entities, both within and without the investigative agency, are discussed and treated as part of the overall issue. This is the main thrust of the book; a major crime is not handled by one unit, or for that matter one agency. The success or fail-ure of the investigation depends on the coordinated teamwork of a multitude of disciplines. The old, old idea of a single superdetective working a major case is long dead in theory, almost dead in practice, but still lingers in the souls of too many police officers. The public and the professional image of the police require that major cases be handled correctly, rapidly, and with expertise. This requires a plan, knowledge, and cooperation, but most of all a system of keeping it all together.

This book hopes to accomplish that.

I suggest you start by having a tape recorder or a stenographer's lined notepad with you when you read. Throughout the book, ideas and issues will set off triggers in your mind regarding a situation within your agency that you may want to capture for reference. You will have questions; write them down and note the page from which they arose. Organize the notes in your own style, but organize before you have to reorganize; this advice comes from experience gained with the seminars.

Objectives of a Criminal Investigation

The conviction of the participants, and the ending of criminal activity, is the true objective of any criminal investigation. The mere arrest is not sufficient to the community's needs. The slowing down of an organized criminal enterprise by arrests is only harassing the organization and does not necessarily end the criminal activity.

These objectives must always be foremost in the minds of the case leaders, and although in many cases the objectives will not be fully met, they should be the targeted goal. There is always debris in a major case; use it to build new intelligence, other cases, and best of all, new informants, contacts, and sources of information.

The objective of this book is to identify major-case investigative phases and the people or groups that perform the work and tie them together in a coordinated and well-managed effort to improve the effectiveness and efficiency of major-case investigations.

September 11, 2001, added a new dimension to police work. **Information** is needed more than ever. The old method of handling discoveries of interest during an investigation, but not connected to the investigation, used to be handled informally by contact between officers, or sometimes by a memo to a specific office. Today the department needs to capture that **information** and digest it into the main system for future retrieval or assignment. The "trick" will be not to contaminate, delay, or cause terrorist information gathering to interfere with the process of "normal" collection, or cause a "wall" to be erected between the two objectives.

Reactive Cases

I

Definitions

1

Precisely defining a "major case" can be a difficult task, but it is of paramount importance to collect the factors to use as a guide. Major criminal investigations obviously include murder, but not all murders, and property crimes, but certainly not all property crimes. Drug smuggling comes to mind in a state such as Florida, but may not qualify in Liberty County, Montana. Some robberies, assaults, or frauds could be classified as major criminal events. Continuing criminal conspiracies in certain cases could also qualify.

In order that we may understand the scope of a major investigation, a statement is necessary. A *major criminal investigation* is defined as:

- An investigation requiring extraordinary resource commitments over an *extended* period.
- A team effort requiring dedicated personnel assignments to the case to the exclusion of all other work for an *estimated* period (could be from a few days to more than a year)

Included would be most murder cases where the criminal is not in custody and his identity is unknown (whodunits). Kidnapping cases, burglaries with thefts involving five- or six-digit dollar values, and thefts of rare art pieces or jewelry may qualify as major cases. Robberies with serious assaults or major sums of money; drug-smuggling conspiracies involving large organizations; multimillion-dollar transaction frauds having complicated schemes or vast sums of money at stake, such as diamond sales frauds and stock, mortgage, and land frauds; condominium "bust outs"; and criminal gangs or cartels are all good examples of major cases. Almost any kind of criminal activity that requires resources as defined in the preceding statements meets the criteria of a major case.

To establish a concrete definition of a major criminal investigation would be a task in itself. There are too many variables in all criminal cases; therefore, maintain some flexibility in case definitions. Understanding the general sense of the definition of a major case will suffice for the purpose of this book. The preceding statements provide that definition. **Command judgment, as always, is the key.**

Major criminal investigations can be separated into two distinct types, proactive and reactive:

A proactive investigation is a planned law enforcement action against known or suspected criminal activity.

A reactive investigation is the police response to a crime that has already taken place and is of such nature that immediate law enforcement action is required.

The differences are clear. In the proactive case, the police select the target. The criminal, or his organization, is usually unaware at the initiation of the investigation that the police have targeted him for investigation. The police, through *intelligence* or other means, have decided to investigate a criminal enterprise or a targeted criminal, identify the case objectives, place an investigative team into operation, and commence their work.

In reactive cases, the opposite is true. A sudden unannounced incident takes place that requires a rapid police commitment of resources to contain or investigate a particular crime that has already been committed. The management and control methods for these two types of investigation are different and will be fully discussed in later chapters.

Resources used in any criminal investigation are manpower, equipment, time, and money.

Throughout these chapters, we will discuss various organizational groups. Four main groups are defined for clarity; they will be referred to throughout this book.

1. *Command:* Persons who establish policy and guidelines and provide direction to ensure the department follows the mandates established by law. Department commissioners, directors, chiefs of police, sheriffs, executive officers, superintendents, and their staffs constitute the command level of agencies. Responsibility for the overall direction and guidance of an organization is part of the command duties.
2. *Command Staff:* Persons who implement department policy within the established guidelines in order to achieve specified objectives. Included among the command staff are the bureau chiefs, uniform and detective unit heads, and field supervisors with managing responsibilities as opposed to operational working involvement or active participation in the work commitments of the agency.
3. *Supervisor:* Persons who direct and control the resources. Squad or team leaders (first-line supervisors) are the personnel referred to as supervisors. Sergeants and Lieutenants are the normal ranks used in this classification. However, the wide disparity of rank responsibilities and spans of control among police agencies throughout the

country must be recognized. The term "supervisor" means the person responsible for the actual operation, coordination, and control of the worker(s) who directly perform the tasks.

4. *Line/Support:* Persons who accomplish the specified objectives and tasks. These are the workers, the detectives, deputies, patrolmen, troopers, investigators, technicians, analysts, dispatchers, and all of the other titles in use to describe the men and women of the line/support services.

Principal Entities

In order to discuss major criminal investigations, the principal entities involved in such cases should be identified. It is these identified entities and their titles that will be used throughout the book.

Department Command: (Command) chiefs of police, sheriffs, executive officers, directors, etc.

Detective Command: (Command Staff) investigative unit leaders and their staffs.

Uniform Patrols: (Line) all uniform services.

Supervisors: (Supervisory) first-line supervisors, sergeants, lieutenants, special agent supervisors, senior investigators, team leaders, etc.

Dispatcher: (Line/Support)

Investigators: (Line) detectives, agents, deputies, troopers, specialists, investigators.

Crime Scene Units: (Line/Support) technicians, photographers, identification units, and investigators assigned to crime scene duties and their support personnel.

Other Agencies: all uniform personnel, detectives' crime scene units, support personnel, and supervisors not from the case managing agency.

Laboratory: (Support) service providing bench analysis of evidence and some specialized field work. FBI laboratory, state or local crime laboratories, and health department or medical examiner labs.

Medical Examiner: medical examiners, coroners, pathologists, and doctors associated with the investigation.

Prosecutor's Office: all attorneys associated with the prosecution of the case, whether they are state prosecutors, state's attorneys, district attorneys, county attorneys, and their investigative staffs.

Defender's Office: includes public and private defense counsel and their staffs.

Public Information Officer (PIO): (Support) the department spokesperson, whether a civilian or sworn employee, who acts as the press officer and handles the department's public, press, and television company relations (if the department does not have a PIO, then a designated officer should be assigned as the major-case contact).

Support Services: technical unit, such as wire intercept technicians, communications specialists (other than dispatchers), aviation units, scuba units, data processing or record/files, training, school resource officers (a great source of gang and juvenile crime information), communication center personnel, radio and terminal operators, emergency center personnel, patrol controllers, etc.

Victim: the deceased or injured party; relatives of the deceased or injured party; a corporation, group, or individual who was the target of the crime under investigation.

Each of the listed principal entities plays a significant role in major criminal investigations. The degree of participation will vary from case to case, and in some instances the entity may not enter into a case, such as the medical examiner in a nonmurder investigation. Each of these entities, and the list is not all-inclusive, holds a position of influence in the investigation, and it is the managing agency's responsibility to coordinate all of the participants' activities to ensure the stated objective of the case is achieved.

The methodology of this book requires that each principal entity be discussed in detail, defining their functions and relationships and how the managing agency can coordinate all of the activities into a well-managed and coordinated investigation.

Television police shows tend to portray criminal investigations rather simplistically. A plot is developed, a cast of characters is invented to support the plot, and evidence is easily found with conclusions drawn rapidly that lead the police to the criminal, with time out for commercials. I will not discuss the blatant violations of procedure and law that routinely occur on those shows. Real life is different, much different. Often plots or motives are not confirmed until the end of a case, if then. The cast of characters can be overwhelming; most have little or no useful information or participation. Much information is biased or misleading; truth and facts have to be validated and proven. Evidence is often "just there" and of no real investigative value in identifying the criminal, although once he is identified, it often ties him to the crime. There are no rehearsals, no retakes, no written scripts. When the case is closed, there is always much information missing or matters still unexplained.

This is both the frustration and the challenge of a major-case investigation.

Investigative Phases

2

Criminal investigations, like most problems, can be separated into phases or chronological units that have a logical and, sometimes, orderly progression toward an objective, the solution. Case milestones can be identified and pointed to as being in a particular phase. The strategy is to synchronize all of the principal entities' investigative activities within a phase so progress toward the next part of the case moves smoothly. For example, during the crime scene phase the problem is the coordination of the crime scene unit, the detectives and uniform officers involved in the neighborhood search, and the uniform patrols' duties in the area, along with the alarms and broadcasts to other agencies and the coordination of their activities. All of those tasks must be accomplished in a controlled manner in order that the case may progress through the crime scene responsibilities and move on to the investigative phase.

Major investigations have been defined as being one of two types, reactive or proactive. Each type of investigation has its associated phases.

Reactive Cases

The **preparatory phase** is not an active phase of the case as much as **it is the preparation required by a department to be able to conduct a major investigation.** This phase includes all preparation of rules, regulations, procedures, training, and equipment, agreements with other agencies, teams, assignments, report requirements, and other preparatory matter. It is the basis for the rest, and it is the most neglected.

The **response phase** is the time from the initial call reporting a major crime to when a crime scene is firmly established and the case control moves from the dispatcher to the field/shift supervisor, to the supervisor at the at the crime scene.

The **crime scene phase** begins when the detective unit supervisor and the crime scene unit arrive at the crime scene and assume control of all activities at the scene and immediate area with its parameters established. This phase continues until all evidence is marked and packaged and the crime scene work is declared complete by the working units and is approved by the case supervisor.

The **investigative phase** is that portion of the case that evolves out of the crime scene and moves to the actual pursuit of the criminal. The investigative phase may be coincidental to the crime scene phase, and both usually continue simultaneously for a period.

The **arrest phase** begins just prior to the arrest of the perpetrator(s), continues with the arrest and interrogation, and ends with the booking of the defendant. There are cases where the investigative phase continues after arrest and into the trial phase. Evidence and proof supplements are normal. Sometimes unarrested crime partners are still loose.

The **trial/appeal phase** includes the preliminary court appearances, the trial, sentencing, and all appeals.

Proactive Cases

In proactive investigations (the targeted cases), the phases are slightly different and are described as follows:

The **preparatory phase** is essentially the same as in reactive cases.

The **intelligence phase** includes the gathering of facts and information about a target, subject matter, or an identified criminal enterprise, the evaluation of that intelligence, and the decision to initiate, or not, an active investigation. The identification and gathering of resources necessary to work the case are part of this phase.

The **investigative phase** includes the investigation of the targeted objectives, identifying spin-off cases and the documenting of evidence. The investigative phase of a proactive case may also include one or more crime scenes.

The **arrest/indict phase** is at the successful culmination of the intelligence and investigative phases of the case at the point where prosecution commences. This can be a time and place arrest, or a "pick 'em off" tactic of selective arrests to stimulate further information or case investigation avenues.

The **trial/appeal phase** is important because many proactive major cases will result in appeals after conviction. The investigative work and coordination must continue in this type of case to the very end.

A second **intelligence phase** is critical to the end of all proactive major cases. This will serve as more than a simple case critique. The time for a complete review of the massive wealth of information gathered during the investigation will be worth the resource commitment. The review identifies any case procedural snares, equipment failures, and personnel problems. More importantly, the review identifies new or reworkable intelligence. Spin-off cases that may or ought to be pursued often come to new or renewed attention.

The ground rules and definitions for this book are now well established.

For the want of a nail, the shoe was lost,
For want of a shoe, the horse was lost,
For want of the horse, the rider was lost,
For want of the rider, the battle was lost,
For want of the battle, the Kingdom was lost.
And, all for the want of a horseshoe nail.
Early English child's rhyme

—From John Gower's *Confessio-Amantis* (Approximately 1390)

Re-Active Case Development Cycle

	Preparatory Phase	Response Phase	Crime Scene	Investigative Phase	Arrest Trial Phase
Resource Growth					
Major Case Activities	Planning	Uniform Patrols	Evidence Collection / Witness Interviews / Detailed Search	Neighborhood Interviews-Leads Arrest / Backgrounds / Press Info	Press / Prosecution / Appeal / Case Critique

Figure 2.1 Reactive case development cycle.

The Preparatory Phase 3

The primary responsibility of the command staff of any police agency is to ensure that the organization is, at all times, prepared to respond and effectively control any situation or event that it confronts. This requires planning, structure, rules, procedures, training, and routine inspection.

Another way of saying the aforementioned is: "You have to work at it to make it work, then when it works you have to work at it to keep it working, then you have to work at it to make it better, and flexible enough to change as needed, which is work."

Organization Responsibilities

Police organizations have generally accepted the principles of management by objectives (MBO). It should not be necessary to stress the usefulness of a good MBO program, but experience tells us otherwise. There are still far too many police managers who do not set objectives, still more who do not fully understand MBO programs, and some who merely pay lip service to such programs, which they apparently implement for "show and tell" purposes. **The error many police leaders make is a simple one. They attempt to borrow a private-industry model and adapt it rather than** *take the principles of an MBO plan* **and construct it for a specific police program.** The wrong way is the equivalent of trying to navigate a space ship through an asteroid belt towing a ferryboat. Industry MBO plans address production; police systems are problem solving oriented. Consider labeling it something else to remove the MBO taint. Try crime suppression program (CSP) or some other delightful name. Call it something different if you must, but do it.

If police commanders are to be successful in their major-case investigations, they must rate their command responsibilities for organization control and policy development as a high priority. I apologize to those of you who do that, but it must be said. Facade building has become a bad habit in some places. You know who they are.

There are real MBO programs and then there are "show and tell," sometimes referred to as "cover your ass," programs. Walk into any police department and read its "mission statement," hopefully a temporary fad that will rapidly fade, and you will be able to identify whether the department's leadership has been able isolate its internal matters from direct political structure or the person(s) politically in charge.

The CYA approach will read, "The Everytown Police Department strives to protect and serve our community by ensuring the peace and tranquility, so rightly deserved, will be at the highest levels, consistent with modern and constitutionally guided law enforcement. We constantly engage in programs designed to carefully attend to changing crime patterns and circumstances arising within our community," … yadda … yadda … yadda. I did read one that said, "We find criminals and jail them, then follow them when they get out. Then we arrest them again and jail them again." It is all in the perspective of the writer.

The professional leader will write a memo:

To Station Commander 3rd Pct (Zone, District, Post, County)
Subject: Increase in Burglary-Commercial
    Commercial burglaries have increased in your area of responsibility by 34% over the past six months. Patterns and MO are: smash & grab, front door breach, cash and electronics stolen—estimate 10 minutes on site. Fri. & Sat. Nights – 9 p.m. to 2 a.m.
    See attached map of locations and order of burglaries.
    You are hereby directed to formulate a plan to reduce or eliminate this problem within three months. A 50% reduction is the anticipated result. Priority Category "C." Your plan is due within five days. Identify the problem, design a solution, and produce a plan of action.
    (The plan includes, but is not limited to, uniform patrol use and direction, loose surveillance, recheck of patrol reports for past six months for information, and suggestions of beat officers. Specifically check radio logs for "hits and wanted," vehicle checks, recorded traffic activity; set forth your investigative approach, including "fences," pawn shop checks, parole and probationer records, informants, associates of, and drug users, specific surveillances, etc. … That, along with a little street pressure, intimidation, and so forth with schedules, assignments, etc.). You understand the idea. Let's identify the mutts running around out there and press them.

A good MBO plan for a specific or general purpose takes about two to three pages. Responses are a requirement. It is simple; you gather the information, identify the problem, identify the means and methods to achieve a result, gather the resources, and implement the program. Police Business 101.

The *department command* is responsible for identifying and setting each functional unit's objectives. These objectives must be clearly stated and defined. Direct the Commanders of each unit to apply their resources toward the stated objectives. Some additional command responsibilities are as follows:

Investigative priorities should be set forth in writing. Set the priorities by class in order that available resources can be directed toward the higher priorities. Police organization human resources are usually insufficient to address all the agency goals and objectives. Unless the work is directed and controlled on a priority basis, effort is wasted and results are often inconclusive.

Without priorities, it is possible for an investigative unit to be working at 125% of capacity due to a series of robberies or murders and have no personnel available for surveillance or other critical case work while uniform forces are responding to "barking dog" complaints or monitoring local high school basketball games. Somewhere **in every chain of command, there is one specified individual responsible for the direction of both the uniform and detective units. He or she is responsible for coordinating both units to achieve objectives. He or she is also responsible for seeing that all information collected by both units is preserved, shared, and directed to the proper place, person, or other agency.**

The *chain of command* should be clear and unequivocal. People should know for whom they work and what they are doing. Fix responsibility at each organizational level of supervision. The table of organization should reflect the command chain *and* responsibilities. A major-case investigation utilizes all functional units within an agency, and unless command lines are clear, difficulties erupt at a time when it is detrimental to a case. It is counterproductive to take time out during an investigation to solve what are administrative problems. (This is a good place in the book to start seriously thinking, based on experience, about the various bits of information that come to the attention of uniform patrols and investigators during their normal workday. Start thinking of the way your department currently collects that data. Then, think of a way to improve how you connect those bits and sources into an efficient format, particularly the reporting, in order to enter the useful bits into your information systems database. We will speak later about getting something useful out of that and changing it into intelligence.)

Next are some management systems to consider.

Manpower allocation systems should be developed in order to assign personnel to work on the agency's priorities. This is an administration feature and not directly a function of major-case workers, but they must have input into its design and construction to shape it or the tendency of administrators to administrate prevails, ad nauseum. Develop the system by using a statistical data collection format that identifies the time that personnel devote to each type of activity. Most police agencies collect statistical data. Unfortunately, a lot of it does not have serious merit, or impact, as work measurement or manpower allocation information. Few statistical systems were developed to meet a specific departmental work objective. Most of these statistical "systems" are products of evolution—part of the "we always collected that stuff" syndrome. Management must look to the future; part of that is collecting specific and pertinent case data. Or for that matter, any statistical data collected must be for a specific management use or purpose. Design the statistical collection package to reflect investigative activities, and use it to identify current and future resource needs. Police organizations accomplish this by human resource case or activity reporting. The main purpose of all data collection is to improve department internal efficiency. The second "main purpose" is to collect strong data support to prove to your political controllers that you are efficient and require resources to produce what they demand: good service. The third purpose is to collect data required by your operators for their purposes, or by other government agencies for their purposes, such as budgets or the FBI crime statistics report. The trick is to make those three important issues compatible with the least pain, unnecessary duplications, or waste of time. Consolidate the collection paper/inputs and disperse any resulting reports to your heart's and management's content.

One source of time and activity data collection that is often missed is administrative, including instructor time. New police officers spend the first six months of their career in school six days a week; without reporting that, thousands of hours are not accounted for to your controllers. Many of the permanent administrative positions do not report or break down their time; thousands of spent hours are lost from your budget projections and reports to your controllers. Those controllers often extrapolate other figures, sometimes from different sources, and miss that point. They think all your statistics represent the work of all your officers. The result is an error of perception; they think those officers are included in the overall work report, making productivity per officer figures grossly unbalanced. Count and use all the time spent to show the "'lost to the field'" time of all sworn field personnel, and separate, but count, civilian personnel time as well as the sworn administrators not working field assignments. It is easy to capture; use it. An administrator sitting behind a desk every day for eight to ten hours is one category of "lost to field" statistics.

Human resource case reporting is a management tool that reflects data gathered on a periodic basis to provide management with accurate accounting of its resource expenditures. It is used in state investigation departments or bureaus that mainly deal with major investigative cases and in large police departments with high numbers of major cases under way at any given time. It is slightly different from a general data system used by state police agencies or the medium-size or smaller departments. Highway patrol departments generally deal with traffic issues, transportation, or vehicle-related crimes, which limit capabilities to assist police agencies with crimes or events. Your department may decide in which category you fit, or take the best of both to fit your specific needs. There are similarities and generalizations within all systems that you should know and use to make your own judgments.

At a minimum, this reporting should include:

1. Number of cases opened and closed
2. Number of cases in various priorities
3. Number of arrests and convictions by case classification

4. Amount of property recovered or confiscated, along with its location or disposition
5. Expenses per investigation, including confidential sources, mileage, etc.
6. Hours per case, including investigative and support by agency unit(s) (some include activities of assisting law enforcement agencies to show the controllers the lack of in-house resources)
7. Resources expended per Uniform Crime Report (FBI report or its substitute) category by functional unit
8. Resources expended in priority by each functional unit

This is in addition to all of the department's regular statistical or reporting data, such as the traffic division or any other units you may have working. The files collate the data by department unit and provide each with data summaries as well as collate with internal files and provide individual officer data accounts. The state investigation bureaus, often, do not deal with "street" crime, traffic issues, public nuisance complaints, misdemeanors, and isolated or unorganized low-level felonies.

Generally, a time- and activity-reporting instrument tailored to meet the agency's needs (objectives) will meet most needs for smaller departments. The data may be cumulative, such as total traffic arrests and total time expended on traffic arrests, or specific reporting on a single case, such as a drug-smuggling investigation, which could consume thousands of hours. Most police agencies that change from manual to computer data collection will need computer system specialists to deal with the complexities. That raises an important issue. The police agency must have someone with the ability to speak with the "computer geeks." This person must be able to direct with explicit, clear directions the department wants, needs, and how they intend to utilize the data. In addition, this person must know what and how credible is the raw data now collected. This person is called a very experienced police manager. You must avoid the situation where your traffic captain tells the computer people to "Put all this stuff from the accident reports and traffic tickets into the computer so we can predict where the accidents will happen" —only to watch the computer guy put his hand on his chin, think, then say, "hmmmmm," walk over to the computer, open the case, stuff a traffic ticket and a traffic accident report form inside the computer, close it up, and say, "Done; anything else?" That makes for a really quiet conference room.

The *case-tracking system* is an organizational method developed to track a specific activity, such as a major case, that will provide management with continuous administrative case and evaluation data. The system may be tied to a criminal justice tracking system that follows and reports a case status through the entire justice system, from the police to prosecutor to court to correction to parole or probation and back to the police. That next to last item, parole and probationers, is a seriously neglected source of information. Many police departments still do not know, or contact if they do know, criminals who have returned to their jurisdictions from correction departments. This is a bonanza of information if properly worked. It should be routine. You may take some "'political correctness'" heat doing this. You may even get a few objections from the various probation agencies. So pick, assign, and direct a couple of smooth people to work that out, but do it.

Another matter to keep in the back of your head is a future goal—that is, meshing pieces of your intelligence system with uniformity to integrate or communicate with other police agencies, an absolute within your state. Eventually, nationwide uniformity or intercapability, along with the ability to connect with every other state, the FBI, and through the federal filter (some say portal), Homeland Security, the CIA, and the military. Thirteen northeastern states started this "'sharing'" in the early 1930s, and that evolved into the National Crime Information Center (NCIC). The New York and Pennsylvania State Police led that effort, with a big boost from the New York City Police and New Jersey Troopers. In addition, consider Canada, where data exchange works very well now, the Bahamas where it works satisfactorily even if sporadically, and Mexico where there are still some problem areas. Agencies who routinely work out-of-territory are well versed in the details of those problems. Have your command officers who visit or vacation in foreign countries drop in on the "locals," establish contact, trade business cards, continue the contacts, and use them as best you can. It works fairly well with street-level crime and fugitives and sometimes even with the bigger cases. A note of caution: use all the usual precautions. Moving on:

For major-case management, the tracking system should include:

1. The department priority orders
2. Case justification criteria (reactive case)
3. Precase justification criteria (proactive case) from the intelligence workup
4. Case-opening reporting: case number(s), personnel assigned, nature of the case, administrative data, and report due dates or structure
5. In-progress reports with deadlines, actions taken, time and resources used
6. Supervisor's evaluation of resource use and progress with resource expenditure estimates for the next reporting period
7. Arrest/confiscation reports
8. Case-closing evaluations
9. Any additional items you need for your use

The proactive case tracking system always should include a synopsis of the case, the target, the expected results, investigative problems, anticipated resources, progress toward the case objective, personnel assigned, identities of criminal activities, and subjects involved.

On a reactive case, such as a murder investigation, this tracking system should be implemented as soon as possible after the initial response and settling-down period. **A command-level supervisory decision is needed on reactive case management systems; sometimes the department normal and routine systems are adequate.** On a proactive case, this must be implemented prior to case-opening approval.

A *management systems approach* recognizes that all functional units interrelate. A department organization should be structured so that all support (staff) functions support the operational (line) units, not the other way around. Carefully design report routing and filing locations. The master file is the place where all original case documents are filed, including all notes and/or any matter relating to the case. Field folders may contain copies or duplicates of the master file for working purposes. **A department cannot permit personal files, or worse, two files**—the master or official file, and a working file with material not contained in the master. Failure to control all files invites case abuse and loss of management control. Very serious disruptions have occurred, especially with exculpatory evidence, due to departments having that problem. Copies of investigative notes must also be in an identified file and noted in a selected manner, by either inventory, numbered, or hand notes in a folder in the master file, particularly in those states that permit discovery of case files by the defense attorney. In addition, these investigator notes and other case flotsam in possession of officers, laboratories, medical examiners, prosecutors, experts, courts, and shipping companies must be continuously tracked, accounted for, and noted in the master file. Case notes, memos, and the like should eventually reach and remain in the master file.

There could be a whole book on just this problem; for example, in state investigative agencies, the "master" file may be in the state capital, far removed from the work site. Some use regional offices for such masters; some gather the case materials later for the one "'main'" master while tracking such things as the case progresses. As more sophisticated computer programs develop, this problem should be eased a bit. I will go no further with this matter in this book. If not done correctly and efficiently, this is an area where an agency can bury itself under a warehouse of paper and computer files, or create material for a comedy show about administrative madness.* Most agencies would need specialized help to achieve this if they start from a scratch position.

---

* See also: record management systems, mobile data terminals, the Integrated Automated Fingerprint Identity System (IAFIS), the National Incident-Based Reporting System (NIBRS), DNA databases, looking for systems integration information; e.g., Los Angeles County has interfaced over fifty law enforcement agencies with prosecutors and courts; and continues improvements.

The department name file (the index) should be centralized and coordinated to meet agency objectives. For example, the index file within an agency should have a "flag" system that will automatically report to any case investigator all queries or other information reported to the department files, currently in the files, or arriving for filing post case event. If a .22 caliber revolver is turned in to the police as found property, the "flag" system will inform any case investigator interested in .22 caliber revolvers, whether it was already in the files or entered during or after the case entry. Along with designated supervisors, the flag will also alert the case manager of any outside queries made regarding .22 caliber revolvers. Your case analyst or manager will make queries to all other file systems deemed necessary if your search for the .22 caliber revolver is not automated within your statewide/national communications system(s). The Los Angeles Police Department (LAPD) had this problem erupt in the Manson murder cases. Their system did not have flag or connection capabilities.

In addition to the aforementioned, a department that captures raw *information* from the "street" must ensure it is collected, reported, sorted, reviewed, analyzed, and changed into intelligence, then assigned to a specific unit for action or stored in a retrievable system for future availability. **This is where an information system capability for internal use becomes a necessity, not a luxury.** Work hard for this to happen. If you are a small local agency, get the state agency responsible for your interstate, intrastate, other agencies, and federal communications to provide that capability or expertise.

Essentially, the remaining *information* is stored for a designated period to catch any future flag hits and then periodically destroyed. Or, forward any new *intelligence* to a specific unit for action while keeping it available for inquiries or response when a "flag" is waved. More later regarding the destruction of information and intelligence. Careful handling is necessary given the current political excitement about retaining information on citizens, other nationals, and stateless persons.

Pick and choose from the systems just outlined, mix and match, or create your own management system.

Inspection of internal systems is management's way of determining compliance with existing procedures and identifying method improvements. There is an old saying, "If it isn't broke, don't fix it." Inspection is the way to find out if something is "broke." Inspect periodically, announced and unannounced, for case investigation flaws as well as administrative procedures, both with the attitude for improvement, not punitively. Management must routinely inspect the department's preparedness.

There are police and sheriff's agencies out there that write all of the appropriate and neatly printed order books or manuals in order to receive "certification" from someone for whatever purpose they need that piece of paper. It is a nice idea to bring police departments into the twenty-first century, but many do not observe their own rules or care to follow them. Inspection, formalized and reduced to writing and demanding corrections, is one major key to reducing that problem.

A good inspection process keeps units up to date and on their toes and identifies personnel who should be "fast tracked" for greater responsibility and those who need "reeducation." That is another book in itself.

Establish Jurisdictional Guidelines: This means do not fight at a crime scene over jurisdiction with another agency. Interagency agreements identifying and fixing jurisdictional and case responsibilities must be determined at the command level. It is a particularly difficult matter when police officials make decisions based on political factors rather than professional factors. Regardless of the difficulties, this problem should be faced and worked out. The matter should be resolved in favor of the agency with the greatest capability of reaching the objective, with appropriate support from other agencies affected. This is particularly true in states with large, full-service state police agencies, as opposed to highway patrol departments or small state investigative bureaus. The issue is the overlapping jurisdiction of state, county, city, and town police departments. Some sheriff's departments are large enough and have major case-capabilities, while most rural counties are not capable, resource wise, of absorbing the extra strain.

This can be difficult when you have to judge a department's capabilities; sometimes the smaller police departments were created to fix poor investigative services in the larger department. Many small cities cannot produce twenty to thirty people in various specialties in short order with efficiency, if at all. Small township police departments, village departments, are usually way out of their league if they attempt a major-case investigation without help. In the Preface of this book, I mentioned deferring a case to higher authority when your agency is not capable, resource wise, of handling a major case. This suggestion, if followed, will allow you to fully participate in the case, play an important role, and share major credit if successful and only minor blame if not.

High-population states without strong state police forces (Florida is one example) cannot seriously claim to have a "police system" operating with effectiveness and positive results. Until the various governors and legislatures of the large and growing states address this problem with a management perspective instead of a political perspective, law enforcement managers must work it out among themselves.

Internal jurisdictional and interagency matters *should be settled by written policies and procedures.* Decisions of who does what work must be made in writing by managers of each agency involved, not the worker or supervisor; most importantly, these decisions must be made before a case begins. The reason I suggest "in writing" is to ensure stability when management changes occur or a new leader is elected or appointed to office. It is better to have an in-place system as the starting point of any new discussions regarding this issue.

Internal Preparation: Preparing an agency for major-case coordination requires that managers plan for the use of support functions such as:

1. Crime scene units
2. Polygraphs
3. Equipment
4. Technical units

I selected a few support groups or items at random to remind you of the detailed thinking required for all preparatory work. Let us think a moment about civilian staffed crime scene units (CSUs). Their titles and pay grades are administrative matters, not entitlements to run a case. They make excellent contributors to criminal investigations, and I highly recommend their special skills in this area, but they are controlled special skills.

The CSU must clearly understand that they report to the investigator at the scene who is in charge at that moment. It may be, under rare circumstances, that the original responding officer is still in charge until a detective or supervisor arrives. Only a supervisor of the uniform or investigative command should have the authority to override that order and then only after he or she understands the situation. When the CSU and the case supervisor have a dispute over a procedure, there must be a designated person within the department administration to whom they can immediately appeal, without rancor; that decision is then final for the case in dispute. Follow-ups to that issue should be routine to fix or settle that matter quickly but later.

Never allow CSUs from two different agencies to work the same scene together without designating which one is responsible for the collection, identification, retention, reporting, and site control of all evidence under the direction of, and supervision of, the investigation case manager. The controlling agency should provide the submission documentation, evidence control numbers, case numbers, forms, and evidence containers (if possible), and these must be used by both CSU units. The original CSU case evidence inventory is the master, and a copy is for the participating agency. Everything goes on one inventory with the normal case file ability to show who collected, where it was collected, etc.

Crime scene photography rules must be in place. Evidence has a habit of mysteriously moving about. It is tough to explain why and how items appear in different places without procedures that control that problem. Whether you decide to have the CSU do the photography or have a photographer/investigator perform that task is a decision you make according to your agency's structure. The critical thing is to have your crime scene form(s) package designate a place for time of arrival of the photographer, weather, and other conditions at the scene, and a place to note the decision for the reason and manner in which the photos were taken. Further, if you adopt a form for photography, get an additional use out of it by connecting it to the department's inventory system for photographic materials. Check with your bench laboratory to determine what they require for evidence collection. Then consider what the individual CSU collectors wish for their specialty and the reasons; if reasonable, mesh them into the system. Today's digital cameras make for explosions of pictures at crime scenes and the attendant issues. Each individual "chip" from a digital camera goes into case evidence inventory and off the department's inventory, the same as for film evidence. In states with open or limited discovery rules, it is required that you produce them for the defense to examine or copy, or both. In nondiscovery states, they may become a court order issue. Let us not even consider what issues unsupervised and unaccounted for photos bring to life. Let us not even consider what havoc an individual crime scene collector, or any officer, who brings personal chips to a scene can wreak. We do not have to worry about that; we have supervisors at the scene; we have rules in place about that. We do not have such items on our CSU materials inventory listed as consumables.

If you do a video walk-through, you need a place on the form in use for the time started and path taken, notating any things or items that have been disturbed and the reason(s) therefor, such as moving items to clear a path to a prime spot at the scene. An audio track that routinely explains evidential issues as they arise will usually suffice for the courts. If you take stills, insert a place for the time *each* photo was taken and conditions at that time in addition to the normal what, where, and who. Be flexible in your written directions to allow the case supervisor to order things done according to the conditions he or she observed at the scene. A court will require that you observe the rules of evidence before admitting evidence into the trial. The forms ensure the information is captured for a proper evidentiary foundation. These forms should meet the requirements of your local prosecutor, or in state police or regional police departments, meet the requirements of the state prosecutors association. Then, all the CSU needs to do to satisfy a court is show that all things done were for a legitimate reason and purpose, and that is captured by the format of evidence collection.

We could go on about problems with two different people taking photos, or the CSU taking photos as he or she picks up evidence, or a multitude of other problems that we have all experienced at crime scenes. The point is that each agency should have a crime scene order or rule coupled with a crime scene form package that is formatted to explain what conditions were, how and when the evidence was collected and/or photos were taken, and who collected the evidence and/or took the photos, what and where the evidence is or went, all prepared, distributed, and ready to go. Identify who was at the crime scene, time in and out through one point of entry and exit—those kinds of details. Evidence control is a major issue. Collection and retention rules, place of retention, security of that place, transport and shipping, access control, inventory control, weight measures where appropriate, inspections, destruction issues, court control issues, … enough!

The New York State Police had a serious problem in one of their regions due to a flaw in the system. Complacency could be identified as the cause; they had many, many years of a "no problems here" aura of confidence that resulted in neglected closer supervision. A bad apple wreaked havoc and caused untold damage with planted evidence. Corrective surgery by the NYSP consisted of a hatchet to the bad apple with a ripple effect up the chain of command, many a career went down the tubes, and the system had to be restructured.

At one of the managing seminars mentioned in the Preface to this book, an Orlando (Florida) Police Department attending detective supervisor informed us that his agency decided to call the master log the Crime Scene Contamination Report; this quickly reduced the number of scene "rubber necks" from the department staff.

Every crime scene has different needs and problem issues; therefore, you need flexibility. Working at the edge of a swamp during a tropical storm requires a bit different approach than one in a top-floor condominium apartment overlooking the pool on a sunny Saturday afternoon.

All information must find its way into the report, then into the specific case index, and some of it into the department master name index file. In the development of your forms, identify which goes in which index and which goes to both.

Expand your thinking to include laboratory requirements and their suggestions or advice regarding evidence submission. Consider the court rules of evidence regarding admissibility and standards. In addition, think of rules to control defense counsels' actions regarding their examination and testing of your evidence when a court permits them to investigate your case. Some states have full discovery rules, some states have limited discovery, but all have access to courts to demand disclosure of certain evidentiary matters. Prepare yourselves to have evidence made available for defense investigation and testing under your terms or court direction. Usually, if you have reasonable and tested procedures, courts will allow them instead of the defendant's wishes. Expand your occasional "think tank" sessions to include laboratory and legal people.

Many agencies periodically review their procedures via a "think tank" session and update the system. Problems are identified; then procedures and forms are changed. That is done to eliminate confusion, improve efficiency, consolidate forms for ease of use, or break up forms for the same reasons.

Speaking of forms, have a fixed form control procedure. Identify every form in use within the department; approve it or remove it; consolidate forms wherever possible; use them to further the department's data collections; periodically check their usefulness via inspection. Recognition or discovery of unit "localized" forms to meet a local unit need should be examined to determine their usefulness and treated accordingly. If they are useful, integrate them; if not, get rid of them.

Technical units must go through a similar process. The decision to have scuba teams, aircraft units, electronic intercept capabilities, etc., is a command-level responsibility and decision. The *controlled use* of those items is what you must address in the "preparatory phase" of major-case management.

Polygraphs and equipment were mentioned to get you to think of the infrequently used items that should have controlled use standards or guidelines written into your investigative procedures, for both regular and major cases. We have all seen the overuse of polygraphs for "elimination" purposes; or loss of control over body wires or vehicle trackers within detective units. I am writing about investigator, not command or supervisor decisions about where, when, and against whom those items have been used without supervisor awareness. That error is usually the result of open or easy access to the equipment. I am aware of some agencies using electronic equipment without that use showing up in the official reports of the case. Those agencies are walking through a maze of trapdoors secured by the strength of a matchstick and do not recognize the sound of the hungry alligators underneath. Worse, there are instances where commanders were aware of that situation and mumbled, "What's the big deal?"

The reason I select a specific unit to raise these issues is to suggest that every such unit in your department needs a critical assessment. What item(s) do they possess; for what use or purpose do they need each thing in their possession? Then you must decide whether controls, looser or stricter, are needed to improve efficiency of use within each unit, all meshed to the department's overall structure of purpose, budget, inventory, field objectives, internal rule making, and other matters. Major-case management must always consider these necessary integrations, in addition to solving a case. I do not wish to get too deeply into departmental structures in this book, but some observations are necessary here and there to keep the wider picture always in view.

Obviously, the size of the police agency is a determining factor affecting the decision of how to address these items, but the department must make provisions for their use and integration into all major investigations. I know of one sheriff's office that consisted of a sheriff and thirty-four road deputies. They lived in a law enforcement paradise; the entire standing order for any major case, or felony, stated, "Call the state police."

Department commanders are also responsible for establishing:

1. A system of internal notification of critical personnel for major cases
2. Time-off policy and recall-to-duty orders
3. Career path training guidelines

4. Provisions for legal guidance
5. Guidelines for patrol response
6. Investigative assignments and/or detective teams
7. External notification procedures
8. Dispatcher duties
9. Supervisory response guidelines for major cases

Management ensures the tracking of all case information flow(s) and retrieval options through a reporting system. All this and much more must be in place before an agency is prepared to effectively and efficiently investigate a major criminal case.

Defining and fixing the responsibilities of individual ranks or positions, as well as functional units, ensures accountability and sees that the supervisors take appropriate action to correct noncompliance and improve efficiency. Failure can be pinpointed and corrected when responsibility is clearly fixed.

The battle of major criminal investigations, while fought and won in the trenches, is often lost in the command offices for lack of planning and preparedness or overreaching the agency's ability, meaning resources, not individual people's level of competence.

Chapter 1 identified the principal entities or functions required to investigate a major criminal case. We will discuss each of those entities or functions and the duties and responsibilities outlined. Department commanders are responsible for ensuring these preparatory items are in place.

Functional Unit Duties

Dispatcher

The communication control room is the nerve center for all police street operations. The multiple and varied duties of a busy communication center require a written policy and procedures. Major-case management and coordination require the use of the existing department dispatch system. It then follows that the design of the system is prepared to handle major events and cases. Written procedures must be in place, along with well-trained personnel, so the radio control system routinely captures certain information and provides defined services. The "Hey Charlie, hold down the radio for a few minutes while I get some coffee" days are over.

Systematize the following:

1. Establish a routine procedure for all initial call recording, including the following:
   a. Time call received

    b. Who called, from where, and the information received

    c. The instructions the dispatcher gave the caller (see Appendix A)

2. Dispatcher's procedures for responding units should include:

    a. The time of dispatching the first and subsequent units

    b. Instructions for responding patrol officer(s), including pre-planned approaches, such as "loud" or "quiet" and fast or slow, plus directions of approach coordinated with other responding units (let's not collide two patrol cars in one intersection)

    c. Shift supervisor notification time and instructions received from the supervisor on certain class or priority calls

    d. Log of all actions and responses taken for the "sequence of events" record; the initiation of the major-case timeline and logbook and in some cases the beginning of the "murder book" (an electronic tape time-marker is helpful; e.g., 8:27 p.m. manual, or 20:27:16 automatic)

3. Items available for immediate reference should be:

    a. Emergency phone listings

    b. Duty rosters of available personnel

    c. Supervisor duty call roster

    d. Emergency situational orders and recommendations (e.g., poison control, hazardous material manual, cat in the tree; you know, the "Just don't shoot it" suggestion)

4. Plans for the initiation of major-crime response tactics are usually handled by a shift supervisor (from a menu available) based on his or her experience. These plans should include in addition to the immediate broadcast routine of the crime to all units:

    a. The actions of nonresponding patrols or their instructions

    b. Field interrogation orders

    c. Escape route coverage

    d. "Flooding" the area with patrol units

    e. Avoiding-the-area orders

    f. Stop-and-check routines

    g. Full-court-press techniques, if appropriate, or one or more blocking rings

    h. Area or sector searches

    i. Establishment checks (bars, restaurants, etc.)

    j. Suspect location checks

    k. Reporting back actions and information

5. Develop the communication system to address:

    a. Notification of fire, ambulance, medical examiner, etc., as needed

    b. Notification of other agencies and initiating their major-case agreements

    c. Notification of internal units or personnel and the time they were
       notified
    d. Recording patrol responses and soliciting information about
       other patrol activities
    e. Switching to special communication channels (if available)

Agencies with sophisticated computer capability can develop programs that will spontaneously pop up any history of the name, address, or events at the place of the incident for information to the responding officer, hopefully prior to his or her arrival. That is also a flag. That is what an automated information system does.

    f. Recording the location and assignments of all units during the
      response phase

Keep this guideline with your poison control, asphyxiation, CPR instructions, hazardous materials manuals, and similar dispatcher instructions. Even the rarest of rare, kidnapping,* usually requires the receiver of the original police call to decide whether to respond with a patrol car or a secret contact with the victim's family. It could be the difference between a live or dead victim. It would be nice if, when that person enters the code or word for kidnapping into the dispatcher computer, a drop-down instruction were to appear to remind the dispatcher of the policy before sending the patrol. In Phoenix, they probably send the SWAT team. In the police business, the devil is truly in the details.

The command level will decide which parts of this information, which is captured and recorded (paper or electronic) in all cases, will be retained at the dispatcher location for supervisory and case manager review, and which is immediately forwarded to the case manager (investigator) in the agreed-upon format. In large agencies that is usually handled by the on-duty supervisor of dispatching. In small agencies that may be referred to the on-duty "street supervisor," or consider the immediate recall of an off-duty supervisor. (Who, we all know, is always immediately available?) Department-encrypted cell phones were truly a miracle for law enforcement. Start cutting the wheat from the chaff immediately, with the ability to review the chaff at first opportunity.

Public records will be discussed in several places in this book. This is a good place to start; 911 calls are public records in many states due to laws, not policy. The time, date, location, and nature of a reported crime and the tape recording are almost universally "public." Set your procedures for the release of those tapes to require a criminal case officer review. Investigative material

---

* Phoenix, Arizona, is now experiencing about three hundred a year; it seems a drug war
  is going on there.

should be redacted or edited out. Directions issued to the caller may be case related or contain investigative material; statements and descriptions of criminals, witnesses, or matters needed for investigative keys may be hinted at if not disclosed outright. Most such early information is case harmless, but some is not. If it is serious, consider challenging the law, as it conflicts with the nondisclosure laws of open criminal investigation material.

Uniform Patrols

The response capability of the uniform patrols is often a highly important factor that determines the success or failure of a major-case investigation. Planning how a patrol will respond requires keen thinking, experience, and detailed knowledge of all the police resources in the area. Surprisingly, contiguous agencies, or those working within a nearby area, are not always aware of each other's human resources, equipment, plans, or other service capabilities. More surprisingly, they are often unaware of what is available on the existing shift in the jurisdiction next door. If you don't bother to collect and use that information, a metro or regional consolidation is in your future.

Uniform officers should be aware of their agency's major-crime response plans, as well as the plans and agreements with other agencies within their work influence area. The officers should understand the department policy and reason for the response procedures. In fact, patrol officers can be of tremendous value in developing a good, workable major-crime response plan. Thoroughly trained street officers implementing the department's major-crime responses are accountable through a strict reporting and recording system. Uniform patrol plans should include:

1. Patrol post assignment orders: Whether your department uses a one-car/one-post system, several cars to a zone, or splits duties within the same area (e.g., traffic cars and complaint cars), there should be clearly stated post coverage rules (see Appendix B).
2. Major-crime response plans: Good response plans call for immediate action upon notice, without orders, from the patrol force on duty. When a dispatcher assigns a unit to a major crime, one that is encountered in progress, one that is discovered routinely, or one that is discovered by original call misidentification (the four of these have differing responses), all other patrol units start a preplanned reaction until directed otherwise by a supervisor. Plans should consider:
   a. Immediate notification of the shift supervisor or dispatching a supervisor to the scene. Once the supervisor is notified and "on the air," he or she decides all.
   b. The number of and which units will respond to the call. The shift supervisor making the call will use a general guideline based

upon his or her judgment, considering the experience of responding officers, their locations, and the nature of the call. Situational responses will suffice. Further, the supervisor will be aware of the past criminal activity in that neighborhood, similar cases currently under investigation, location of the event, and political or internal boundaries in the event a "nearest patrol and fastest response" is required (including other agencies). When you get into the thinking required for these matters, you will discuss routes, car-to-car coordination factors, and more.

c. Orders for all *unassigned* units to stay away from the scene. Stress that all patrols should not converge on the scene and hold those who violate the rule accountable. After three-quarters of a second worth of deep and thoughtful reflection, the sergeant may say, "Two nearest units on this one. All other units … do …" whatever. Then, "Oh yeah, Charlie 3, get Adam 12 out of Gantry Park, he usually parks on the back side this time of night; get him on the street … now."

d. The system of approach to the crime scene—loud or quiet—and route(s). The first unit will go in fast, but maybe a second unit should approach slower with extra alertness for information that may be obtained (license numbers, witnesses, etc.). The in-charge street supervisor is earning her or his pay; experience will tell out.

e. Requiring all units to note their exact location at the time of the original dispatch. All locations are recorded by the dispatcher for immediate use and decisions by the shift supervisor, then **routinely forwarded to the case file.** Require all in-service vehicles to call this in as a response procedure as soon as airtime is available. The dispatcher will inform all other on duty patrols who are or were temporarily out of service. Departments using computer dispatching to in-car computers have the ability to speed this up, and much more. Agencies with patrol car trackers can capture this data automatically. Some can put up a patrol car location display on the supervisor's in-car screen (and have the dispatcher turn on the detective car locators). Neat to have that capability. It helps when everyone knows who is converging on what may be a high-tension deadly confrontation situation, especially if an undercover narcotic officer jumps in without his color of the day on display. Worse if he comes running around a corner with a gun in his hand—they tend to forget why police officers wear uniforms.

f. Plans for recording license numbers, stopping and checking vehicles or persons, checking bars and other business establishments.

If, in the judgment of the officer, information may be of use, he or she captures it in a prepared format that is easily communicated to the dispatcher and case supervisor. It is retained, indexed, and placed in the case file or sent out on a case lead sheet for further action. The case beat and flow is starting, gaps are identified, and review is available for second thoughts. All this while no confirmation of anything has occurred.

g. Movement or positioning of units to cover possible escape routes. This is usually a responsibility of the shift supervisor; if unavailable, the most senior person working under that supervisor currently on the communication net is charged with that responsibility.

h. Use the in-place system for feeding all data (information) to the investigating unit as a matter of routine, not only when or if requested. General decisions regarding which matters are confidential and which can be transmitted are already coming together. The department field identifications and situational checks with record and retain systems should be a routine. Some of the best information may have been noted and recorded by alert patrols prior to the crime.

3. Training for major-case response: The duties of units responding to the crime scene are usually well covered in training programs. Not only should training people update the training curricula or subject matter, major-case managers should also check them. Those of you who rely on other agencies for training must do it yourself if you cannot get the necessary outside training that fits your specific needs.

The duties of units near the scene or routine patrol responsibilities, before and after a major-case call, are often neglected and should be attended to, since their actions are often critical to the success of a major case.

Uniform Patrol Operational Duties: Patrol Post Crime Response

Zone	Scene
Rule	Area coverage
Boundaries	Position for escape
Duties	Check persons and vehicles
Crime Scene Duties	**Next-Shift and Next-Day Duties**
Secure	Recheck area
Broadcast	ID witnesses and deliveries
Record information	Recheck escape routes

Experienced uniform supervisors are worth their weight in gold. Quick decisions implementing crime response actions can be a critical factor, particularly when based on sketchy information.

The street supervisor or officer in charge of the shift is responsible for deciding which of the many options available to use, such as flooding the area with patrols or working an area perimeter for the purpose of "forcing a break" or obtaining information. Whether you have a one-patrol department, ten patrols, or hundreds, someone will be vested with this responsibility. In addition, all that preplanned activity **must be in the department's index format.** Items or pieces of information developed are then routed to the case manager for his or her review, selection or rejection, or further case use, and then placed in the case index. The department case file or database retains all of that information; then, eventually, all of it is entered into the department's main database. Reports on matchbook covers are indicators of a problem.

Patrol car equipment should include the normal emergency roadside flares, reflectors, lights, batteries, rope, axes, fire extinguishers, and such things. In addition, supply geodetic survey maps for rural areas and detailed city maps for urban settings. The immediate need for those arise when a search takes place for missing persons, especially children, or a crime scene grid, mapping, and neighborhood searches become necessary. Some agencies have plat plans for developments and rural areas with ownership indicated. They are available from your tax appraiser's office. These are of use for flag indexing named locations and addresses. If that becomes too much of an upkeep problem, at least supervisor vehicles must be equipped with the basics. Some departments use portable drawing boards with plastic overlays for marking, then transfer the markups to the maps for record preservation.

As you can see, we are delving into minutia. My purpose is not to tell you a box is needed to carry this stuff in your patrol cars with your hazardous-material manuals, or first aid references, but to start the thinking process of what is needed and where it is to be kept for preservation, availability, and replacement.

Other Agencies

Agreements with other law enforcement agencies prior to an actual case are of vital importance. Nothing is more ridiculous than police agencies at a crime scene trying to settle who will do what or who is responsible for what, or worse, squabbling over jurisdiction. Agreements and coordination move the case forward. Law enforcement agencies must work together. Agreements must be in place and workable, whether they are made between the New York City Police Department and the New York City Transit Police, New York City Housing Authority Police, or the New York Port Authority Police, or in Seminole County, Florida, between the county sheriff and the Winter Springs Police Department.

Agencies that work with, for, or next to each other should agree on:

1. Jurisdiction and responsibility for major cases. Those agencies working in dual or multiple political jurisdictions still using the "whoever gets there first, has it" system had better sit down and negotiate a working agreement. Worse, if whoever gets there first drags the body across the boundary line to the other guy's house. We all know of a few abandoned stolen-car recoveries that get pushed around town a bit before someone relents and has it towed.

2. Roadblock plans (used if appropriate to the area), stop-and-check routines, information recording (license plates, names, etc.), and **the method of routinely feeding that information to the case-controlling agency.** Roadblocks are essentially useless in urban or suburban areas, but major traffic arteries and choke points can be surveilled, or at least some of them can. Patrol officers know how to intimidate traffic—that is, look for and make eye contact with drivers to see if a reaction can be provoked. All "the usual suspects" move around and patrols do know them. Have them pass the information back into the case without being asked, information such as names, who were together, sometimes descriptions, and certainly motor vehicle registration numbers if you do not have the time or opportunity to stop selected drivers.

3. Response to crime scene criteria. Stay away or assist. Either way, let the controlling agency know what your patrols are doing, accept directions from the controlling agency, and **submit all information to the controlling agency rapidly in the agreed-upon format.**

4. Crime broadcast procedures. On publically committed major crimes, broadcast as soon as reported, rebroadcast as soon as confirmed, with or without complete information, and feed descriptive data as soon as it is received, even if it is piecemeal. Always remember that each case is different, and your street supervisor or officer in charge may change or correct the procedure to be followed based upon his or her judgment. **The key words are flexibility, judgment, and experience, in both controlling and assisting agencies.**

5. Reporting of information (without waiting to be asked) to the controlling authority (a big problem). It is easier if the method of reporting is preset as to place or person to whom it is to be reported. This is usually the case manager or, in a large case, one of his or her assistants. The case manager is then responsible for seeing that the data is fed into the case and regular report system. This is one of the case manager's duties, along with managing the investigation itself.

If not in place, the responsibility falls back to the street supervisor to inform everyone, including all other agencies, how to accomplish that task. Quickly.

We will talk further about this, but you can see a shell or structure being built. The investigators or street officers are using their normal tools: department form interview sheets, investigative lead sheets, or regular note pads. Whatever is your norm. We are directing that information to case storage and retrieval systems as well as the normal department systems. We will continue to move toward tying it all together with the theme of input, storage, notice to the players, and distribution to the interested parties. All this is **within a frame of administrative control and data collection for multiple other purposes.**

6. Even if routine, the importance of assistance agreements on the sharing or use of personnel, technicians, specialists, and equipment, such as:
   a. Crime scene specialists
   b. Polygraph operators
   c. Manpower reserves
   d. Investigative files and similar crimes information
   e. Intelligence information
   f. Establishing working relationships
   g. Agreements on who reports to whom and in what form
   This is just a matter of sitting down and fully discussing the issues and deciding on the circumstances and factors in your working area. Commit this to writing, pass it around your command, and keep it updated. Information must flow.

7. **Press agreements.** Press agreements, or information control agreements, ensure some tranquility among law enforcement agencies. **Only the agency controlling the case may release information to the media.** Any law enforcement agency assisting another in an investigation must refer all press inquiries to the managing agency, without comment, not even a news item confirmation, not so much as a peep or winked eye. This agreement must be kept at all costs. **At this stage, every piece of information must be held within the police community until the controlling agency has decided upon the investigative keys they wish to protect.** Sadly, this is one of the most violated "agreements," particularly by individuals or agencies that are politically or egotistically motivated. Reduce this agreement to writing and take immediate disciplinary action against violators. There is not much you can do when the "violator" turns out to be the head of another agency, except maybe just get him drunk and shove his ass into a 'gator pond.

Detective Command

The primary responsibility for the conduct of a major case investigation rests with the detective command. The chief of detectives is required to have a competent, highly trained staff of investigators or access to expertise from other agencies. A complementary team must be available, or gathered, to perform major-case investigations properly. The commander must be aware of each individual's (or team's) skills, talents, or deficiencies. Detective commanders must structure their operation not only to handle the everyday matters, but also to immediately move on a reactive major case. They must also be prepared to accept the initial response team as it is constituted from the on-duty street shift. This raises a uniform, detective, and dispatcher schedule issue. It is not a good idea to have an all "rookie" or low-seniority personnel on the night shift. This is one more item that fits into the preparedness phase. This, in turn, leads to the major-case on-call list. Which leads to vacation schedules, training lists, which lead to … etc.

In order to prepare an investigative unit for the managing of a major case, the detective commander should implement certain procedures. Some of these are:

1. Responsibility for the supervision of a major case, which is always assigned to one person. In small departments, the detective commander may have to assume this responsibility. In large agencies, this person may have the responsibility for more than one major case or a major-case unit.
2. Contingency plans to reshuffle personnel, rapidly, according to unit or agency priorities. Which lead to labor union and contract issues, which lead to … etc.
3. A directive that requires selected command personnel and supervisors to respond promptly or immediately to a major crime according to a classification or scale of seriousness.
4. Agreements between the investigative and uniform units within the same agency that set forth guidelines or orders on response procedures, coordination of crime scene functions, and interunit assistance according to priorities and assigned duties.
5. Procedures for advising the detective commander of the assigned supervisor's response to major crimes and the status of investigative reports; a part of the normal information flow system.
6. An availability roster and a recall-to-duty system, which lead to overtime issues, contract issues, restrictive off-duty travel issues, etc.
7. Procedures for notification of investigative personnel, supervisors, and/or case specialists. This should be a detective command internal system, **initiated by investigative personnel,** *not a dispatcher.* Once

a dispatcher notifies the appropriate person within the detective unit, responsibility for further selective notification should rest with the investigative unit. **Information is passed on with instructions that are particular to the case under investigation.** No investigator should respond to a crime scene without needed preliminary information for his or her specialty, even if it is only "observe and report" matters, such as abandoned vehicles, license numbers, delivery vans noted, or bring the coffee and donuts. *Direct notifications save a great deal of time and confusion; besides, the dispatcher is busy.* Consider conference calls if you are recalling multiples of officers. This, of course, leads to equipment issues, overtime policies, etc., etc.

8. Agreements that address the working and coordination conditions with other agencies. These are more detailed than the policy agreements negotiated by the agency heads. These deal with **the details of work and how each will report to the other and in what format.** For example, if you assign routine neighborhood interviews to another agency, specifically inform them of items you wish covered and what you insist on being observed of the persons and conditions at the interview location. This requires an assessment of the competency of the other agency personnel prior to the current case involvement. See, no one said this would be easy. As in your own department, you do not assign personnel to tasks they are incapable of performing at the required standard.

9. Inspection and readiness of equipment, one of the most neglected areas in detective commands.

10. Procedures for evidence handling and a crime scene unit's work plans. Input from detectives, managers, and CSU people should be utilized and agreed upon with flexibility, and a clear understanding that the detective-in-charge is the final authority and carries all of the responsibility.

11. Agreements with prosecutors and medical examiners. Murder, arson with a death (murder), kidnappings, robberies with shooting or life-threatening injuries, or problematic legal issues that arise, such as search and interrogation issues, demand that a prosecutor be assigned from the beginning of the case until it is turned over to the prosecuting attorney's office. Experienced investigators and prosecutors will know which cases need that service. When in doubt, ask that a prosecutor be assigned, particularly when dealing with an elected prosecutor office. The assigned prosecutor must be experienced and not just out of law school. Young lawyers cause more trouble than a Navy ensign with a clipboard and pencil.

12. A procedure for keeping all of the preceding up-to-date and appropriately distributed.

Detective commanders also have the responsibility of training and developing their unit. They should nurture investigators to full bloom by exposing them to as many situations and types of cases as possible. Training and experience mean improved effectiveness and efficiency.

The responsibility for their personal, as well as unit, awareness of crime laboratory capabilities, procedures, and the lab's key personnel is vested in detective commanders. They must maintain a liaison with their laboratory and develop a close working relationship with the laboratory managers.

Most detective commanders have implemented, in one degree or another, many if not all of the aforementioned procedures. It is also true that most detective commanders are seriously deficient in their contacts with the medical profession, business and trades people, and social services. Detailed knowledge or highly developed skill in these professions is not necessary, but detective commanders and their staffs at selected levels should have at a minimum a working knowledge of the rudiments, or at least be in contact with and be able to intelligently converse with, experts in:

Medical profession:
   Gynecologists
   Psychiatrists
   Traumatic-injury specialists
   Cardiac units, medical laboratories, and pharmacologists
Business and trade: An example of a good person to know outside of your own department's employee experts is a high-level manager of a phone company or communication company. They would be able to inform you of the inside abilities of their business, such as their retention times of phone call records, whether they record who calls and is called from throwaway phones, the details of how they trace and track calls, signals or towers, or what your department needs in order to peek into their records in addition to the warrant information issues relating to the phone company. This often speeds up police matters. When you need something in a hurry, it pays to have a good contact.
Bankers, securities specialists, and accountants: In addition to knowing and contacting such specialists within the state structure of insurance departments, banking regulators, and stock and security brokerage regulation (many if not all states regulate stock brokerage under the $5 million cap; the federals take the others), get to know private experts in those fields. They often give you a broader and somewhat different take on those professions. Make sure they are of the capitalist mind-set and not just opportunists that use capitalism as cover for their operations. You are liable to wind up investigating them just after you had them over for a party. Not good form.

Labor relations experts: at the command and staff levels.

Special trades: Jewelers, antiques dealers, pawnshop owners (which are an interesting group of people)—most wind up somewhere in the informer or interested citizen category, depending upon their backgrounds. Some, of course, are simply dealers in stolen property, along with other charming business activities and trades. Car rental business and credit card managers at banks and credit card companies are excellent sources of inside information.

Social services: particularly the bureaus that deal with abused children or battered spouses.

Clergy

Psychologists and behavioral scientists: Personal experience with psychologists has been uniformly unproductive. They have been of minor value. You may have had better experiences with that field. I recommend caution, and sticking with psychiatrists. However, I recognize those are tough businesses; guessing human behavior from statistics, case studies, or similarities to other people, then applying it to an unknown but specific individual is fraught with complications and error.

Mental retardation and disorders services

Juvenile services

Research biochemists: These should not be from your own laboratory. Choose someone to sit and talk to in comfort. You will get a real understanding of things like deoxyribonucleic acid—which some people call DNA since, like me, they cannot pronounce the word. Deeper understanding is extremely useful. Further, innovative knowledge of the advancements and testing capabilities is of greater interest. This carries forth to all such subjects.

Maritime specialists: This is important if a port is in your jurisdiction. Learn maritime and admiralty law, such as jurisdiction over foreign-flagged vessels, the fact that ship registration changes of flag often occur while at sea, and the difference between 3, 12, and 200 mile limits of jurisdiction. Consider helicopter response issues to underway vessels approaching or leaving a three-mile jurisdiction, and investigation of crimes against U.S. citizens on a foreign-flagged cruise ship in a U.S. port.

In addition, federal interests may arise, along with state interests in crimes and some civil actions. Onboard crime by Americans in port is one thing; at sea is another. Search warrant issues and basic knowledge of extraterritorial jurisdiction would be of interest. Inland rules of the road are different from the international rules.

There are many more such examples, but that is for you to work out to suit your agency needs. Think of two instances where you needed some guidance on a special issue. Time's up. Add those two contacts.

Some agencies develop advisory groups of interested citizens to support their department along the lines stated previously. People of all walks of life are fascinated by police work. They become interested and are willing to help. It is voluntary citizen participation in what, to them, is an exciting and interesting public service. Do not bring them to a late-running retirement party until they are ready for that exposure. Do consider inviting them to a once-a-year party to meet with all of the major-case functional unit leaders, including other agency heads and prosecutors, medical examiners, laboratory people, and other useful bodies—maybe a couple of judges. A Saturday afternoon in a park, an ice tub of beer, a little soft guitar music in the background, and you would be surprised at the high-level enjoyment your advisory group(s) would tell you they had. The expansion of their personal knowledge of the police business would be of enormous benefit to your agency. **Do not invite any media;** they are not part of the team, will not obey your privacy wishes, and will attempt to develop snitches. If they show up, politely ask them to leave, informing them that it is a private, nonofficial gathering of friends having a get-together, not a violation of any government in the sunshine rule, where those exist.

Conduct quasi-official meetings with your advisory group(s) on occasion and discuss vexing problems or ask for information or advice. After you are satisfied some of them meet all of the required "tests," consider discussing a particular case with them to assist in expanding your own knowledge.

Development of the commander and his or her investigators in the rules of evidence, law, the constitution, and investigative technique improvements is a continuous program. The investment of time and money in training and education programs is necessary. Many state police or state investigative agencies have programs to see that mid- and high-level officers are schooled in specific fields of study: accounting and financial transactions, Indian affairs, education with concentration on testing, constitutional studies, and public administration. Spread the developed skills throughout the department as part of a career development program. They are worth fighting for with the agency money; it is through efforts like these that the police will accomplish their mission.

Now the control side: these contacts are all reported contacts and listed by name and specialty. The specialties of each contact are available to the whole department through an assigned officer. Anyone on an investigation who needs quick information may contact that officer and request whatever he or she needs. Further, all case managers are fully aware of that information and that it is available 24/7. In addition, any request made due to a specific case under investigation is listed as a lead investigative inquiry and placed in the administrative side of the case file since it is general information, not an investigative matter. The response is usually background and administrative; if the response becomes case relevant (a rarity), it becomes part of the investigation, indexed, and added to the case.

General inquiries made for personal knowledge are not filed in any specific case file. Whether you track that information at the command level is a matter of discretion, your choice.

Investigators

The officers assigned to do the actual work of investigation should be prepared by nature of training and experience. Investigators should have the education and mental capacity to deal with and perform at all strata of society. Constant training and education improve these abilities, but experience is the tie-breaker. Competent, experienced officers are important for major-case work and an absolute requirement for the supervision of a major case. The experience level is not one of mere "years on the job." We all know of officers with twenty years of service that translates into one year's experience (and vice-versa).

Experienced officers not only quietly and effectively work through the investigative "puzzle," they are the ones who:

1. Are always ready to roll on a case.
2. Developed a good and reliable group of informants and interested citizens. (Informant identification and control is another subject and will not be addressed here.)
3. Assume case supervision responsibility and act until a supervisor arrives.
4. Are aware of all interagency and internal agreements and their applicability to the particular situation at hand.
5. Are aware of the investigator-uniform officer relationship and cultivates it in a positive manner. They recognize the value and usefulness of the uniform force and are never negative toward them.
6. Most of all, are aware of their agency's limitations and are not afraid to seek help. These people recognize the value of cooperation.

When detectives are born, they usually have from four to seven years service in some combination of police work and formal college education. The best experience is that of a hard-working street cop. They have participated in many initial phases of felony investigations, have made numerous felony arrests, and have investigated from start to finish untold numbers of misdemeanor-level work. They have had felony work assigned to them as special tasks by investigators. They have worked the fringes of felony cases as a first responder. They have attended uniform officer in-service training classes. They have experienced search warrant enforcement, surveillances, scene searches, and neighborhood interviews, developed informants, and attended autopsies. These individuals have well-developed person-to-person communication skills at all strata of society. They probably have delivered investigators safely to their homes after the euphoria of a "case critique" session upon completion of a successful closure of a major investigation, which happened to be held at the "Club Wild Turkey." A reminder that good management knows when to turn a blind eye.

After all that, new investigators' first assignment is to go back to school. They must be exposed to a minimum of a three- to four-week intensive (135–180 hours), focused, and informative review of:

Criminal investigative techniques
Interview formats and techniques:
    Witness interviews
    Suspect interviews
    Citizen interviews
Recognition of the sixteen personality types, as well as approaches to, handling of, and dealing with each
Crime scene technology: must be able to perform all CSI trades, for example: photography; fingerprint lifts and classification; procedures for hair, blood, DNA, and semen; submissions; etc.
Laboratory capabilities and requirements
Laws of evidence updates, particularly:
    University texts on evidence
    Burden of proof (including the necessary elements of each crime). The investigator must be aware of the meanings of the various case evidentiary "burdens": reasonable and articulable suspicion, probable cause, preponderance of evidence, clear and convincing evidence, and beyond and to the exclusion of reasonable doubt. The investigator also needs to determine the value of the evidence being collected.
    Presumptions and inference
    Relevance, competency, and materiality and the trial admission rules for both direct and circumstantial evidence
    Hearsay
    Res gestae
    Admissions and declarations
    Dying declarations
    Expert opinion evidence
    Documentary evidence

Excuse and justification, such as accident or misadventure, and the use of deadly physical force (the last is usually covered in the normal in-service firearms requalification and self-defense training)

Laws of arrest updates

Trial and testimony procedures and updates

Statement and interrogation procedures and updates

Report writing, forms, and information system updates, including the regular case management control system as well major-case control actions. If you still do this manually, let the trainee build an exercise "murder book," as it is called in some jurisdictions.

Criminal-case law reviews, especially probable-cause thresholds, stop and frisk, detention without arrest, field interrogation, and custody issues. Note: State police departments report criminal law court case decisions, which influence police operations. All changes, nuanced decisions, even a shaded by circumstance case comes down the internal communication system to be read and initialed by every sworn officer in the department. Some smaller local departments do not have the funds to do this. If the local prosecutor or department legal service does not routinely assist, get on the state police distribution list.

Investigation unit directives, rules, regulations, and procedures

States with full-service state police departments often "save" a few seats in their classes for small local police agencies. In states without that special service, some have "universal" courses available through whatever police training facilities are available. Most of those are inadequate but better than none at all, since that would leave you only with "on-the-job training" (OJT). Controlled OJT builds off a directed base and is focused on applications of the learned material, as in probationary officer postacademy training. That is how one gains "experience." But experience is different from experiences. Some university and private seminars are available, but you usually have to attend about a half a dozen to get close to what you need, and they tend to be drawn out and cost more than the value received. Private seminars are best suited for the special issues you have, addressed to keep your staff current in the business.

Good training is a problem; I once offered a "seat" at the Henry Williams Homicide Seminar put on by the New York State Police to a relatively small Florida sheriff's office, about 175 deputies; they declined without ever realizing that seminar is the improved version of the renowned Harvard University Homicide Seminar for pathologists and police officers. The NYSP, and that seminar, has an international reputation as being among the best there is, and a worldwide waiting list for attendees that extends into years.

When I retired, and my wife and I were preparing to sail away on our schooner *Pisces*, I offered a life's selective collection of instructive material to a high-level Florida police official. The collection included medico-legal works recommended to me by Dr. Michael Baden, former medical examiner for New York City; lecture outlines with all supporting materials for arson, murder, child sex crimes, rape, and sexual predators; a series of lectures on white-collar investigations, police manuals, order books, and administrative procedures from about five large and very good police departments; and much more information, such as essays written by experts in various fields—two 4- by 7-foot bookcases full of compacted knowledge. He declined. "It would take up too much office space, and besides, I'd never get around to reading all that stuff." "Put it in your department library," I said. "We don't have one of those," he said. He never recognized I was offering it to his department to spread around and use.

I guess what I am trying to say is that training is just a term sometimes used to fill some kind of void that says, "We are trained." It is meaningless unless it really happens, and it takes an understanding leader to ensure the training is real, effective, and of a high degree of value. There are places where this does not happen.

Crime Scene Unit

The crime scene unit is an important and integral part of most major-case investigations. The handling of evidence and the understanding of what must be done with evidence to further the investigation and to have it examined by a laboratory in order to gain introduction into a court should be in the forefront of the evidence technician's mind at all times.

In order to prepare for a major case, crime scene units require:

1. Detailed training and experience in their craft. This includes some formal education requirements and specific law enforcement instructions. Evidence technicians obtain experience by working directly under a qualified certified instructor at actual crime scenes until the department's specified, formal procedure of exposure, instruction, and the required qualification level is reached in order to work alone.
2. Inspection routines to ensure the readiness of their vehicles, evidence kits, and evidence packaging material. Each department must decide what each of its vehicles carries—uniform, detective, supervisory, and special vehicles such as the crime scene vans/trucks. All are equipped differently depending on the needs of the agency; this is decided by what they wish to be delivered quickly anywhere in their

area of jurisdiction, from additional firepower and ammunition to hot coffee for a beat officer working in a freezing rain.

3. Tools and equipment. That includes items at the mundane level, such as geodetic survey maps for rural areas and plat plans for urban areas, and those items like computer capability to draw architectural building plans to match a scene. Consider aerial photography for all conditions, when relevant. These are sometimes necessary to identify with specificity locations and addresses for case indexing and information systems if you have developed one of those for internal record searches.

4. Training updates as well as investigative, forensic, and specialty bulletin acknowledgments (read and initial documents). By the way, *copies* of these initialed documents are retained in the individual's personnel folder's training section and in the department's training section folders and are indexed in the personnel section master index. Personnel matters are kept out of the department's main record index in automated files and are kept separated from the manual systems.

Crime scene units should operate under the command and control of investigative units. They should prepare plans or agreements with all investigative units they service (some states and counties offer their CSUs to local police) with specific plans in place for:

1. Evidence collection methodology
2. Site control procedures
3. Coordination and control of evidence systems
4. Method of scene searches (This is a general methodology; each scene has its own problems, and decisions are made accordingly.)
5. Recording of who and what **comes into and goes out from** the scene.
6. Evidence-tracking capabilities and records (chain of evidence and receipts). Try for mutual compatibility with your forms, or adopt a standard for the region. If you use a state police CSU, it is usual to accept theirs or listen to a polite "you can probably do it yourself anyway … call if you need further help." One purpose is not to confuse a jury. Prosecutors are having enough trouble with juries by the spread of TV crime shows' penchant for misinformation and error.

Crime scene units are a support service to the investigators, not the main characters of the investigation. There must be a strong liaison and understanding between investigators and crime scene personnel. This is particularly important in the agencies that use "civilian technicians" instead of police personnel. Specialized civilian services within police organizations tend to focus their work and interest to the narrow spectrum of their skill and sometimes lose sight of the main goal. One result of using "civilians" to perform the crime scene technician duties is a general lessening of police investigator knowledge of these skills and procedures. Supervisors must guard against this within their commands, or the tail will soon be wagging the dog. Remember, we hired civilians to do the important but specialized and repetitive work at crime scenes because they cost less than a detective, certainly less than a laboratory bench analyst, and have the abilities to focus on the one task.

CSI is an entertaining television show, mostly because Grissom is a unique character; the other two CSI shows are not up to any standard. The shows are a good vehicle to point out how real CSI units *do not* do things. Real units do not interview witnesses, execute search warrants, chase criminals, carry guns or arrest people, or constantly place themselves into personal conflict-of-interest situations. Nor do they haphazardly handle evidence, allow walk-in traffic to their "lab space," or conduct serious bench analysis of evidence. Some will do field tests for identification to achieve probable-cause requirements or assist the investigation with immediate information. CSUs collect evidence, record their collection, and store it until the case investigator has it sent to laboratories. Case supervisors have to guard against their crime scene units attempting to go beyond their duties, unless they are sworn police personnel operating within the case as police officers under the direct command of the investigator-in-charge.

Laboratory

The functions of a police laboratory are often misunderstood. They are for the examining of evidence and scientifically reporting the results of those examinations. Laboratory technicians are usually bench workers, skilled in a science, not crime scene technicians, not police officers, and not identification workers. Many people, and sadly some police investigators, expect laboratory personnel to function as they are portrayed in so many television police shows. As the saying goes, "It just isn't so." TV writers make quantum leaps. Give a TV "lab" a clump of grass and dirt, and they will tell you which farm or dirt patch it came from, how many people stepped on it, and their age, sex, and favorite breakfast cereal.

Reality makes us recognize that laboratory services support the investigation and offer proof by scientific examination of the items submitted. Good laboratories perform some truly outstanding feats, but it is the prosecutors and the police that must use this data to move their case.

Laboratories should provide and investigators should be familiar with:

1. The facility location and personnel to call
2. Laboratory handbooks listing:

     a. Specialties available at the laboratory or through the laboratory

     b. Services and requirements for evidence submission

     c. Statements of "how to," and "do's and don'ts" for evidence collection

3. Agreements, with all agencies they serve, on case examination priorities and procedures for evidence examination within each case. This is where the laboratories will ask you to tell them exactly what you want examined, what they should look for, and whether the search or examination is necessary at this stage of the investigation. They will also ask you to determine exactly what the prosecutor intends to use at trial before they examine evidence for no purpose at all. Time is a commodity that a bench service laboratory does not have in overabundance. Work with them on these issues; discuss your problems with them. You will get better service as a result.

4. Police laboratories will have a list of all available outside experts in all disciplines for discussion of specific evidence with investigators. If you use a private laboratory for some purpose, inform your normal police lab first; they will be glad to help you with capabilities information.

5. Twenty-four-hour availability of personnel and recall status for special cases

6. Information service for special handling of unique or unusual items

7. A memorandum of understanding about testifying at trial, stand-by times, availability for trial, insertion into the trial to testify out of order if a trial is running late, and other matters that will free up the laboratory examiners to return to their backed-up caseloads

A **detective commander** is well advised to speak (it usually winds up to be mostly listening) to the chief judge of the circuit or district in general terms about police, prosecutor, and court trial cooperation. Never raise a specific case with the judge, unless asked by the judge or you receive permission from the judge to address a specific matter. Develop a working relationship with the chief judge and do not rely solely on the prosecutor to handle the court.

A word of caution to smaller police agencies attempting to operate "labs" independent of the state laboratory system. The smaller you are, the more trouble you will have. Departments must get their laboratories certified by the best source available with complete independence from the department. Have it ordered by, scheduled, and paid for by your political controller as assurance to them that the laboratory is proper and functioning at a high degree of professionalism. Let the controllers inspect you. The department laboratory will be challenged by defense lawyers for personal association with the investigators, agency bias, along with the process, equipment maintenance, etc. etc. The prosecutor will demand proof of educational foundations, clean university degrees, and certifications and assurances of specific experience of the examiner's qualifications before confidence is achieved. Most of all they want an examiner to be able to testify to a jury in a manner that will be understood, in English. This is an area where political correctness has no place.

Laboratories require highly qualified professionals, each personally trained and certified to conduct forensic examinations. This is a long and expensive process. Inspections that review quality of equipment, procedures, independent sampling of tests, and examination to validate the laboratory findings are among the things that must done, routinely and within acceptable periods.

Medical Examiner's Office (ME)

For cases involving murder, some serious-injury cases, suicides, unattended deaths, and examination of found body parts or suspected human remains we have the ME system. Coroner and medical examiner offices run the gamut from the local undertaker to complete organizations with medical staffs, equipment, facilities, and laboratories. Whatever the situation is within your jurisdiction, you should establish a working relationship and major-case agreement. If you work in a jurisdiction without professional medical examiners, your agency should have a political goal, expressed through your controllers, to see one created.

There should be agreement between the police and medical examiner on:

1. Call status and availability of medical examiner personnel.
2. Autopsy agreements, including which forensic pathologist will perform the autopsy and testify in court. Major cases should not be the training ground for pathologists; hospitals provide that in noninvestigative deaths. Avoid, if possible, hospital pathologists without medicolegal training in forensic pathology. Pathologists must testify in and should have a good command of the English language. This is not a negative point of view concerning the numerous foreign doctors in the field, just practical common sense. Juries need to understand the testimony, clearly and with precise presentations of facts as to the cause of death.
3. What information should the news media be able to get, and by whom? Medical examiners may release the cause of death in a statement with very few details, identifying whether the case is a homicide, suicide, or natural death. **Unknown causes must always be reported as "still under investigation or review" without further explanation.** There should be no speculation, opinion, or preliminary "guesses" by either the police or the medical examiner about

the cause of death, nature of wounds, or condition of the body prior to the autopsy, especially if another field of examination like toxicology, anthropology, or the like is not yet completed. Inform the medical examiners that the press will question them about case matters in order to get the police to open up with confirmations, denials, or obstructive answers. Examiners should not let themselves be used by an aggressive press; tell them that investigative keys have not yet been decided upon and revealing information will damage the case, maybe irretrievably.

4. Immediate and timely reports to the police on the autopsy findings and conclusions. The verbal report should come as soon as possible; record it, or at least carefully note it for the record.

5. Preliminary findings resulting from the medical examiner's examination of the body at the crime scene. The medical examiner reports these to the case manager, who notes or records the findings, then immediately reports and copies them to the investigation supervisor, who reviews them for any further investigative actions and files them in the case folder. Index all and provide a case reference number for the location.

6. Laboratory findings. Report these findings to the designated investigation supervisor as soon as confirmed (the agreement should identify this procedure; the case coordinator will ensure he or she is the contact with the laboratory); and do it by direct contact. Index and file laboratory findings in the same folder with the medical examiner's report. Review, copy, certify, and sign the reports and inform the case investigator.

7. Arrange oral reports and how they will be followed up in writing to fit the circumstances. Prioritize major-case medical lab tests and examination reports, with a copy of the list sent to the prosecutor. If the final body examination report will be delayed, the examining physician's protocol notations should be made available to the police.

8. Property control. This should eliminate confusion over who retains the property of the victim. In murder cases, the police control the property since it may be evidence or provide investigative leads. Exchange inventories of property and receipts. The police will cooperate with the medical examiner with this evidence; some of it may be helpful to the ME for his or her needs, but the police retain control. Any possession by the medical examiner is temporary.

9. Notice to a victim's relatives is the responsibility of the police for investigative purposes. Inform medical examiners why they should not contact anyone for notice purposes. Get it in the agreement and hold them to that rule. The purpose, of course, is to have that handled

in person by an investigator with the ability to observe the person, question, and look around the location.

10. Responsibilities for the investigation. The police will investigate the crime and the medical examiner will determine the cause of death. If coroner's inquests still occur in your jurisdiction, secure an agreement to ensure they are conducted in cooperation with the prosecutor and the police. Independent inquiries by the medical examiner should be discouraged unless they will result in materially furthering the investigation and are conducted with participation and cooperation of the prosecutor, who in turn consults with the police.

Prosecutor's Office

Since the objective of any major-case investigation is to convict the criminal(s), the prosecutor's office is as critical to the investigation as the police.

Agreements between police departments and prosecutors offices should:

1. Provide a duty or call list of available prosecutors who will respond to certain major cases, such as murder. They recognize the value of personal observation and the value of supporting the police with direct participation. Prosecutors who are dedicated to their tasks will try to have an attorney respond. Further note that in proactive cases, make agreements to prosecute before the investigation begins; police priorities may not be in tune with the prosecutor's priorities. They may be a little reluctant to prosecute some proactive major cases due to the personnel time drain. Jurisdiction of the case prosecution is part of the case selection and decision process. Many proactive cases have the luxury of jurisdiction selection; use it to keep away from the "political" and contentious prosecutors. That is particularly easy for federal and state investigative bodies. Local agencies may use it to advantage with contentious prosecutors in some reactive cases if there is an out-of-jurisdiction connection. Call the state police or state investigative agency; they may have a solution.

2. Agree that the assigned attorney will respond as quickly as possible, even if it means leaving the Saturday night country club party. At the crime scene, the prosecutor will:
   a. Give legal advice on evidence.
   b. Assist in preparing any legal papers.
   c. Provide legal advice on custodial interviews or other legal matters, factoring in the situational facts and information available.
   d. Observe the crime scene to assist themselves in trial preparations at a later date.

Prosecutors must remember they are there to assist and to protect the prosecutor's legitimate interests, not to run the investigation. (There are some jurisdictions where prosecutors' investigators do assume a case investigation responsibility, but these are rare and usually the result of inadequate police investigative capabilities discovered in prior events in that jurisdiction.) The "do not try to run the case" agreement does not stop some of the personalities those lawyer jobs seem to produce. If you find yourself in an irreconcilable situation, just do not call them until later. The detective commander or top supervisor on scene makes that contact; put it on a speakerphone for the enjoyment of your case supervisor who will be present, but always work toward an agreement. The vast majority of prosecutors are great people to have around, really, but a few are first-class irritants.

3. Provide a mechanism to routinely advise the police administrators and all sworn personnel of recent court opinions, and in some cases law changes, affecting police investigative techniques. In some of our larger states, the state police routinely provide this service to their personnel and, without charge, to all participating local agencies. These are "read and initial documents" for all personnel sent by official communication terminal messages or e-mails.

The police should develop a system to have officers routinely advise police administrators of the prosecutor's performance at trial, case preparation, and case filings/charging. The police administrators should then provide the prosecutor's office, in routine private discussions, of individual prosecutor performance and written notices of any internal police evidence or crime scene procedural changes. This *should be done* on an agreed format with criteria to avoid personality clashes. The prosecutors, in turn, *should be asked* to reciprocate regarding trial, investigation and case preparation abilities, and faults of the case officers. This corrects matters that need to be corrected and may control a cancer before it causes damage.

Press Officer (Public Information Officer)

One of the most difficult areas of major-case management is often the manner in which you handle the news media. The instincts of all professional police officers run against discussing law enforcement investigations with the media. This is a very proper attitude and does not stem from any nefarious motives or schemes to hide corruption or incompetence. Professional police officers believe in their responsibility and duty to conduct investigations free from a circus atmosphere. Recognition of the right to privacy of the victim and witnesses is a virtue, and a more important public relations issue than any temporary and fleeting relationship with the media. Certainly, a criminal defendant has a right to a fair trial that takes place in a courtroom, not in the press. The media tend to get hysterical when they feel their "right" to gather and sell news is endangered. On occasion, the media should be reminded that they are not the guardians of civil liberty; the courts are. (Although the press has achieved some notable victories in this arena, for which we must applaud them.)

Let us place this issue in its proper perspective. First, there is no legal right of the public or media to know anything about or of an active police criminal investigation. Even the most liberal of "public records" or "freedom of information" laws concede this point. There is certainly no constitutional right of the public or press that the police must furnish information about an active police investigation. Second, the media are not restricted to the rigid rules of evidence or search-and-seizure procedures as are the police. The information the media publish, and the manner in which it is presented, is often prejudicial. Opinion, speculation, and theories about crime investigations make interesting reading, but their revelation is not conducive to good investigative techniques. The press track record in considering these matters prior to publication has not been a good one. The tragic part of this problem is that some of the prejudicial information, abuses of privacy, damage to innocent reputations, misinformation, and speculation we so often read or see in the media come from the police themselves.

Yet we must recognize that the press can have a very positive impact on police operations. The public should know what their police are doing and the manner in which they perform. The police should cooperate with the press and inform them of selective and limited factual information concerning criminal cases. If this is not done, the press has shown a tendency to speculate or conduct a separate investigation and further complicate an already muddy problem. Actually, that is a total lack of responsibility and professionalism on the part of the media. You could tell them that, but a very high percentage of them would not understand, and if one of those nonunderstanding ones should rise above the rest and get it, he or she would not care.

When a major crime is committed, the news media may be furnished with some basic information. Evidence that, if disclosed, would harm or hinder the investigation must not be revealed. Items that, if disclosed, would reveal interrogation keys must be jealously guarded. **Do not identify witnesses or suspects not charged.** (See Appendix C for suggested press guidelines.)

Establish clear internal controls and guidelines for the handling and dissemination of information. Designate responsibilities and implement controls for press contacts via the public information officer.

Police agencies should:

1. Designate who in the department may release criminal-case information. Identify a spokesperson as the media point of contact. Strongly discourage the media from developing their own sources (snitches) within the department. The public information officer can often act as a buffer between the press and the investigators. This will relieve a lot of pressure and leave the investigators with "deniability" for printed errors or press "misquotes" at trial time.
2. Develop a comprehensive set of guidelines on what information may be released, and implement firm rules on what information may not be released. The rule must be written as a department order with "will not" or "is prohibited," not with "may not" or "should not" or "can," which are passive suggestions, as are those that appear frequently in this book. Write your orders as though they were statutes. Write your rules as though they were statutes. Write your regulations with a little flexibility as though they were guidelines, and leave room for judgment. Write your agreements and memorandums of understanding as a synopsis of recollection of the matters discussed. And, as an aside, get your "understandings" delivered to the other person before he gets his to you.
3. Develop a written policy on information releases that encompasses all personnel within the department, nonsworn support and sworn officers.

   Once a public information officer is designated and the rules established, use him, and have procedures that will involve him at the beginning of a major case. These procedures should:
   a. Provide for press officer notification and guidelines on his response to the crime scene or other point of contact—preferably to the crime scene, where he will assist in keeping the press off the back of the investigators, which by the way, precludes on-scene investigators or crime scene personnel from talking to the press.
   b. Establish media notification procedures. Try to delay that as late into the response phase as possible to give the investigators a reasonable head start.

I know of one triple-murder investigation, assassination style, hands tied and shots in the back of heads, where the state police managed to keep the killings a law enforcement secret for almost a day and a half. A leak from another agency alerted the press; they freaked out and did not calm down until later, and then only after learning the killers' vehicle was under police surveillance in a neighboring state. As it turned out, the murderers were arrested while getting into their vehicle hours after the press, radio, and television stations were going ballistic with the news. The killers, it seems, did not read papers, watch TV, or listen to radio news.

I would note the state police agency in that case made no effort to appease the press; in fact, they condemned them face-to-face, one-on-one, one at a time, and without reporting that to the media at large. They took the public/media "heat" for the news delay without further comment. When asked, they responded, "Sorry, we do not comment on how we conduct criminal investigations." Turned out they were right not to explain themselves; from the letters and comments submitted by the public, it was clear they fully understood and agreed with the police.

4. Establish procedures to deal with the media when they arrive at a crime scene.
   a. Keep them separate and away from the immediate scene and away from any command or control post.
   b. Keep them away from where they can overhear any investigative conversation or capture video of the detailed process. Large tents or shelters can help limit press aircraft video recording. The orderly collection process sometimes appears to be the opposite to an uninformed prospective juror. Remember, juries are TV *CSI* trained.

Press officers should be shielded or prevented from learning too many details of the case. If possible, they should have only information that may be released. Press officers should understand the reason for this: leaks cannot be attributed to them; they can be truthful and maintain their credibility with the press. In this case, a certain degree of ignorance is bliss.

Summary

The principal entities and their general functions and suggested procedural guidelines have been identified. Next, we move on to the actual criminal investigation. As we "run through" a case, discussing the roles of the principal entities in the investigation, further support for the preparatory system will emerge.

First, a slight side issue. I am moving it off the main message because it develops fundamentals we must keep in mind during our focus on the specifics of case managing and the new arena in which we now find ourselves working, which presents a new problem. Since the new issue, terrorism, is beyond the scope of this book but directly related, it must therefore be considered if you intend to build or renew your existing information system. For views of the information and intelligence arguments currently in Congress, consult the Congressional Research Report (CRS) titled *Fusion Centers: Issues and Options for Congress.* Read it at your leisure; I do not wish to interrupt your train of thought at this point in the book. It can be obtained online. Some discussion appears later.

Fusion Centers have been introduced into our lives, the direct result of the terrorist attack of September 11, 2001. At this writing there are 58 such centers, with more planned and others under construction. The Fusion Centers are developing a path or route for intelligence sharing among federal agencies, through the FBI, states, state police or other designated agencies, and a few local police departments. When the bugs are worked out, newer computers and programs will speed up the old process. **We must think of major-case controls with these centers in mind.**

Communication intercept rules require continuous updating to suit modern technology capability. It is reaching the point where all conversations "travel" through dedicated wireless communication transfer equipment (satellite, microwave, cell phone, etc.). Individual phone calls transferred via wire were easily separated from the batches of calls. Nowadays, calls are not only bundled, they are packeted, and only reseparated and singled out at the receiving equipment. It is becoming very difficult not to capture all or most calls made while looking for one single caller. In addition, technology allows one terrorist to call one or more persons via throwaway phone cards, throwaway phones, and varied e-mails from numerous addresses from one or more computers. Sometimes I wonder if the drug rings hold classes for Islamic terrorist cells as they do for the Revolutionary Armed Forces of Colombia (FARC). The laws and courts need to recognize more latitude with minimization, sorting times, retention until checked capabilities, but most of all speed and procedural ease, not requirements, of obtaining warrants, even if temporary until made permanent. The process of obtaining a warrant with a recorded phone call to a judge followed by e-mail confirmation is easily captured, reduced to writing, and then entered into the case and court files.

The Patriot Act has made giant strides toward clearing the way for these capabilities. What many of our political leaders do not understand—wait, they do understand but failed to inform the public at large—is that a great portion of the act that increased *federal* intercept and business records' availability merely reinstated to them what state law enforcement already had, legal methods to obtain much of the aforementioned without warrants. In the late 1970s, Congress, through the Foreign Intelligence Security Act (FISA), restricted the FBI from easy access to such material. Further, the intelligence "wall" between the FBI and CIA (famously presented to the public by the 911 Commission) also came into existence, by federal law.

If your state rules are more restrictive than the new federal rules, attempt, again through your controllers, to bring your state's restrictions into line. Then, when new methods are developed by the terrorist groups to evade, hide, or substitute methods of information exchange, include a rapid mechanism to be able to legally get on to that new method. **One big improvement would be to allow the intercept of all communications** *of a person or entity,* **regardless of the method of communication or location of the phone or communication device, or access to the phone or device by other persons not included in the warrant.** In addition, more leeway is needed for code and encrypted communications, **all with enhanced privacy control procedures and unlawful-disclosure penalties.**

We must keep integration of information with this new sharing tool in mind with any changes to our record system. We will talk about this later in this book.

We are continuing the development of a major-case system now. The prior chapters have set the stage to enforce your thinking and continued consideration of the system you currently have, with the added scope of subject matter when changing or improving your particular major-case control. We will present the structure carefully and within constitutional and statutory parameters. A specific methodology will be the department's choice. Efficiency, scope, integrations, and step-by-step process development will be controlled by the department. Available development resources will determine the value returns.

The Response

4

Before discussing the response phase, I would like to introduce a method of emphasizing the case coordination reasoning. Making a point by examples of case problems will help validate a system of coordinating and managing major criminal investigations. The telling of "war stories" or personal anecdotes is one method, but that will not be used here. Stories and anecdotes are often inadequate to make certain points and always lack sufficient background information to make competent judgments about them. A second method of using examples is to identify well-researched and widely circulated publications that provide sufficient information about major-case problems. This is one of the methods that will be used in this text. Examples will help relate understandable situations to the proposed major-case management system.

There are two dates in the annals of U.S. law enforcement history on which crimes of such magnitude and notoriety were committed that critiques of the investigations still occasionally flare up. They are:

- November 22, 1963, at Dealey Plaza
- August 9, 1969, at 10050 Cielo Drive

The assassination of John F. Kennedy in Dallas, Texas, and the "Manson murders" in Los Angeles will be long remembered.

Two books were published that are excellent for their information; in addition, they are well written and easy to read. I use them **because they are outdated** and all the "old wounds" are either healed or buried. Further, many of the same problems still exist in too many agencies.

Helter Skelter: The True Story of the Manson Murders, written by Vincent Bugliosi (the prosecutor of the Tate-LaBianca trials) with Curt Gentry (W. W. Norton & Company), and *The Day Kennedy Was Shot,* an uncensored, minute-by-minute account of November 22, 1963, written by Jim Bishop (Funk & Wagnalls), are both recommended reading for police commanders, supervisors, and investigators. (The Warren Commission Report also has some useful information.) These books should be read not just for their information value or to rehash the criticisms, failures, successes, or commendable actions of the Dallas and Los Angeles police. Read these books from a management perspective. Focus your attention on the case control problems or errors, and visualize what rule, procedure, supervisory review, or organizational change would have prevented or minimized the problems. We can see the value of strong systematized case control by identifying the case management problems of the Dallas and Los Angeles police. You can then develop procedures within your agency to avoid similar problems.

We are not picking on the Dallas or Los Angeles police. Both are fine organizations and, frankly, few police organizations in the United States could withstand such intensive case reviews without similar criticisms. In fact, it should be noted that Lee Harvey Oswald was arrested 80 minutes after he assassinated President Kennedy. That is not a bad piece of work. Moreover, members of the "Manson Family" of killers are still (as of 2010) in California prisons.

Duties of Responding Units

The normal beginning of a major case is the phone call reporting the event to the police. We hope the forces of the police are unleashed in an orderly and previously planned manner for the investigation. We know the patrol will not be buck naked at a local swimming hole taking a quick, cooling dip, or that the sergeant is not sleeping in the back row of an X-rated drive-in theater. Certainly the detectives are not playing gin rummy in the back booth of Charlie Bookmaker saloon. Those things cannot happen; we have supervision, with rules and procedures!

The Dispatcher

Initiate patrols.
Broadcast.
Log.
Notify.
Control information flow.

The routines in the radio control room ensure that the dispatcher records the time, date, who called, the number called from; notates the information reported; and issues instructions to the caller.

The dispatcher also, as preplanned, is expected to:

1. Dispatch patrol.
2. Notify the supervisor or commander on verification of a major case.
3. Notify the investigator on call after confirmation.
4. Receive patrol reports.
5. Broadcast a radio notice (alarm) even with only limited information.

6. Account for all other patrol units within the vicinity and log where they were and what they were doing.

During the initial phase of a major case, the dispatcher is the information flow control point. Is your agency system prepared to start feeding all data on request or as preplanned, and do you have adequate logs to precisely account for all information? Do your plans or systems ensure that a separate major-case log notes information, assignments, NCIC checks, license data, record checks, name checks, and information requests? Alternatively, is this information at least separated or check-marked to differentiate it from routine traffic, all to be recaptured later and forwarded to the case manager? The Los Angeles police thought so, but there is still some confusion as to what happened to the original calls on the Manson case.* Strong evidence indicates that the first of three calls to the police were made at 8:33 a.m. The LAPD recorded one call at 9:14 a.m., a forty-one-minute discrepancy. Further complications arose *at the trial*. When you consider the following sequence of events, note the time discrepancies:

8:33 a.m.	The testimony reported that the first call to the LAPD was made at this time.
? a.m.	This is the second call to the LAPD.
? a.m.	This is the third call to the LAPD.
9:14 a.m.	LAPD records show that the first unit was dispatched at this time.
9:05 a.m.	The first officer on scene testified that he arrived at this time.
9:15 to 9:25 a.m.	The second officer on scene testified that he arrived at this time.
8:40 a.m.	The third officer on scene testified that he arrived at this time.[†]

There was an obvious problem. Is your system adequate? Would your department's case review and control system catch these discrepancies at the initial reporting or at the trial, as in Los Angeles? The trial prosecutor has now been confronted with the seed of doubt about the credibility and competence of the police officers. This is a deadly seed at a trial and can grow into a jury virus.

It is clear that the start of the "Manson case" problem was the start of the case itself. Police agencies do not have people sitting around waiting for something to happen—no squads of people, no one sleeping upstairs, washing or polishing equipment, or playing cards. Officers are all engaged in

---

* Vincent Bugliosi with Curt Gentry, *Helter Skelter* (New York: Bantam, 1995), 11, 12.
† *Ibid.*, 14, 20, 21.

other work. The disengagement and rapid reassignment of resources is the "routine" start of most major reactive cases.

This is why we have systems, as routine, that permanently capture information in a format for retention and distribution in the correct place. The old use of sticky notes or plain paper notes morphed into formatted event or complaint pads, then serialization and better designs to assist and continue as part of an officer's report. This, by the end of the officer's shift, was routed to the supervisor, case file, records section, or a case investigator for open files.

Today, computer-forced forms for data collection are available and in use in many places. This is also the data entry point for the start of major cases as well as the routine work. Collection of this initial information is a forced format, which starts the original flow into the major-case "funnel," where it all comes out in the major-case folder controlled by the case supervisor. The system continues to collect everything from every person involved, which may be numerous and scattered from many sources. They are connected like a spider web, with a case manager at the center, aided by the index and case manager-controlled flag system, available to all in the spider's net. The case manager is the spider and the index his web. The department supervision apparatus is connected to all.

Uniform Patrols

Get there.

Control and preserve. Our well-prepared and trained officers arrive and immediately set their critical observations, questions, and separations into operation. You know the drill; in a murder case it is the "person who found the body" routines that are so critical to the investigation that are initiated, along with the myriad of all other matters that require attention. The immediate observations set the officers' priorities according to their experience and training. The Investigation is under way.

Broadcast.

Call for assistance.

Accurately record.

Inform detectives.

Be alert.

The key to success in many major crimes often lies in the action the responding units take in the first few minutes. The uniform officers must make multiple and rapid decisions as they proceed to the crime scene and again when they arrive. In addition, the actions taken by nonresponding units may be critical. Of course, the type of crime determines the response. If a murder victim is found in a vacant lot decomposing, there is not much to get excited about during the response. However, if the call is, "Shots fired, officer down, two males fleeing on foot in different directions," the response is decidedly different.

The decisions made during the response to a crime must be correct or at least not wrong.

Usually there is a maximum of two officers for the initial response (unless the criminal is still present). The crime problem is quickly identified and sized up. The officers secure the scene and detain all persons present, take care of any injured, and quickly determine resources immediately needed to assist in crime scene security and witness control. The officer(s) must then call for that assistance and broadcast any information regarding the criminal and escape method.

Street supervisors decide which preplan is implemented. Their training, their experience, and ultimately their best judgment determine the choice. They may decide to flood the area with roving patrols, trying to "force a break" to cause a reaction that will identify the criminal(s). Supervisors may want certain area nonresponding patrols to cover likely escape routes and stop and check logical suspect vehicles, or just surveil traffic and record license numbers. They may order all or none of the aforementioned.

In Dallas, Texas, after shooting President Kennedy, Lee Harvey Oswald left the Texas School Book Depository. He walked away from the crime scene for four blocks; boarded a bus, which retraced part of his walking route, then turned and carried him an additional two blocks. Oswald got off, walked another block and a half, and entered a taxi. He rode to a point near his city rooming house. He changed clothes, picked up a handgun, and left the rooming house, walking. Officer J. D. Tippit of the Dallas Police Department was performing his assignment, patrolling his assigned sector. He was prodding and trying to force a break. Tippit came upon Lee Harvey Oswald. The patrol intimidation worked, but, sadly, Oswald shot Officer Tippit to death. The "second response" by the Dallas PD resulted in Oswald's arrest shortly thereafter.[*] The Dallas police used a closing ring of patrol cars to squeeze Oswald loose. It worked, but it cost J. D. Tippit his life; as we all know, this seems to "go with the territory" in our business.

The Dallas Police organization had a patrol response system that provided for a strong and visible police presence and applied pressure that resulted in "forcing a break." Oswald panicked; he was captured.

Patrol response plans should include a time limit during which the first arriving unit is required to broadcast, or call in, information to the dispatcher. If the patrol unit does not call in within that time, the dispatcher

---

[*] *Report of the President's Commission on the Assassination of President Kennedy.* (Washington, DC: U.S. Government Printing Office, 1964), 20.

must contact the unit by any means available. Decisions and actions are delayed without information. Make every effort to obtain it.

Preliminary interviews, controlling, and sorting out witnesses are started by the uniform patrol. The names and information collected must be in writing and turned over to the detectives in the department format. Even if the original information is passed on orally, follow up with the written report in department format for indexing and review.

Additionally, the dispatcher alerts non-crime scene patrols with available information pertinent to identifying and locating the criminal(s). The patrols need only information to which they may react; insignificant details are not necessary. Log this information and all additional information as it becomes available; it should be broadcast to the patrols. If a change of shift is occurring, the preplan system should keep the information alive on the street. This activity is part of the timeline.

Police units not assigned to the crime scene must stay away unless they are called for a specific assignment. These units should be keeping the pressure on the streets, trying to "force a break," or on other assignments. Some departments violate this rule so often that it seems the last car to arrive at the scene is assigned to get the pizza and cold drinks for the gathering.

The key to this problem and many others is the first-line supervision. Major-crime response should automatically include a supervisor. The more serious the crime, the greater the supervisory responsibility; and, appropriately, higher levels of supervisory response are in order.

Supervisors ensure that the department's procedures and orders are carried out. The duty supervisor directs the patrol response as well as the crime scene supervision at this point of the investigation.

What is the uniform supervisor doing during the response phase? He or she is implementing the department's prepared plans. The supervisor will:

1. Use his or her judgment for use of area patrols, deciding their best value.
2. Ensure that all patrols and other agencies receive all pertinent information.
3. Implement crowd and/or press control measures.
4. Identify and gather needed additional resources. For example, officers may be needed for an area search on foot or a crime scene search.
5. Establish control of the investigation until relieved by higher-level supervision. This may entail implementing area grid or circle searches or motor patrol searches. If a search is implemented, it must be systematic, with direct assignments and instructions to the officers involved. The assignments and instructions are reported on the department format for timeline, indexing, follow-ups, and review. Some supervisors carry tape recorders for the later paper records.

According to Jim Bishop, officers of the Dallas Police Department, including a sergeant, converged on the Texas School Book Depository immediately after the shots were fired at President Kennedy. Yet Oswald was observed by an officer and allowed to leave. Other persons were milling in the area. The building was not sealed or guarded for at least seven to eight minutes, until Inspector Sawyer arrived and ordered that no one be allowed to leave.* This, regardless of the pressure of the event, was a supervisory lapse.

Keep written notes of all assignments and instructions. Ensure that all officers involved in the investigation start feeding back information followed by written reports to the supervisor.

This is the realistic beginning of the case information flow. Capturing as much information as you can during the initial response is a wonderful idea, and on occasion produces much of value. **However, prioritizing, fully and accurately identifying the issue, and securing what is left to secure is the primary action.** The uniform supervisor is responsible for seeing that all information obtained and all assignments made reach the proper parties to the investigation. All of these actions must be documented in the department's format. For example, if a patrol is told to physically search an area for evidence, such as a weapon, crime proceeds, discarded clothing or masks, etc., a report should be submitted indicating who searched what or where the search covered, the time, what was found, and the disposition of any item(s). This could trigger a "secondary" crime scene. Other information, such as persons encountered, license numbers of parked vehicles, the point of crime location, circular search for the probably abandoned escape vehicle extended outward to the point of the supervisor's judgment, etc., should be included. Submitting this information on matchbook covers or laundry lists is to be strongly discouraged. Preprinted formatted paper is required; filling out a lead sheet is the simple method. This improves the index and review and is the accountability tool to ensure you get it all, or at least as much as you can.

Some officers may be assigned to visit and check open business establishments (bars, laundromats, service stations, etc.). They must include in their written report the names of persons encountered, the time, descriptions if pertinent to the case, and any other information obtained.

The uniform supervisor is responsible for seeing that the proper crime response is made, controlling the activities until relieved, and ensuring that all actions and information are promptly passed on to the investigators orally and then followed up on in writing.

---

* *Ibid.*, p. 8.

IACP—Patrol Operations

Proceed to the scene promptly and safely.
Render assistance to the injured.
Effect the arrest of the criminal.
Locate and identify witnesses.
Interview complainant and witnesses.
Maintain the scene and protect the evidence.
Interrogate the suspect.
Note all conditions, events, and remarks.
Arrange for collection of evidence.
Report incident fully and accurately.
Yield responsibility to follow-up team.

Other Agencies

Notify patrol units.
Implement planned agreements.
Submit all information through the prearranged method and format.
    This should include the negative reporting as well. If a patrol did not
    see or notice anything, at least the officer's location(s) and timeline
    must be transmitted to the control agency.
Cooperate.
Do not hold back.

The managing agency's communications personnel alert the other agencies about the major crime. Those are the police organizations working within the same jurisdiction or same geographical area. The planned major-case response agreement should be implemented. Remember, the agreement may run a scale from complete, to specific, to no direct participation, depending on the managing agency's capabilities to investigate the event. The notice alarm goes out to all agencies within the area, regardless of cooperative agreements.

The other agencies' area patrols should implement the prearranged road blocks (if any) and searches (if feasible) and check possible escape routes.

Information obtained that would be of immediate value to the managing agency must be passed to them immediately. Supporting or assisting agencies must submit all information concerning the case without reservation and without holding back any item or lead. Remember the rule: no going off on your own investigation without direct contact with and approval of the managing case agent or supervisor.

Submit all information in writing even if an oral report was made. Submit the information to the controlling agency in the agreed-upon format and to whom the planning agreement states.

This principle ensures that information will get to the intended person. This person is usually the detective supervisor or his or her designated coordinator. **In effect, the information reaches the person who has the responsibility for ensuring that the matter is acted upon and entered into the case index.**

Information may well go astray without a system or agreement about how information is passed to another agency.

Detective Command and Supervisor

The following are the duties of the detective command and supervisor during the response phase:

Implement plan.
Respond.
Fix responsibility.
Coordinate and establish a liaison.

Major criminal case investigation is one of the primary responsibilities of a law enforcement agency. Therefore, police commanders should respond to the scene of major cases to see that the department is meeting its responsibility. Obviously, the size of the agency and nature of the major case determine the level of command response. There is no simple rule of thumb to follow; your agency determines who will respond. In large agencies (over 1,000 personnel), you may limit the response to operational (line) commanders. In small agencies (under 250 personnel), policy makers, chiefs, or sheriffs may wish to respond to major cases. In those medium-size agencies (250–1,000), the response may be a combination of line or policy-making positions.

Murder gets a higher-level command response than robbery cases. One guide should be established that is firm. That is, every investigation designated a "major case," as defined in Chapter 1, should have a commissioned officer respond—a lieutenant or higher rank regardless of whether the officer is a detective or uniform commander.

Command-level response to major cases is for ensuring that:

1. The major-case response plan has been implemented.
2. A supervisor is assigned and responsibility fixed.
3. All activities are working smoothly, in the case-developed order, and systematically.

4. The scope of the case has been determined, all required resources involved are moving fast, and all internal notifications have been made. (This is the time to "kick butt" if needed.)
5. Other commanders within the agency are contacted and produce needed extra resources.
6. Other agency commanders are contacted for coordination of resources, if needed.
7. The coordination and liaison with the following are implemented:
   a. Prosecutor
   b. Medical examiner (if required)
   c. Press officer (if needed)
   d. Laboratory (if needed)
8. The cooperation of other law enforcement agencies is working. In spite of plans and agreements, difficulties often occur at the scene of major cases. This is particularly true where elected police officials' jurisdictions overlap other agencies' jurisdictions. The commander is there to ensure agreements are kept.

History tells us that, regardless of agreements, difficulties will occur. The command at the scene should make immediate efforts to implement the agreements and make a strong effort to cooperate if possible, even agreeing to team up investigators. The rule should be:

Team up rather than fight.
Fight rather than permit two investigations.

If you should be unfortunate enough to reach this sorry state of affairs, inform the prosecutor; he or she may prevail in settling the matter.

Another responsibility of the command-level officer who responds to a major case is to ensure that the major-case investigative team is structured properly. The commander must also ensure that the team is flexible, with one supervisor assigned responsibility to coordinate:

1. Uniform activities
2. Evidence and crime scene control
3. Research and case records
4. Intelligence matters
5. Immediate interviews and statements
6. Lead development
7. Case index
8. Feedback of all information

Commanders must remember that they are there to see that the case is moving according to plan, not to participate in the investigation (unless the size of their agency requires a dual role).

Investigators

Get there.
Secure information.
Inform the supervisor.
Assume control and act.
Listen to instructions.

Investigators must get to the crime scene rapidly, debrief the uniform officers, and inform the detective supervisor accurately of the scope of the investigative problem, the current situation, and what efforts are under way. They should also estimate the resource requirements and assume investigative control from the uniform officer(s).

Public Information Officer (PIO)

Respond.
Establish a press center away from the crime scene and command post.
Control the press.

The PIO or the designated person to be the press officer should respond to the crime scene and establish contact with the detective commander. He or she listens to the decisions on how and what information will be released in this particular case. The PIO should establish a media area away from the crime scene and command post, keeping the press outside of the crime scene and case control perimeter. The press should not be able to overhear discussions of the case and, if possible, should be shielded from crime scene activities.

The press officer will not call any media without permission of the detective commander and if possible should wait until the crime scene has been cleared.

The press officer handles all information releases to the media with care not to divulge any information that would be harmful to the case. The PIO controls the press, preventing them from starting their own investigation. The press officer may use delay tactics to hold media representatives at the press gathering point. This keeps the media from bothering the neighbors and the case investigator from having to reinterview the neighbors. In addition, it eases the rereview of TV news report tapes to check them against the case file for contradictions and/or additional information, or to correct or rectify neighbors' "new" statements.

The more planning an agency does, the quicker the response and the sooner the confusion of a major case is clarified and then dealt with. The initial actions are of the knee-jerk variety to the event. The faster the response phase is brought under control and ended, the better the case coordination.

As the case settles into its routine, the case manager is gathering together the information. The reason it all goes so smoothly is the preparation, which resulted in the uniform officer and investigators arriving with their equipment and formats at hand. They have a form or forms on which to report their activities to the patrol post file, case investigator, and, if a "flag" reports a "hit," that specific case manager's file and the intelligence unit. In addition, the copies of the forms in the patrol book contain the past sixty days' activities , the same forms that are used for any major case. You immediately recognize the advantage to having that information; it saves hours if not days of back-checking. We will be discussing this in the Index chapter (Chapter 15) in detail. After its sixty-day retention period, the patrol post file goes into the trash bin, where it cascades to its demise.

The stop-and-check activities of any police department can, at times, be controversial. The legal issues surrounding "stop and frisk" policies along with the "stop and ask questions" problems resolve themselves with the "reasonable and articulable suspicion" and "probable cause" rules. Where appropriate, common sense and reasonableness are used when a straightforward police "stop and request information" issue presents itself, which, of course, may escalate to "frisk and grab." The public relations issues of confidence in the police and suspected racial harassment remain. I suggest you resolve those head-on with the specifically concerned community. Deal with the neighborhood leaders, clerics, and political people. Inform them of your policies and reasons. They are for that community's protection.

It is good manners to be polite when you ask, "Excuse me, sir, I've noticed you driving in a high-crime area and wonder if you have seen any suspicious ...," or "Sir, I see you live a few blocks away, ... as you know we are having problems... ." On the other hand, "I wonder if you can help me and the neighbors ..." or "Sir, I'm looking for ... (person, place, or thing), can you help me?" Ever since the television and movie "police officer" actors turned nasty, we have a problem training our new officers. We have to tell them that they do not start a conversation with, "Hit the concrete, scum bag" (TV) or "Assume the position, shithead" (movie). Alienation does not recommend itself to good practice and sometimes results in a few bruises and wounded egos. Courtesy, even at an arrest, has a place in human discourse that can be nothing but positive in its results. I know that sometimes that can be really difficult under some despicable circumstances, but it is the professional way. Sometimes courtesy can be difficult for the detainee, since it is unexpected and a experience he has rarely encountered.

In reality, we are engaging in the same method of conversation as the violent-felony squad looking for someone in a tough neighborhood, with warrant in pocket. Everyone knows that routine; nobody knows your man. Get the person who is as close to resembling Danny De Vito as you can. Put horn rim glasses on him and send him "in" alone asking, "Excuse me, sir, I'm from the lottery commission and we owe Mr. Jerk a check (showing an envelope stamped 'unknown at address') and it keeps coming back address unknown …,"etc. You get to wait and arrest your violent felon at his annual bowling tournament after you sit behind him for a while, making him nervous, watching, until midgame. (There are two men out there who, if they read this, will laugh until they cry, knowing that full story.) We do have some good days.

Your patrol post file will carry the record of all post activity, whether city, county, or regional. The record will show that stops for "driving while white" are higher than the reverse, black or Latino. The record will also show that stops of whites in black neighborhoods are greater, proportionally, than the stopping of blacks in white neighborhoods, particularly in the poor neighborhoods with rampant drug trade street sales. That, of course, assumes the police are operating and stopping people for professional reasons, not racial. The post book notes all contacts and stops; nonentries are rule violations. Supervisors review all reports, including post activities. Racist patterns will emerge from the total and individual statistics if such things are occurring.

Police departments with good supervision and inspection of internal activities will discover and remove any racist found. They will quietly investigate all such complaints. Racists in police departments are an anathema to the public, destroyers of organizations, and definitely in the wrong line of work. Get rid of them and report that to your controllers, orally (memo to file) or in writing, your choice.

Here is a way to sum up this chapter. Congress, egged on by the media, made a big deal about the army during the Iraq War "not having a plan." Without a plan, the army managed to collect the navy transports and carrier groups, the air force attack wings, one Marine division, and a few army brigades, all surprisingly trained and equipped with the right tools and supplies, and outstanding rcady, willing, and able personnel. Half were assigned to go in through Turkey from the north; that changed after Turkey disallowed a previous agreement to permit the army to cross through Turkish territory, while the navy ships were off the Turkish coast, preparing to disembark one-half of the attack force. The army switched routes and the order of battle overnight, requiring everyone to take the southern Iraq approach, over the one and only usable road. All of you who understand military logistics know that was impossible. Everyone showed up at the right place and time; they proceeded to destroy a larger army in six weeks, stopping and waiting only for gas to show up over the crowded highway. The troops moved too fast to build an additional road, which they were prepared to do. Only one problem that they could not reschedule occurred; the troops assigned to secure Baghdad arrived a week late. The assault troops, necessarily, moved too fast; they held an enemy by the nose while kicking his butt (George would be proud). Reality and priorities rule; the army took the "political hit," listened to the media and congressional opportunists decrying the "looting of a city by its own citizens," very calmly knowing that Congress is overloaded with idiots, which is a kinder definition than the alternative. They did not care about the media, recognizing there is not anything you can do about mere distractions.

All this to have a media report about the "no plan" at all levels. There was one notable but ridiculous question. A correspondent (that is what reporters call themselves overseas) asked of a young Marine lieutenant at the front about to lead a platoon assault, "What is your battle plan?" The lieutenant gave him a strange look and answered, "How in hell do I know … I'll decide when I get to grips after I see what I'm up against." That is the definition of the response phase: be ready to deal with all the unknowns.

The case now moves into the crime scene phase.

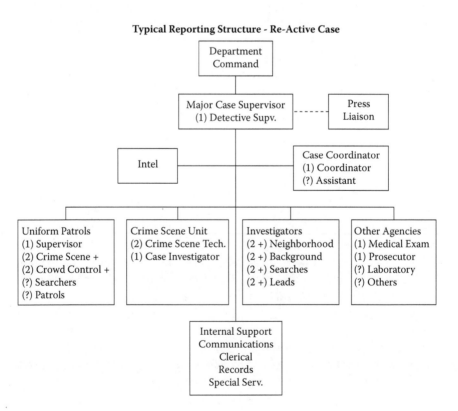

Figure 4.1 Typical reporting structure—reactive.

The Crime Scene

5

There is no precise point in a major case where the response phase ends and the crime scene phase begins. Many activities attributed to particular phases overlap or are conducted simultaneously. I am separating the activities into phases in this book to clarify case control systems. This is not to imply that all investigative activity be slotted into phases, or indeed that the phases themselves must be in order. There are too many exceptions in real life to insist on an investigative order.

For our purposes, the crime scene phase begins when the scene is secured and the examination and processing has started. Let us then review the roles of each principal entity during this phase.

Department Command

Stay out of the way.
Do not run the case.
Settle priority or manpower issues.

Commanders should respond to major cases as often as possible and show interest in the work. They may stand by and look important, but should stay out of the way.

Commanders may:

1. Ensure that responsibility is fixed with the detective supervisor, and let him or her run the case.
2. Listen to reports and suggest to detective commanders any missing or forgotten items.
3. Settle any manpower disputes or priority difficulties.
4. Brief personnel and let the press officer deal with the media.

Commanders should not make any press statements at this time. If they are forced into making a statement by some special circumstance, it should be general and within the established guidelines. Make an absolute rule: no statement that indicates any promises of early solutions or other such nonsense, and no statement that identifies any details of the case other than as appears in the stated sample policy (see Appendix C).

Department commanders must not run the case or get personally involved. It is not their job. When department commanders violate this rule, the results are often disastrous. High-level command involvement causes confusion, delay, and loss of motivation and initiative at operational levels where it is critical.

Most command blunders of the no direct case involvement policy are inadvertent. When commanders order an investigative lead or operational activity, they may only be trying to help, but at that instant, they have just assumed case operational supervision and thus operational responsibility. The problem is compounded if several high level commanders involve themselves. The actual or intended detective supervisor is no longer sure of the case control or of his or her duty or status in the investigation. Please remember that a committee cannot conduct criminal investigations. When this type of leadership failure occurs, matters are often made even worse when, after a few hours, the commanders "walk away" from the case to return to their real duties.

There is a difference between inadvertent meddling and intended interference. In the latter, the department or detective commanders recognize serious case control deficiencies in the case supervision and move to correct them. By doing so, they effectively relieve the supervisor of his or her duties and either replace the supervisor or assume the responsibility with full knowledge and contemplation of their actions. In this instance, roles change but the case "chain of control" remains intact.

Remaining aloof from a major investigation is often difficult for police commanders. Most of us are like old fire horses; when the bell rings, we automatically get into harness and race to the fire. It is natural to want to be involved to "lend our experience," or one of the many other excuses for being caught up in the case. However, the evils of command-level meddling are far greater than momentary personal gratification.

Dispatcher

Control patrols.
Clear radio traffic.
Make notifications as directed.
Log all case information calls.
Do not talk to the press.
Institute record searches as requested.
Feed information to the detectives.
Feed information to the patrols as requested.

All of the aforementioned is captured and reported in the appropriate department format and forwarded to the case manager in the dispatch retention format previously developed to handle both routine and major events. The index is developing as we move along through the case investigation. This is the rule, whether the system is manual or computer generated. This allows the normal department records to remain true to their form while providing the case coordinator and/or manager a copy to enter into the case file, including the case index. Early on in the investigation, the case manager's decision to create an individual case file index will be made. However, the process automatically starts and continues the same route feeding until the decision is made that the independent file **is not needed,** rather than going back and rebuilding the file. Such decisions can change with introduction of new information; it then follows that to have all case index management flows up and running is a lot easier that starting over. If special case management is not needed, all that is lost is the extra copy paper or computer space.

Then, of course, remember that the press and public are listening to radio traffic. Consider getting your radio operations encrypted as soon as possible—particularly if you are located in an area that is subject to a terrorist attack. You need that as a partial defense, to respond to diversionary attacks, and for a host of other reasons. If "they" cannot tell how you are responding, you may gain a slight advantage and limit lives lost by avoiding such things as secondary explosions at the first scene or running into an awaiting ambush.

At some point near the end of the response phase and during the crime scene phase of a major case, the role of the dispatcher changes from "the point of control" (requiring preplanned actions) to a support role of supplying information and providing specific communications upon request for the case investigators. Usually the dispatcher's relative importance to a major case starts to diminish during this phase. There are still certain duties to be performed, and these must be considered in the department's major case control system.

The dispatcher is still the control point for information that flows to all patrol vehicles and some detective units. The dispatcher's duty manuals should address the requirements of logging (the time, name, address, instructions) of major-case communications. The dispatcher should accept and log all communications with special attention to:

1. Criminal-history checks
2. Lists of special files such as wanted, missing, or escaped persons in the crime area, by name and address if the department has that computer capability
3. Roadblock and patrol roll calls for information
4. Other agency assignments and their feedback of information
5. Forwarding patrol assignment lists to the detectives (lead sheets)

Most important is a procedural requirement that all information be documented and forwarded to the detective case manager through the established department system. This is done with lead return sheets, in car computer patrol and detective activity or equivalents from whatever source, sent to or from uniform patrols and detectives and returned to the detective case manager through the one of the established routes. Every lead sheet initiated within the department, including the dispatcher or from any source, has a copy sent to the case manager by the most immediate communication method in a continuous feed.

Many departments are now using off-net communications for detectives and other special units. Before you do that, make sure you put in place a method to capture all the information, orders, leads, and replies that were previously captured by the dispatcher. Further, cell phones create a tendency for officers to bypass the case manager and speak directly with each other. This is permissible for its convenience and time-saving capability, but with a caveat: that case information and actions are recorded and reported in the manner in which you decide. If you are fortunate enough to have a small enough agency where the same team seems to be working together all the time, the recapture task is easier by ensuring you have a very strong supervisor in control

In addition, the dispatcher(s) must be able to secure extra personnel if the case is going to overburden the communication system for more than an hour or two. Consider an indoctrination program, wherein civilian hires come aboard, spend the first week assisting the dispatchers, then traffic, then personnel, etc., before they sit at the place they were hired for. The department then has a ready backup supply of workers available on shift or call back. It is also a great morale booster for the civilians to know what they really do to support the department.

Dispatchers must continue to feed all information to the detective supervisor or his or her designated coordinator and log it. They must make the notifications to the medical examiner, clergy, and prosecutor, as directed by the case supervisor. The major-case radio log should be kept separate, or marked (tagged) if taped, and recaptured from the routine communications recording. Further, if you have sufficient radio channels, one should be designated or cleared for major-case work during the initial rush phases.

As a major case develops, numerous telephone calls from the public or other agencies sometimes occur. Some of these calls are cranks, some frivolous, and some have real information. The responsibility for receiving the calls, logging the calls, taking and passing the information to the case supervisor for decision purposes rests with the communication section.

The department system of information control should stipulate that major-case calls are logged at the normal intake point, documented, and forwarded to the case supervisor. If an officer or civilian employee receives a call from a friend, informant, or any other source, the system should require that information to be accepted, logged, and passed to the case supervisor through a central feed point, usually the communications unit, and then on to the case manager. Failure to have such information control will result in lost information. Having the system will not guarantee that information will not be lost, but it will reduce the chance of loss and provide a method of fixing responsibility if "lost" information later comes to light.

Finally, communications personnel should not be permitted to talk to the press at all; they are too busy. All calls should be referred to a press officer. No "uh-huh" or "nopes;" no talk, no utterances of any kind should be permitted. A simple "I will refer you to the press officer" is sufficient to answer all major-case inquiries. Communications officers must also remember the press and public are listening to their radio broadcasts.

Uniform Patrols

Preserve the scene.

The uniform force preserves the crime scene from contamination until the crime scene unit arrives. The uniform officers then usually provide the resources to keep the scene clear of unauthorized persons. (See Appendix D.) This is a straightforward duty. The Los Angeles Police Department felt their crime scene duties were clearly stated and that their officers were trained. Yet, at the Sharon Tate residence, site of five murders, a pair of horn-rimmed glasses was moved six feet and two pieces of a gun grip were moved from an entryway to a place under a living room chair. In addition, an LAPD officer superimposed his print over any other that may have been there by pushing an electric gate-opening button with clearly visible blood on the button.

Enough said.

Other Agencies

Stay away from the crime scene.
Carry out preplans.
Inform the controlling agency of actions and follow up with a report.
Do not talk to the press.
Cooperate.

Again, we must address the delicate subject of interagency cooperation for those areas of the country where police jurisdiction responsibilities have not been legislatively settled.

During this phase of a major criminal investigation, a supporting or assisting agency should respond to a crime scene only if requested. Discourage officers who go to a crime scene out of curiosity or to "rubber neck;" they are often the source of leaks. The case-controlling agency should be informed of the actions supporting agencies are taking, as agreed. Supporting agencies, when their assistance is requested, should expect to handle the minor case chores, such as traffic or crowd control, supplying resources for searches, etc. They should accept this lesser role without complaint. It is a proper role and not subordinate. From a practical standpoint, the minor roles usually mean you can assist another agency and recover your resources in a hurry—the best of situations.

Supporting or assisting agencies must strictly adhere to the following:

1. Never try to usurp a case.
2. Never try to grab a quick arrest merely to beat another agency.
3. Never ever conduct independent interrogations or interviews unless they come to you inadvertently. Even then, call that along with the circumstances in to the case controller immediately and seek instructions. Investigative actions that occur outside the control agency's knowledge or directions are usually disastrous to the case and interagency cooperation. The instant that such activity takes place there are two investigations of the same matter under way. This of course must not occur.
4. Never talk to the news media about another agency's investigation, even if the supporting agency is a major participant in the investigation. This rule is an absolute. I cannot think of an acceptable exception. The supporting agency should not confirm a press statement or reveal its own activity in the investigation. Media people are experts at dividing and conquering. Many stories are built by picking pieces from different sources. This matter is a serious problem among law enforcement agencies, particularly those that are more political than professional. It should not be so!

Detective Command

Respond.
See that the system is functioning.
Liaise with other agencies.
Take and give suggestions.
Have no personal involvement.

Detective commanders' role is only slightly different from their superior's. They must ensure that their case control system is functioning. Appropriately, the detective commander is the best point of liaison with other agencies or principal entities to ensure smooth interagency coordination. The detective commander has a responsibility to:

1. Brief the department commander(s).
2. Brief the public information officer.
3. Listen to the detective supervisor's reports and suggest actions to correct errors or omissions. The detective commander should not become personally involved in the investigation for the same reasons department commanders should not. If detective commanders must involve themselves in actual investigative actions or controls, I suggest your agency is either not prepared, or designed, or large enough to handle a modern major criminal case with its own resources. Alternatively, the detective commanders have leisure time on their hands and may not be necessary; this does happen in overstaffed departments. And yes, there are overstaffed departments. Sit down and reflectively review the internal productivity standards of your operations to be sure your department is not in that class.

During the crime scene phase, a detective commander should chase stragglers (or officers there only out of curiosity) from the scene or assign them to a unit for some duty. He may wish to keep one as a "go-for" (i.e., go for coffee, runner, etc.).

The detective commander should be prepared to support the investigation with other resources or units if necessary. For example:

1. Aviation units
2. Scuba units
3. Marine units, etc.

Crime Scene Unit

Establish contact with the detective supervisor.
Identify parameters of the crime scene.
Establish the reporting system (chain).
Decide the scene methodology.
Provide preliminary reports.
Show and discuss all evidence.
Log all actions.

The crime scene technicians are either officers or civilian employees acting as a crime scene unit or other agency specialists that arrive to perform what is historically the crime scene function. This consists of the mapping, photographing, searching for, and collecting evidence of the crime at the scene for identification, laboratory examination, and ultimately as evidence that leads to arrest and entry into the court system. The crime scene unit should be a well-trained and experienced unit dedicated to the job of handling a crime scene. Units so dedicated have their system of searching, collecting, and presenting evidence—all of which should have been worked out in precase agreements with investigators, laboratories, and prosecutors.

The main effort of the crime scene unit is, of course, to maintain the integrity of their work and to coordinate their findings with the investigators.

Crime scene units:

1. Establish contact with the detective in charge.
2. Receive a briefing of available information and find out the parameters of the immediate crime scene and any other area identified as connected to the crime. Accept the direction of the detectives in this matter and record the instructions issued for future reference.
3. Identify the case reporting system, including to whom the crime scene unit will report immediate findings.
4. Identify the case investigator who is assigned to the crime scene unit, coordinate the plans for a method of attack of the crime scene, agree, and get to work.

   I recommend that case investigators be assigned to the crime scene unit while they perform field work on a major criminal case. This can be the vital link that ensures a complete two-way flow of information and instruction. There has been a tendency for case supervisors or coordinators to check the detail work of crime scene units, but other pressing duties often distract their attention.
5. Work the crime scene methodologically.
6. Report any information to the assigned case investigator or coordinating detective immediately (for leads).
7. Provide preliminary reports to the detective supervisor.
8. Control evidence for packaging and retain it.
9. Make detective supervisors or case agents sign for any evidence they may wish to take control of or remove (after sealing and packaging).
10. Log all actions, steps taken, findings, etc.

The crime scene unit should be equipped and prepared to:

1. Perform all fingerprint duties at the crime scene, including classification and identity matches when necessary (from **Henry Classification** to **AFIS,** to **IAFIS,** to the current department system; if readers are not familiar with the systems, check the Internet under the preceding boldface terms for an explanation).
2. Make all print comparisons and examinations in connection with the case and take all control prints. Provide a list of those immediately to the case supervisor/coordinator; it avoids duplication or missing people who, later, may be difficult to locate.
3. Take photographs of the crime scene, autopsy, and arrest, particularly if the arrest is made immediately. The prisoner in fact becomes a part of the crime scene as far as evidence collection is concerned (clothes, fingernail scrapings, DNA swabs, etc.).
4. Prepare all evidence for laboratory examinations.
5. Report to the investigator/coordinator or supervisor all preliminary results, examinations, or information developed at the crime scene or autopsy in memo or report form. (Oral reports are made as soon as possible.)
6. Arrange for aerial photos, if needed, as soon as possible, usually the first flying day.
7. Provide a minimum of three persons for a crime scene. This would include the case investigator assigned to the crime scene unit.
8. Discuss and show *all* evidence to the assigned case investigator/ supervisor.
9. Mark all areas as "clear" once processing is finished. This permits other investigators greater access and thus a view of the crime scene. Interview teams should be cognizant of the crime scene and evidence gathered as soon as feasible.
10. Have a procedural checklist and identify all persons present. (See Appendix D.)
11. Search the scene thoroughly: floors, walls, ceilings, and furniture. Items in a room should be carefully examined, noted, and photographed.
12. Make sketches and take measurements, etc.
13. **Leave a copy of the inventory with the case supervisor or attending investigator prior to leaving the scene. Account for every item or piece of evidence and its location at this point.**

Crime scene units from two different agencies should not work the same crime scene. Methodologies are different and duplication occurs, or worse, a lapse takes place. It is analogous to permitting two photographers to randomly photograph a crime scene; we all know the evils of that mistake. If help is necessary, the case-controlling agency decides which crime scene unit to use. If a mix of units is unavoidable, the control agency's procedures and orders must be followed, including their forms. This will aid prosecutors in their presentation to a jury. It may avoid having two experts from differing laboratories testify using two different methods and inserting contradictions into the prosecution, before the defense attorney introduces one, two, or more confusions.

Laboratory

Assist as requested with the following:
Experts
Special equipment
Unusual circumstances

Crime laboratories are not usually involved in crime scene work, but there are circumstances or conditions where their assistance may benefit a major case.

Laboratories should be notified of major cases when extraordinary burdens may be placed upon their resources, such as collecting large volumes of evidence for examination, or other unusual circumstances prevail.

Crime laboratories should send competent personnel to a crime scene upon request when:

1. Specialized needs for evidence examination exist, such as when evidence is of such a size it cannot be removed and transported and examination at the crime scene is necessary.
2. A body is to be excavated and extreme care is required to avoid damage or loss of evidence.
3. Special laboratory equipment is available, is needed, and its use is not within the capabilities or expertise of the crime scene unit.
4. Crime scene units require assistance due to their expertise falling short of an acceptable standard in a specific task, the laboratory assistance is requested by the case control agency, and personnel are available.

It is appropriate to mention that you should not feel anger at an organization that says no to your request for assistance. Human nature makes it easy to condemn or fault others for your agency's inadequacies (they exist or you would not call for assistance). Recognize that there will always be times when rejection occurs. Accept the problems and move on to realistic solutions, not condemnations.

Medical Examiner (When Needed)

Pronounce death.
Arrange for body transport.
Prepare the body.
Confer with the detective supervisor.
Arrange for the autopsy.

When a major case involves a death under circumstances suggesting murder, the medical examiner's primary responsibility is to investigate and report the cause of death. This responsibility requires a medical examiner presence at any crime scene with a body.

Medical examiners should:

1. Arrive and pronounce death.
2. Make preliminary examinations of the body after it has been photographed as found and its place marked for measurements and position.
3. Arrange for controlled transportation of the body to a secure place. At this point, the body is evidence, and chain of custody rules prevail over culture, family, or religious customs.
4. Prepare, or assist in preparing, the body for transport—for example, the placing and securing of plastic or paper bags over the hands and head, and seeing that the body is placed in a new cotton or rubber body bag. The CSU should be prepared to perform this task.
5. Ensure that property is accounted for and exchange receipts with the case investigators. The police should retain all property until it is identified and they are satisfied it is not evidence.
6. Report all preliminary findings to the case detective supervisor.
7. Arrange the time and place of autopsy and agree on a pathologist.
8. Confer with the prosecutor at the scene.
9. Ensure that relatives are notified **by the police.** In a murder case, the police should insist on their making the family notifications and then do so promptly with specific instructions to the officer(s) making the contact. The reason is, of course, that the family may be directly involved or be capable of providing investigative information. The police should never pass up an opportunity to view people, note their appearance and reactions, and hear immediate comments (basic criminal investigation 101). Passing items like this off to others indicates a lack of personnel and raises the question of whether

the case itself should be passed up the ladder. Time and distance factor in this decision; if you must pass the notification off to another agency, large and medium metro area departments are usually reliable, and state police are very reliable. State investigative agencies are shy of available personnel for such matters but are very reliable for special notification circumstances. Unless you know that highway patrol departments have been specially trained in these matters, try other methods first and avoid small departments unless you know them well. If you must use an unknown, submit your request with detailed written instructions to them via an e-mail or state communication net. Otherwise, you are depending on luck and hoping the notification will just be another unrelated event, as is normal.

Medical examiners should refrain from discussing the case with non-investigative personnel and particularly the news media. There is no confirmed information a medical examiner can release at a crime scene. In fact, it is usually days before any sensible statement can be made available. The best rule at this point is not to say anything. **Make sure the medical examiner consults with the case manager and the prosecutor's office before any release of any information.**

Prosecutor

Respond.
Check in with the case supervisor with some hot coffee.
Offer legal advice when asked or if he or she notices a legal matter that needs attention.
Observe the crime scene and the evidence.
Watch the evidence handling.

Prosecutors should respond to major-case crime scenes involving murder and other types of cases where significant evidence collection will take place. The attorney assigned should be responsible for the case to its court conclusion, if possible. If this person is not the trial attorney, make sure he is competent at criminal law and of an agreeable and cooperative nature. If he is young and inexperienced, have one of the unnecessary commanders entertain him so he stays out of the way. The prosecutor is responsible for training and exposing his own young staffers to crime scenes; they should come to a crime scene under the tutelage of a senior attorney.

The assigned prosecutor should discuss the case in detail with the detective supervisor and crime scene technicians. Discussion of the case should focus on:

1. The evidentiary points pertaining to the case, stressing the value of negative proofs and making sure every exculpatory fact is included.
2. Legal advice concerning searches, seizures, custodial interviews, and eavesdropping warrants if such are appropriate to the investigation.

   Police officers are often in haste under the pressure of the immediate opportunity to search for or seize material under circumstances that later cause courtroom difficulties. A prosecuting attorney can often assist in identifying legal circumstances, acceptable thresholds of probable cause, and when "legal paper" is needed. A basic assumption is that the assigned attorney is legally enlightened and sufficiently aggressive, not a young, inexperienced lawyer, fearful of being overruled on borderline decisions.

   Prosecutors at the crime scene may also:
3. Observe the crime scene and offer any comments or suggestions to the detective supervisor, particularly about the legal significance of evidence or information and the **absence-of-evidence** issues. This is important and often overlooked early in a case. Certain circumstances often indicate something should naturally follow or be present and is missing. Beware the ides of March.
4. Check all critical interviews and/or statements for completeness, problems, or legal insufficiencies. The sooner errors, omissions, or other problems with statements are cleared up, the better the chances for a strong case.

Public Information Officer (PIO)

Set up the press center.
Debrief the detective commander.
Keep the media from the crime scene.
Limit media contacts to one person (press officer).
Keep information general.

The crime scene duties of the PIO are important, not in the sense of furthering the investigation, but in keeping details within the agency and out of the public arena. The public information officer, or person acting as the media contact, has a critical responsibility to protect the investigation from an aggressive media corps. It has been said that the first casualty of war is truth. The media has a sorry track record for accuracy and objective reporting at sensational events. Speculation and rumor are often printed or broadcast for momentary media satisfaction at the expense of an investigation or a person's privacy or reputation. The press speculation at the Tate killings in Los Angeles's now infamous Manson murders is a story in itself. Many sources led to the speculation, including an LAPD sergeant who made the statement: "It's like a battlefield up there."* Another officer stated: "It looked ritualistic,"† referring to the crime scene. Those statements in themselves are relatively harmless; the problem is what the press turned them into, ritualistic killer cults roaming the area, and worse.

If you need to be convinced of press speculation, go to your library and review the Los Angeles papers for the period after August 9, 1969. Since then, the press has honed the practice into an art, along with TV talk shows that thrive on that theme.

Or ... take another example with a radically different situation, at Attica, New York (September 9–13, 1971), when the New York State Police retook the state prison from the 2,200 convicts in control. Toward the end of the event, a correction department *officer heard that* "some hostages [correction officers] throats were cut;" the press, already in full ballistic mode, went public with that, then speculated and made several incorrect assumptions. They picked up that information from an unauthorized and uninformed source and ran with it without confirmation. (It was unclear whether correction officials repeated that rumor.) They knew there was a New York State Police (NYSP) spokesperson available for inquiries regarding the prison retaking and were instructed to use that person regarding "inside the wall" information. The press erroneously reported that some of the *dead* correction officers had their throats slit—an assumption.

None of the bodies of the ten dead correction officers in the morgue that day revealed any such thing; the *medical examiner reported* that to the press. The media feeding frenzy went out of control with accusations of a state "cover-up" (governor's office, NYSP, and correction department). Logic alone identifies that as ridiculous. Neither the NYSP nor correction department ever made such a statement or claim, but it didn't matter. The NYSP had no evidence any throats were cut on any of those bodies, while the trooper-inflicted shotgun damage to nine of the correction officers was obvious. However, due to the body conditions, they were awaiting cause of death confirmation from the medical examiner, as they do in every case.

To this day, many around the world believe that no throats were cut but that the state attempted to cover up the shootings with a false statement. That belief is factually untrue. The troopers killed twenty-nine prisoners, shot and wounded another eighty or more, and killed nine correction officers dressed

---

* Bugliosi with Gentry, *Helter Skelter*, 11, 12.
† *Ibid.*, 14, 20, 21.

in prison garb who were mixed among the prison inmates, all in the middle of the prison yard.

The facts are that two correctional officers under the control of convicts had their throats slit. They were among the thirteen hostage officers taken up to the roof of a yard cross-tunnel, each with a convict holding a knife at his throat. All were dressed in disarrayed prison garb. When troopers commenced the retaking of the prison, the convicts on that roof started to slice thirteen throats, but they never finished. All thirteen convicts died at that instant, each with a .270 copper jacketed round through their heads and a knife falling out of their hands; they were dead before their bodies hit the roof. Two correction officers survived serious throat cuts, and ten more uninjured correction officers walked safely to the oncoming troopers and were the first of twenty-nine to walk or be carried out of the prison, with a trooper. A ricochet off the yard tunnel roof handrail killed one correction officer. Troopers had two rifle teams on an adjoining cellblock roof, about 100 yards away. The "throat cut" event was separate from the yard event, by time, distance, and context. That incident was video-recorded by the state police.

The "report" started somewhere among the crowd outside the prison where twelve now-free officers were being taken to a hospital for further examination. The two with throat cuts were already stitched up by standby doctors at the temporary aid station set up outside the prison walls. The original "rumor"—it cannot be called a statement—was literally correct but seriously incomplete. In retrospect there was probably no way on earth to prevent such errors under those conditions, but it is a good reminder that the press no longer rates facts or accuracy as the primary requirement before going public; they are in a race to be first to go public. They need to be controlled as best you can; they are irresponsible and do not care. Multimillions of tax dollars were spent by the state commission and two grand juries "investigating" that event over four years—several months on just this one issue.

That is a case where the press disregarded the PIO, who had confirmed correct information. The media chose rumor rather than wait forty-five minutes for that confirmation.

Or … you can wait until there is a major event in your area and watch the media.

Continuing.

At a crime scene, the PIO officer responsible for handling the news media should:

1. Set up a "press" area away from the crime scene, away from any temporary investigation command post, and away from any area where case officers may be overheard.

2. Arrange to be briefed by the detective commander or case supervisor and agree on what information may be released to the media. The PIO may release:
   a. the time the investigation started.
   b. victim identification in death cases if relatives have been notified; then consider keeping the identification from the public for another couple of hours, giving families time to pull their needs together. In "newsworthy" cases, meaning sensational, the press will go park on the family front lawn.
   c. the names of agencies involved in the investigation.
   d. the general nature of the matter under investigation. Do not discuss evidence, wounds, witnesses or their statements, theories, suspects, descriptions of wanted persons at this time as the information is often inaccurate, or any material fact of the case. Do not release the identity of any witnesses, particularly until they have had their statements taken and the detectives have had the opportunity to advise the witnesses that they do not have to talk to the press and suggest that they should not discuss the case with the press.

   The press officer should:
3. Never go "off the record" or provide "background" or make statements "not for attribution."
4. Never permit the media access to the crime scene under any circumstances. Sometimes it is necessary to shut down a street for a relatively short period until it is searched and cleared; use that as the barrier for the media. Never make any promises, deadlines, or suggestions regarding the probabilities of solving the case or implying the rate of progress.

Major criminal investigation news media contacts should be limited to one person, at least until the case settles down, and preferably through the entire case. Other officers and employees should be barred from discussing the investigation with the news media. If actual case workers violate this rule, I recommend their immediate removal from the investigation. Most police agencies prohibit discussion of any matter under investigation with nonauthorized persons, and the news media are not authorized to receive investigative information except as provided by the department control procedures.

Failure to keep investigative information out of the press often results in lost investigative keys, muddied information, and undue public speculation and fear.

There are suggested press guidelines in Appendix C.

The Investigation

6

The crux of the matter is at hand. So far, we have developed a picture of all the principal entities involved in a major-case investigation. We have discussed their roles in the investigation and some of the system requirements needed to make these entities function automatically, but under control, in response to a major reactive case. Now we must manage and coordinate all of the case activities toward the objective, conviction. Remember, everyone wants to help with activity and information, but **the case manager must know who, what, where, when, and how the work is progressing and, more importantly, that the work is under his or her direction.** This requires a control system and a case organization structure.

This is where we now begin to speak of information—its origin, date, time, location of an event or interview, assignment, action, review, retention, indexing, and retrieval, along with flags to notify the case managers of information connections.

This is where we now begin to speak of the case managers' assignment, priorities, investigative acts, and their reporting—lead sheets, indexing, tickler notes, reports due, reports overdue, and how to fix the coffee machine.

While we do this, think of the preparatory issues we have discussed and associate them with timelines, evidentiary rules, evidence and testimony admissibility rules, and how to fit our coordination to reduce the problems inherent in "inevitable discovery." Also, think of matters regarding searches, warranted or nonwarranted, or regarding interviews, when they turn into custodial or remain noncustodial.

We need to know about every event, every item touched, and every person spoken to, in relation to "what did we know and when did we know it?" Think about one detective discovering evidence that would make a different interviewing detective immediately recognize that his interview would be custodial if he were aware of that information, and the ramifications of that. Think about a detective seeing an item, passing it by due to an unrecognized relevance, and later finding out a serious need for that item, now requiring a new warrant for an item already cleared from a previous warrant or gone missing.

We are shutting down defense attorney arguments, cracks in the evidentiary trail, and lost investigative and court time by using "in the course of ordinary business" formats within our system. We are going to win the case on the battlefield and not in a prosecutor's office discussing a peace treaty with the defendant's counsel.

Aw shucks, you say, here comes tedious, detailed form and format building. You are lucking out; I am not going to do that. I cannot; that is the stuff and result of serious think tank sessions, where you build a system suitable to your specific needs. Remember, we spoke of those—where you shout and throw erasers at each other for a couple of days.

Another word about capturing the timeline: **consider a requirement that *every substantive* (nonsubordinate) paragraph in the report start with a lead line reporting the date, time, and location of the contact or interview being reported at that time.** In addition, a name or informant number must identify the source of each piece of information received. Index the informant number or code name and number; it is how that person is referred to in all correspondence, except in his or her locked identity file. Clearly indicate that the person providing the information is speaking from personal knowledge, not hearsay. If it is hearsay, indicate that, then identify its source as best possible. Each person interviewed gets his or her own date, time, and place paragraph(s). Scream if you get "I spoke to Andy, Betty, and Clara and they said… ." That requirement is in addition to any such references to dates, times, or locations within the paragraph as part of the substance of the subject matter event. It eliminates the confusion of "What did you know and when did you know it and exactly who knows?" as opposed to the "who, where, what, when, etc." reported within the overall context of the case investigation. Then consider, on the report form, a "Reported To:" space box, or check box with Date, Time, and method (oral, paper, e-mail)—whatever you use. Part of the accountability items, as well as being useful, are vital regarding exculpatory and custodial issues. This is a formatted interview sheet or return lead sheet.

Let us continue and see who is doing what.

Department Command

Continue to look important, but stay out of the way.

Dispatcher

Perform routine duties.
Be alert for related incidents or information.
Be alert for notices.

Dispatchers normally start a return to their routines by the time a major case reaches the full investigative phase. Dispatchers should continue to maintain an awareness of the case, paying attention to notices or items in other jurisdictions that may be similar or connected to the case in any manner. Supervisors keep this process alive over as many shift changes as they deem necessary. Put it on your "Read, Initial, Time" clipboard at the dispatcher's seat. No dispatcher, or dispatch point, should be unaware of any ongoing major reactive crime or event.

The system (procedures) should provide the mechanics of bringing such dispatcher-obtained information to the attention of the case supervisor in a written format, such as a complaint or lead sheet report. This will be done at the beginning of the case at the first opportunity by the dispatch supervisor after review for completeness and accuracy. The supervisor is responsible for checking each item and ensuring its delivery to the case manager. Thereafter a delivery system is agreed upon and carried out until the case slows down to a point of normal flow. The case manager decides when that occurs.

Uniform Patrols

Do second-day follow-ups.

Obtain field identifications from new witnesses with an immediate oral report followed by lead return sheets.

Perform stop and interviews, by lead sheets or field interview forms.

Do loose surveillance, on lead sheets or department surveillance logs.

Interview informants, on lead sheets by informant number.

Do citizen interviews, on lead sheets.

Feed all information to detectives in the agreed-upon format. We see the "lead sheet" label a lot now; it can be a simple format, but include the return on the lead sheet or have a separate return lead sheet. It is the department's decision and should fit within its regular formats.

The uniform force also starts disengaging resources as the case settles into an investigative routine. However, there are still important functions to be noted. For example, sometimes it is prudent to leave a uniform officer to guard a crime scene after processing is finished to:

1. Maintain control of the site in case reexamination is necessary.
2. Provide security or privacy to a crime victim from curiosity seekers.
3. Guard unprotected premises or property on a temporary basis.

Officers assigned to this duty, depending on the nature of the case, may be either highly visible or concealed. They should be instructed to be alert for persons who may have information or persons without legitimate interest or who reveal an unwarranted curiosity about the crime. Perpetrators have been known to "return to the scene of the crime." Some crime scenes provide targets of opportunity for other criminals. Neighbors often discuss the case more freely in the informal atmosphere that develops after the crime scene processing is finished and could provide information not recalled earlier. The uniform officer must recognize that every "chat" with a neighbor about the case is a reportable event. I suggest you use an experienced officer to separate the chat from information; they recognize negative useful information as well as real facts.

Persons legitimately conducting personal or business affairs in the vicinity can be identified for possible leads or information. Instruct the officer about all the information opportunities available and provide her or him with a means to funnel any information obtained to the detectives. Lead sheets are best used for this report. Further, your experienced officer can recognize what to call in immediately and what can wait until the end of the day. This is where you find that Mr. Chatter tells you he told Joe Bigmouth all about the case since Joe was away when it happened. The index reveals that Joe said to an interview team that he witnessed the crime and elaborated in minute detail. Problem? Not really; it was just resolved or, better, avoided.

Uniform officers should:

1. Be used for second-day and -night follow-ups, with fixed or loose surveillance of the crime scene area.
2. Stop and check travelers, commuters, or regular delivery route persons for information or to find possible witnesses.
3. Submit all field identification reports, or lead sheets, to the detectives through the department system.
4. Stop and interview persons at bars, laundromats, gas stations, and business establishments in the neighborhood. They should prod and push for information, particularly information that became known after the case detectives interviewed these people during the neighborhood sweep. That means these officers should be briefed, advised to be attentive for contradictions and sources of information, and collect and verify new information—all passed on to the case coordinator.
5. Contact and interview their street informants.
6. Perform expanded area searches for weapons, proceeds, etc.

   Remember that the uniform officers are the eyes and ears of the detectives, so a report mechanism is necessary to get their information to the detective in charge of the case, for that matter, any case.

Investigators

Take charge from the uniform force.

Conduct interviews of *all* officers present; inform them their written report is due.

Arrange for witnesses' written statements—immediately or later.

Call for any additional resources.

Start the neighborhood work.

Start the background work.

Start the investigative work.

The Scene Team

The coordinator informs them of the due date of their scene report or memo.

As investigators arrive at a major crime scene to join the team, they will find, because of the response and crime scene procedures of the department, many activities taking place. Investigators know they will be part of the investigative team on the case. Having knowledge of the department case control system, they can move quickly into the coordinated structure of the case. The preplanning, along with a clearly defined chain of command, ensures a rapid and smooth buildup of case resources.

The working case investigation team will develop into a group consisting of:

Detective supervisor (1)

Assistant (if needed) (1)

Case coordinator (1; may be the detective supervisor; judgment prevails)

Crime scene unit (2 or more, maximum of 5)

Investigator (1, with the CSU, plus as needed)

Uniform officers (2 or more, crime scene guards)

Uniform neighborhood search in patrol cars (2, or more if needed)

All other uniform assignments will be directed, such as patrols, roadblocks, crowd control, etc., with the number of officers as needed or available.

Investigative teams form and are placed in action as follows:

Neighborhood interviews (one to four, or more if needed). This can be an area where information slips away. A predetermined plan is best, with assigned routes and scope, getting all persons at each place of interview identified, including persons not present at the time of interview but present when the crime was committed. Lead sheets are immediately prepared as each person or missing person is identified.

Follow-ups will be necessary and obtained as soon as possible; the incomplete lead sheets greatly reduce errors since they are stored with the case coordinator in his or her "to do" or "pending" case file.

Leads/statements (one to four, or more if needed)

Backgrounds/records/intel/analysis (one, or more if needed)

Crime scene/area search teams (four). Use one investigator and three uniform officers for outdoor searches, more if needed. Anymore than four officers requires a search plan and pattern with its appropriate search plan report, sketch, maps, ground markers, stringed plots (as in rural or wilderness searches), or marked aerial photos. In some cases, you might consider calling the waste management company to move all the dumpsters to one parking area for a diving party. After chalking them for original location issues, you know you will find the chalk in your kits since they have been inspected. All as needed, of course.

Indoors, as conditions dictate. In a condominium, you have laundry chutes, elevators and shafts, garbage disposal routes, rooftops, storage areas, bins and closets, to name just 10 percent of the places. Depending on the search, you may require the search team supervisor to report the search, or each individual officer reports his or her search areas and items.

Discretion and judgment are the key. Follow-up searches of the same area depend upon the completeness of and satisfaction with the first search.

Rapid changes of case priorities and availability of resources dictate numerous changes in activity at the outset of major criminal investigations. This is a root cause of coordination problems. Case controller/coordinators must know who is assigned to what activity and its status. They must decide investigative or activity priorities and make assignments by priorities based on their best judgment of the case. Logbook(s) and/or written assignment lead sheets are necessary to keep control of all the simultaneous activities. The completed sheets are reviewed for completeness, indexed, and then attached to the coordinator's original lead sheet or reassigned with a new sheet for follow-ups. That original sheet may be the starting point of several new leads, and each should go out with attached information or briefing of the new officer assigned. The logistics of these methods must be worked out within each department, since all handle these matters differently. The structures of manual and computer operations are radically different from each other. Most modern operations use a combination of both. The field work at this stage is still best done on paper; you can look at four or five things at once, mix and match, reclassify easier, and find things in the "mess pile" easier—all while talking on the phone and writing on several sheets at once.

The "desk management" of the paper method is structured according to your system—a file folder, folders, compartmentalized brief cases, marked drawers, or several chronological clipboard files. Organization is the key, more than the methodology.

Let us put the problem in perspective by reviewing what duties the investigators perform.

A typical major criminal case unfolds this way:

Investigators arrive.

Investigators debrief the uniform officers, ensuring that the officers' comments are from written notes to be formally reported at the proper time and place (department procedure).

Investigators take charge from the uniform officers and assign them, or return them to their supervisor for other immediate case responsibilities.

Investigators assess the situation and call for any needed assistance or resources.

Uniform officers will assume crowd control, crime scene preservation, and order at the site. Uniform officers will also conduct area checks for suspicious persons, vehicles, evidence, and locate, hold, and separate possible witnesses.

The crime scene unit will be at work with one primary case investigator assigned to the unit. The control of the crime scene unit is the investigator's responsibility. During some of my lectures, I have been told by strong crime scene unit advocates that crime scene units can and should be independent of the detectives to ensure that all proper procedures are followed. I disagree. Discussion usually points to the problem of criminal investigators having inadequate knowledge of good crime scene procedures. This is a training problem. All criminal investigators should have superior knowledge about good crime scene and evidence control procedures. The fact that some do not is a sad commentary on investigator selection and training. If the department is blessed with such personnel, do not assign them to a duty they are incapable of performing.

A clear viewing area of the crime scene is established for investigative personnel. Random or curiosity viewing should be discouraged. The scene is shown and discussed, with specific items of interest pointed out so the investigators are armed with basic preliminary case knowledge when they commence their assigned activity.

The evidence control point is established for viewing and discussion with investigators. Nothing is removed from the scene without the knowledge and consent of the case supervisor or coordinator. There have been instances where important evidence was properly identified, tagged/marked, packaged, processed, and removed without investigators being aware of its existence. Those instances are usually the result of the mania for evidence control where the "forest can't be seen because the trees are in the way." Nothing goes into the locked evidence van until the case supervisor or coordinator sees it and initials the evidence tag as approval for temporary storage. This is the point where the supervisor and crime scene personnel resolve issues and discuss the evidence and any preliminary observations made by the technician, even if that discussion had previously occurred with a case investigator assigned to the CSU. Further, this is required even if the assigned CSU case investigator has previously passed the information to the case coordinator or supervisor. Never let an opportunity for checks and balances pass without using it to its full extent; it helps to reduce error and misunderstandings.

Many departments use evidence sheets where a copy is left with the case coordinator for the file at the scene. We are beginning to see the volume of different "pieces of paper" emerge. We are all aware of this, so start thinking of your department's forms, notes, memoranda, yellow sticky papers, and matchbook cover information flows with format consolidation in mind. They all have similar identification characteristics and may serve multiple purposes. This is great for the small departments; now all you need to do is create your forms to fit your purpose and get a laptop, printer and computer program for office/administrative matters. For those departments that still use the "long form" typewritten reports that generally are written from notes after the event, or Dictaphone reports, at least consider forms for routine processes. These will not replace the detailed written report, merely consolidate the information, merge it, and support it.

Those departments that are using various computer-driven reporting systems usually find themselves reducing them to paper at the end of the day for their field working file, prosecutors, and court copies, particularly on major cases. If you developed such a system, even if in stages, with the entire department criminal, administrative, reporting, and statistical process in mind, you are on your way to more efficiency and productiveness. Let us continue.

The crime scene unit does its work under supervision. A case or crime scene command post is established for a central reporting point. This is usually near the crime scene, outside the roped off and/or placarded area, but inside a secure area, away from the crowd or media.

All orders come from the officer in charge. All persons coming and going, reporting of activity, progress, status, information, evidence, etc. pass through this single point and sign in and out on the "contamination sheet."

(The Orlando PD officer who came up with that title was a genius, or got tired of being roughed up at trial.)

Witnesses are separated and assignments made to interview and secure statements. (Identify possible witnesses not at the scene and arrange to locate and have them interviewed.)

The case "report back" procedure is established by the case supervisor/coordinator.

The case continues to unfold.

Investigators and/or uniform officers begin a neighborhood canvass, with two-person teams if an abundance of personnel is available, under specific assignments. This is where inexperienced personnel may be assigned with an experienced investigator. This is where they improve observation skills of persons, places, demeanor, physical marks, general appearance, nervous habits, and such other unusual matters. Open wounds and blood all over the place would be nice to find. The canvass instructions should include the following:

1. Proceed systemically, house to house in neighborhoods, farm to farm in rural areas, apartment to apartment in condominiums, etc.
2. Report significant information back to the central control point immediately (by phone, in person, or by radio if secure channels or encryption are available).
3. Have investigators call back to the case coordinator at convenient intervals, every thirty minutes or after each three interviews or whatever the situation requires. This routine keeps everybody up-to-date on the progress of the case. This oral report must include, at a minimum, the names and addresses of those interviewed, time of report, and to whom made, all recorded on the lead sheet return report. The case coordinator enters the data into the case log, timeline, and/or index in the manner you have set up. That information is captured at that time, whether you use a computer, tape recorder, Dictaphone, or paper. In addition, the substance or nature of the information is noted in the same manner, and the supervisor or case coordinator sets forth any action taken on lead sheets if that is the result. Those are either put into the "to do" desk manager file or immediately assigned out for further action. And, everything is indexed with the available identification. The index could start with one word, a nickname, say "Art." If you are working with a computer, an immediate last name will appear, "Theft aka Lover"—one reason why computers will never take over the human brain and coordinators must see all.
    Back to the investigator.

4. Obviously, get the who, what, where, when, how, alibis, etc. (investigative procedures).

5. List who was interviewed at each location, noting both positive and negative information, and note who was absent and not interviewed. Follow-up teams will be assigned during a neighborhood recanvass to locate the missing persons.

6. Call information in on so-called "hot" leads and await instructions. Investigators should never follow developed leads on their own initiative and never go beyond the scope of their assignment without supervisory/coordinator permission. Without this rule, investigators will go charging off after what they consider important while the case supervisor believes they are performing other tasks. Loss of case control develops rapidly at this point, confusion reigns, and assignments go incomplete. Who knows what information or leads are missed when assignments are changed or ignored without the case supervisor's knowledge? The only exception I can think of is if a perpetrator is located and *immediate action is required* to prevent escape, injury, or further serious criminal activity. Even under the exception, it is usually easy to immediately notify the case supervisor. He or she may have other ideas as to the timing and location of any contemplated arrest.

7. Obtain preliminary statements only if necessary or your investigation situation permits the time needed. The immediate job is to obtain limited identification information in order to take action. Good, readable notes by the detective are required.

8. Detailed statements, when positive evidentiary value is determined, should be taken at a police facility equipped to handle the logistics. Uniform patrols may be used for transport. Suitable interview and statement-taking quarters should be located and used when the police facility is so far removed from the scene that to make a trip would be impractical. The place where statements are taken should be controlled by the police and away from the hubbub of the case. Mobile offices may be suitable if equipped properly; consider them when the identity of the person giving the statement means it is best done in privacy or secretly.

The neighborhood search begins and usually consists of, at a minimum, one case investigator and three uniform officers, who start a careful systematic search. Start the search at a logical place, usually the crime scene, and move out from the original point. The search should be designed to fit the circumstances present; i.e., circle, grid, or linear, and, if at night, arrange to redo the search in daylight. Case supervisors, according to their best judgment and experience, should determine the scope and level of detail or effort of the search.

The investigation into background matters relating to the case begins. Developing information on the victim and/or victim's family, associates, and business relationships, the premises, or other property is usually assigned a priority.

Investigators identify, locate, and interview friends, relatives, associates, fellow workers, and persons who last saw the victim or the proceeds of the crime. Travels and experiences are identified, as are the characteristics, relationships, etc., of the cast involved in the crime(s). Wake up the neighborhood for this type of information; do not wait for "normal business hours."

The in-depth interviews of witnesses start, and their detailed statements are taken.

All of the aforementioned must be done in whatever degree of intensity and selected priority as decided by the detective supervisor according to the nature of the case. These investigative activities must be done as soon as possible, thoroughly, and then systematically reported in detail to the case control center.

Detective Commander
Supervisor
Case Coordinator

Uniform Patrol	**Crime Scene Unit**	**Investigators**
Crime Scene	Crime Scene	Neighborhoods
Crowd Control	Processing	Background
Searchers		Searchers
Patrols		Leads

The detective supervisor firmly establishes the control of all resources and the case investigators. Investigators must know their duties, assignments, and the case system established for information flow and reporting.

The supervisor continues issuing instructions to ensure no one goes beyond his or her assignment without permission. Command will be flexible, not the workers. Make sure the best locations are checked first, that all witnesses and "at the scene" persons are "eye balled" by investigators, and then get to work on the systematic investigation. If possible, assign inexperienced officers or investigators to more experienced personnel so they learn which information is to be gathered, which must be communicated immediately, and which can wait a bit. If your department runs detectives as team partners, this is the place to split them, assuming proximate equal experience. The theory is the expansion of personnel experience to the less experienced.

The case will move away from the crime scene and into the investigative phase. The alignment of resources is already shaping; the scope of the investigation is being identified. Goals, phases, and milestones are being established.

At a very early point in the case, the detective in charge should start charting his investigative course. He must:

1. Start thinking of assignment of personnel for the duration of the case.
2. Set investigative priorities, goals, and milestones, then solve his resource problems of personnel, equipment, and money.
3. Set investigative time frames and anticipate when tasks will be completed.

Do not hold off making the case control and administrative decisions because the case "looks like it will break any minute."

Start:

1. The assignments
2. Ensuring the systematic flow of information and issuing follow-up instructions
3. Recording and case indexing (see Appendix F)

A picture of a typical major-case structure appears in Figure 4.1.

Detective Command

Maintain momentum.
Liaise.
Allocate resources, and control.
Start case examination (probabilities).
Complete all "must do" work prior to resource cutbacks.

During the investigative phase, the detective command is responsible for ensuring that the investigative team is set up according to the established department procedures and that the report mechanisms are working. The role is one of supervision, not investigation. Detective commanders are, or should be, aware of *all other investigations* within their unit. They should require that all possible lead information of value developed from other cases be reported to the investigative team(s). This requires a review, in detail, of all other cases, even squad room discussions if appropriate. Mere oral reports of supervisors or investigators, even with challenging and probing questions by commanders, may not be adequate. Detective commanders should read all investigative reports, or establish a report reader position where work volumes prohibit their individual attention. This not only provides detailed review and information at the command level but also establishes a standard for investigative and reporting quality control.

If your department has a computer index flag system in place, as each item is entered into the major-case file, any "hit" generates a reply and is immediately forwarded to the case manager for information inspection and action. If the department is still on manual record checks, it is more selective and done by the case coordinator as he or she sees fit. **Eventually, but as a high priority, every name, address, and all other information are checked against all other records available**, anywhere. This is where an experienced coordinator is of great use and a computer of greater efficiency. Later in the case, a manual check should be considered to override the computer flaws of exactness. Pick a time to check case nuances, differing spellings, secondary names of places, names, and nicknames, and broader expansion of known associates. Investigators know to what I am referring: all the flotsam of all major cases and the tedious detail that require human thought and reflections. Do not let a computer rule a detective's mind.

Detective commanders should be informed of the progress of each major case and evaluate the probabilities of success in order to make sound judgments regarding continued effort considering their and the department's priorities. They should be aware of all case follow-up work and see that it is completed.

Adequate resources must be kept on the case until all possibilities or investigative avenues that would be lost or severely damaged if not immediately attended to are completed. Resources should not be cut until work reaches the point where time, meaning pressing time, is no longer of importance.

Liaison duties are the responsibility of detective commanders. They see that interagency cooperation and coordination continue to be smooth and productive.

Momentum of an investigation should be maintained. It is just like the NFL, lose momentum in football and maybe lose the game.

When investigative resources get scarce, use other resources from within the department or from other agencies. If commanders are on top of all department activity and know the agency priorities, they can always squeeze additional resources for a short term.

Consider:

1. Using uniform officers for minor detective cases or warrant execution
2. Cutting traffic enforcement and regulation details for a couple of days
3. Overtime
4. Other agencies' resources

5. Canceling training classes
6. Using recruits from training schools for grunt work or postacademy probationers working with field-training patrol instructors

Detective Supervisor

Lead investigative teams.
Give out assignments/leads.
Institute a report-back system.
Do the case review.
Oversee the index (logbook).
Ensure proper information flow.

The detective supervisor is the person upon whom the real case burden falls. This is the person holding "the bag;" whether it is full of candy or not at the end of the case depends largely on his or her ability. All the case operational decisions are his or, as we see more often, hers.

The available resource commitments are his. Only experience and good judgment can pull him through with any semblance of order. The better the person is, the higher the chance of success. The detective supervisor is the key person in a major-case investigation, the responsibility is his, and therefore he must have case decision-making authority.

The detective supervisor also is tasked with the difficult job of keeping his investigators' minds from straying while at the same time encouraging their "thinking process." Investigators must think; they do that correctly by *avoiding* logical fallacies, which are riddled with false assumptions, and simple rules of progression, which all have exceptions. Also, they avoid hasty generalizations—even if one turns out to be correct, they require supportive and admissible evidence—or the opposite, conclusions that do not follow the evidence. Finally, also avoid circular reasoning, which is a devil often lost in the details by issues that seem to provide an answer but in reality do not. This paragraph is more suitable to a course on investigation methodologies than in a case control book; I place it at this point of the book to remind everyone that in many major cases the defendant is often charged, tried, convicted, and sentenced to death. The supervisor carries a heavy burden, and the department is responsible for seeing that he or she is the right person for the job.

The Coordinator

Detective supervisors have three areas of immediate case concern. They must supervise the entire investigative team, coordinate all of the principal entities involved in the case, and perform the actual case leadership, including work assignment functions. I recommend that in a major-case investigation the supervisor delegate the latter two responsibilities. Of course, each case has to be evaluated as to its peculiar needs, complexities, and scope. The responsibilities may be divided, under clear lines of authority, as follows:

1. The supervisor has overall responsibility and supervision.
2. The coordinator works directly under and for the supervisor, keeping track of the case details. ***Everything* comes and goes through the coordinator—a two-way funnel.**
3. The assigned lead case investigator (agent) performs investigative team leadership functions in the field and is responsible for writing and submitting the case investigative report. (Those agencies that consider a "report" to be a collection of memoranda or investigative forms simply placed in a file are sadly in need of further education.)

The scope of the investigation and the availability of resources determine if one, two, three, or more individuals will perform the three responsibilities. I recommend three for optimum case control. Two with some difficulties can accomplish it. When one person must assume the mantle of the three functions, well, as the movie comedian sheriff says as he chases the bandit, "su'm bitch." Tap the clerical pool.

It is impossible to cast in concrete the responsibilities of the three case supervisors' functions. Each police department or prosecutor's investigative staff is structured differently, each has different workloads, each has different levels of resources, and finally, each has different types of technical equipment and systems at their disposal, manual to completely automated. These factors necessitate that you decide how to structure and divide the responsibilities of the major-case investigation team.

Let us examine these responsibilities and look at some examples of case control problems to assist your thinking of things that must be coordinated.

The case supervisor must establish the working contacts and the report flow system for the investigative team, prosecutor, medical examiner, crime labs, and other agencies; not only regional participants, but, as an example, the state or federal Violent Crime Analysis Program (VICAP) as well as the agency's internal support functions (analysts, records, intelligence, etc.).

An example of coordination failures occurred between the LAPD and their prosecutor's office in the Manson case. The prosecutor issued a list of relatively important instructions to the Tate murder investigative team to follow up after Charles Manson's arraignment

(California requires felony trials to commence within 180 days of arrest/arraignment; the clock was running). After three weeks, only one item had been completed.* I am sure each side of this particular issue could be debated, but one fact is abundantly clear: a request (direction) for specific work was made and not done. Would this lapse have occurred with better case coordination/supervision? Let us fix the responsibility. It was an LAPD case and the supervisor was responsible for ensuring that all case items were investigated to secure conviction, not merely an arrest. The fault lies with LAPD supervision. Later, lists of forty-two investigative items were requested, and one officer stated, "But that isn't our job."† Apparently **the LAPD tolerated having work assignments from a prosecutor's office go directly to the case workers.** If the supervisor was not aware of this work assignment, the fault was his. If he was aware of the prosecutor's request, the fault was doubly his. This is a problem everywhere. **Prosecutors return case questions they have or specific additional information they request to *the report writer, signer, or officer who delivered it as a matter of routine, absent specific agreements to ship them elsewhere.*** Good case management requires this to go through the designated supervisor by prearrangement. This should be required for all cases, not just the "big ones." The reason is obvious.

4. Identify the central point of case reporting while still at the crime scene. **All case information from all sources must clear through a central point.** Like a funnel, information and reports flow two ways through this point. The central point is the case supervisor and/or the coordinator wherever they are physically located; beware, they tend to move about or split. This is extremely difficult to achieve, particularly in a "big case" with multiple agencies and units within an agency, including the temporary outside agencies. This is a difficult but not impossible task. In the three-person scenario of supervisor/coordinator/lead case agent, all information that comes to the supervisor and case lead investigator is forwarded to the coordinator for control and indexing. Information coming to the coordinator is kept for control and indexing but shared with the other two via copy or other communication, which is logged. The preparatory work provided the necessary tools and system for the case controller. This is called central desk reporting (CDR), which we will discuss in detail further on in the book. Meanwhile, you will see the initials CDR from time to time to make the point for later discussion.

---

* Bugliosi with Gentry, *Helter Skelter,* 191.
† *Ibid.,* 212.

5. The supervisor or the lead case agent establishes the crime scene boundaries and decides the priority of processing; the coordinator notes and fixes that in the case file.

The coordinator establishes the working relationships and reporting (oral and written) with the crime scene unit, including:

   a. Follow-up reports
   b. Immediate significant-information reports
   c. Setting report submission deadlines
   d. Setting evidence examination priorities and routines

For an example of coordination/supervision failure, let us again use the LAPD Tate murder investigation. The crime scene unit took a total of forty-five blood samples, but, for an unexplained reason, did not run subtypes on twenty-one of them. Problems were caused by this omission.* The failure was not with the crime scene unit, but with the case supervision for failing to see that the subtyping was completed, and with the coordination for not realizing the prosecutor required this work. If a matter is not complete, it is in a pending-action folder, tickler, or however you set up the distinction between completed and pending. In addition, the matter must be periodically checked by the supervisor. A major case is never sent over to the prosecutor like a simple burglary case is; it is hand delivered after an appointment with enough time for the "intake attorney" to get an overview from the case supervisor. Set up a second appointment with the intake attorney for a complete case review after the preliminary review in order to go over the case together, in detail. The intake attorney will decide whether the trial attorney will be present. Do not wait for the prosecutor to do this; they have no idea as to your schedule and time limitations. They usually wait until it is too late to do follow-ups, get explanations, or require further investigation with impossible deadlines. It is the nature of the beast. If it is an important matter, his or her delay and your time crunch sometimes end in a plea bargain, which leaves no happy person at that meeting. Then call the prosecutor who was at your crime scene and yell at him; he will apologize and maybe buy you a beer. If you buy him one back, he may straighten the problem out for future cases.

6. Establish the time intervals for uniform and detective case investigators to call in to the central control point with their progress reports. This provides a mechanism for the case control personnel to be continuously updated and to feed new information and assignments to the investigative teams. Relatively short time periods should be

---

* *Ibid.*, 13.

considered at the beginning of the case and lengthened as the case shakes out and settles down. Exchange sensitive information via the most secure communication capabilities you possess.

Immediate oral reports should be required from any investigator who develops:

a. New facts that shed material light on the case
b. Important new name information
c. Information that should be broadcast immediately
d. Witness accounts (for statement assignments)

The investigator is then advised when each written report or lead sheet is due, immediately or at the first department case report deadline date. Lead sheet returns are usually required as soon as the lead assignment is completed, full reports a little later, and all initial case activities filed with the coordinator within five calendar days—sooner if needed.

7. Make sure the press officer (PIO) is on the scene to handle the news media. In addition, keep the PIO and the press away from the investigators.

8. Start the case administration by implementing the department's case management system. See that:

a. Assignment and lead sheets are used.
b. Case indexing begins, along with the logbook. Some agencies combine these; all that is needed is a page-numbered hardbound notebook with an alphabetical index in it—the same concept as the old time police blotter except everything gets into this file.
c. Selective officer case briefing schedules are started, usually at end of day. If further work is identified that needs action, you have all night. Morning quick updates take care of the detectives and uniform officers arriving for assignment. This is the case manager's decision; he knows what to brief and who needs to be briefed; let him do his job. The departments that run nonstop until the necessities or "hot" leads slow down to the point where you can pause usually set the report-backs by groups or the nature of assignments with special instruction for surveillances. Those are tough and, thankfully, are rare. Coffee ... and cots for decorative effect only. The reason I mention that is a reminder that when people are tired, they tend to take premature actions to end the agony; please try to avoid that. At some point you have to initiate rotation or bring in new people and deal with the attendant issues. Then again, that is why the detective supervisor is paid the big bucks.
d. A detective monitors the case call-in phone and radio at all times during the initial phase where officers are out of reach of their

normal communication facilities. Every call is noted with sufficient information for case file requirements; any action that needs immediate attention is orally reported to the case manager and followed up with the written notations. He does this on the case material provided for him, and so does his relief and any others who may answer in his absence. The logbook may be the instrument used, followed by lead sheets sent or called out. You can communicate with anyone and give him a lead at any time in any manner; he will note the assigned department case number, give you the number on his blank lead or lead return sheet he has in his briefcase. Or, yours. Then when the assignment is completed, he will return the original to you, with the department record room copy attached and one to the patrol post file or the detectives case list file.

e. Clerical help, if needed, is available from the trained and experienced administration offices. They started learning what the department does from the day they started with the indoctrination routine and scheduled exposure to the rest of the department as appropriate.

f. Immediate lead assignments are recorded, and all leads and assignments that were initiated prior to the case control personnel arrival are recorded. At a minimum, they are identified and noted for follow-up control (the response phase work). Capture it while you can.

Street officers are all into the case by now, and when not on assigned work they will initiate their own acts. The normal date, time, and location rules for everything an officer does automatically kick in along with the report requirements. In addition to the lead, actions, or assignment reports they submit, make time at some point to have a case investigator interview each officer to see that you have it all. This catches and captures the unassigned "officer initiative" actions before they go astray.

The administration chores need to be accomplished in order to review, quickly, where you are. The multiple orders, assignments, and myriad of other details requiring attention need to be systematized, or the normal chaos will take a deep hold. Important items are easily forgotten or, worse, believed to have been taken care of but were not. During the Tate murder investigation, one of the five victims was found in a car parked in the driveway. More than twelve hours passed before the LAPD followed up on the car registration in an attempt to identify the victim. Understandably, they were busy, but I fail to understand this lapse, unless the case leads and management had not yet been brought under control.* Consider sequentially numbered lead/assignment sheets or logbooks with check-off columns. I suggest you picture this or build your current process in your mind. Reduce it all to notes and paper before you ask your computer people to do it; you will get better results. Remember, our goal is to reduce this to simplicity with the least number of forms possible collapsed into as many dual or multiple purposes as we can achieve.

9. Set up interview teams. Neighborhood interviews, whether the case is in the middle of a housing project or out in a desert, need to be conducted by a systematic process. Reports, both negative and positive, must be taken, and relevant information worthy of written statements needs to be identified and addressed. Negative reporting is usually an anathema to police officers but must be included in a major case. If a person states "I don't know anything" on Monday, let us be sure it is recorded in the case file by Tuesday before he writes his book about the investigation or appears on a national TV show.

   Exculpatory statements or evidence must be a part of the investigation. If some statement or fact clears or *could* tend to clear a person of suspicion or guilt, it must not be excluded; even a hint of exculpatory evidence (proven, unproven, or proved false) must be brought to the prosecutor's attention. The most difficult part with the exculpatory evidence problem is accepting the fact that the police do not get to decide what that is; the courts do, through the prosecution and defense. That means you are stuck with everything collected and, in some cases, should have been collected; please contact your legal office or local prosecutor regarding how you address the collection and retention process. Legal counsel to the police department is your best bet. Defense lawyers will tell you to save everything, even ideas and the remotest of possibilities; prosecutors will tell you to save everything that is relevant and not be able to tell you what that is.

   The relevancy problem is context and association to the case, evidence, and facts determined. A good-faith investigation, with records that are clear and comprehensive, without missing reports, lost collected evidence, or confusing statements, is the best, safest, and ethically correct position. You have to be the "good guys" in what can only be described as a fur ball. It is like a government regulation, where no one can tell who is right, wrong, guilty, or innocent until after the trial when a judge or civil case jury flips a coin to decide.

   Neighborhood interview teams will develop general information, habits, etc., from residents, local vendors, trades and deliveries, etc.

* *Ibid.*, 22, 23.

(See Appendix E.) The label "team" indicates the number of assignments, not whether there are one or two officers at each interview. That is a case manager decision. Routine matters are easily handled by one experienced investigator. Some interviews may be handled by a two-officer team for safety or witness values; this is usually one experienced officer and one gaining experience, uniform or plain clothes. When you need to intimidate people or split interviews within the location, use a two-officer team; when you need information, use a one-officer team; when you do not know, use a two-officer team until you get a sense of the situation. Then the second officer can go next door while the first continues. Get your supervisors to use this practice until it is department routine, particularly if you still use the two-officer-partnership system. The three-officer team is best used with two or three cars. The interview takes place with either one officer (this gives you a car or two for a back exit watch) or two of the officers; they leave and move a couple of blocks. The remaining car(s), which were in place prior to the arrival of the "interview" car, watches for any movement, departures, or arrival of a visitor of what is probably a suspect or target. This is rare in a reactive case, but since one never knows the situation until you are in it …?

Lead interview teams will locate friends, relatives, enemies, and associates, and conduct personal interviews. Their visual inspection and observations of note will be submitted with the interview forms or reports. Alibis, known activities, identification, and interview of the last known person to see the victim or object of the investigation intact must be substantiated. They will check business establishments for witnesses. Lead interview teams will redo neighborhood interviews as more information that is specific develops that requires rechecking. Problems arise when teams are sent forth to interview and investigate without sufficient information about the case or without detailed instruction. During the Kennedy assassination investigation, the Dallas Police Department and some deputy sheriffs were sent to L. H. Oswald's residence in Irving, Texas. The officers lacked adequate information about details of the crime. They searched Oswald's house (some called it haphazard ransacking) and collected numerous items without purpose.* Many in legal circles believe there would have been some serious Fourth Amendment problems with relatively important evidence seized had the matter reached a court. Although I have heard a law enforcement friend

---

* The matter was never litigated—no harm, no foul.

from Texas jest: "Son, ya'll may have search problems up thar in the USA, but not he'ah in Texas."

I will restate that investigators should not go beyond their assigned duty without checking in and receiving permission (added assignment). It is up to the supervisor/case coordinator to be flexible regarding assignments, not the officers. Failure to insist on this crucial rule will result in detectives developing information and chasing "hot" leads on their own. Neighborhood canvasses then are not completed and interviews are delayed or not completed, while the case control people think the work is being done. This is a very tricky area when you consider all the exceptions to this rule that immediately come to mind; by this time, there have been eight or nine hundred decisions made, what's one more.

10. Make sure the victim's relatives are notified in person, if pertinent. The case manager makes that *decision,* not the uniform service that is normally assigned such tasks.

11. Activate the case/department report system right from the start. Never permit a required report to be delayed by the "It's been a long day, I'll do it tomorrow" excuse. Tomorrow never comes!

12. If missing property is part of your investigation, the case manager will institute the case coordination process with your pawnshop detail. That unit will recheck all their files for nonserialized similarities; serialized property is already in the system. That unit will check all unidentified fingerprints they have lifted from "pawned" property against captured case fingerprints; any DNA lifted from "pawned property" will be checked. Agencies that do not check stolen-property outlets on a regular basis and collect owner-pawnee as well as "taker" prints at stolen-property outlets should consider doing so when time and resources are available. The case manager will also request that the surrounding police departments check their files, prints, and DNA. It is also a good way to use case "downtime or fill-in time" as a resource saver and as a routine process. For a crime scene unit waiting for a crime or to be called out on a case, this is a very good way to occupy their time. In addition, it is a good training ground for new officers. Some states have laws regarding pawn shop retention time and reports to the police of specified pawned items. Besides, it makes the shop owner a little nervous and a bit more careful. He may start storing his stolen stuff in a "cooler room" in a shed or basement. Get a snitch to provide a probable-cause statement; bingo, warrant. You now have evidence of knowledge and intent.

I believe adequate justification for a case coordinator has been stated; nevertheless, let us point out some additional advantages. First, supervisors should be relatively free to move about, particularly at the beginning of an investigation. However, **good case control dictates that a central point and/ or temporary control post is necessary for the funneling of information and administrative control (CDR);** a case coordinator solves this problem. In addition, some jurisdictions have difficulty in having case investigators sit at the prosecutor table during a trial; defense lawyers have them excluded. **Case coordinators do not testify; they perform no actual investigative act and do not take actual possession of any physical evidence.** They direct under supervision, their names do not appear in any portion of the investiga- tive side of the case file, and they report nothing to the investigative file. Yet they know more about the specifics of a case than any single individual, since everything passes through their heads and hands. Their hands touch only paper and phones, all hearsay. **The case coordinator may sit at the court- room trial table and assist the prosecutor; the investigators and trial par- ticipants will be barred, as they are all possible trial witnesses.**

Any good defense lawyer will list every name associated with the case that he possibly can to avoid this very situation; defeat him. He will not list the coordinator, even if a court would allow him to waive any defense objec- tion to hearsay. The prosecutor could then use him. The proverbial "wild bull in a china shop" could not do as much damage to a criminal defense as a police officer being allowed to testify using unlimited hearsay.

One of the major-case preparatory rules I stated earlier was to never per- mit information to come into your department without formal acceptance (written) and a system to ensure it arrives at its proper destination. It is the old tried-and-true rule: "If it is not in writing when it arrived, you write it up … immediately." The destination in a major criminal investigation is the case coordinator/supervisor. During the Tate and La Bianca murder investigations in Los Angeles, two investigative teams (one for each case) were working in the same office only a few feet apart. Twenty-four hours after the Tate homi- cide, two Los Angeles County Sheriff's officers (LASOs) approached the Tate team and advised them of information that led LASOs to believe there were strong similarities between the Tate murders and a murder case they were investigating, with one suspect under arrest. The LAPD Tate team rejected the information.* The LASO had arrested a member of the Manson family! The failure was in case control and administration, but the information was evaluated **and rejected at the worker level;** the Tate supervisor was not made aware of the information. **The contact and interview of the LASO deputies in the LAPD office was case activity. In a case management system, this is required to be entered into the control system and funneled through a case coordinator.** He decides what information is relevant or not. All the

---

* Bugliosi with Gentry, *Helter Skelter*, 33–34.

organizational structuring, pyramiding layers of supervision, and establishing spans of control designed to coordinate activities such as this are defeated by a simple low-level decision. "Nah," said one investigator, "we know what's behind these murders. They're part of a dope transaction."* (A hasty generalization, maybe.) No wonder some law enforcement leaders would like to insert castration under their disciplinary prerogatives. There are consequences for failure to follow known procedures.

I have hesitated to use up-to-date examples to avoid embarrassment to any agency, but they do occur. The depiction of the event that follows highlights a major major-case failure in a large Florida department (over 1,000 officers). The sheriff, although responsible for the case management system, is probably not directly at fault for the reporting breakdown or flaw.

Let me set the scene. A three-year-old child was missing for thirty days before relatives called the police in July 2008, initiating a massive investigation. Searches, tips, inquiries, and multiple agencies, including the FBI and the Florida Department of Law Enforcement (FDLE), were involved. The sheriff's office "had the case" and conducted the investigation. More than 5,600 tips had to be checked, neighborhoods, swamps, and lakes searched. You get the picture—massive control issues.

An area electric meter reader found the body in a field on December 11, 2008, about half a mile from the child's home in a brush, tree, and lowland area. He reported that to the sheriff's department. The mother was in jail at that time and under charges for her daughter's murder.

Here is the case management problem. The meter reader, a persistent fellow, previously reported to the sheriff's office a suspicious bag at the same place he found the body bag in December 2008, mentioning that it **may be the missing child.** He called on August 11, 2008, telling a dispatcher about "something suspicious, a bag, in the same area." He says the responding deputy "was rude and did not make a thorough search." The department public relations officer stated (in December 2008) that the "deputy responded, looks, surveils the area, and did not find anything suspicious."

On August 12, 2008, the meter reader calls again and speaks to a detective, who informed him that the "dogs searched that area in July and it closed out that area;" apparently, no other action was taken.

Then on August 13, 2008, again the meter reader spoke to the dispatcher and the responding officer who cleared the area with no further action. Something about "encountering a large snake" was mentioned; the deputy turned back and cleared the call. The "snake" was not confirmed, at least publicly.

* Ibid.

The ground water-level conditions were apparently better in December when, out of his continuing curiosity, the meter reader actually relocated and went to the bag, which was at the same place. and opened it. There was the bag just as he originally reported. He picked it up and a small human skull rolled out.

A case management system would have prevented the officers involved in the August 12th and 13th reports from having their careers go up in smoke and their butts kicked all over the squad rooms. The case coordinator would have read the August 11th dispatcher's and deputy's reports the same day and called the responding officer wherever he may have been and demanded, "What does cleared mean, what was in the bag?" You and I know that absent a satisfactory answer, and there could not have been one, that child's body would have been found within sixteen and a half minutes after the skies opened and thunder and lightning struck. The time delay would have been due to the case coordinator sputtering incoherently for a few minutes. It is no excuse that deputies found and opened without results more than 300 garbage bags prior to this one.

The location has an identifiable address that would have been indexed and flagged along with all the other area grid or dive searches the department conducted, which in turn were mapped and entered into the case file. The three reports generated from the meter reader calls would have been submitted to the case manager the same day they were reported.

If the report or reports came to the sheriff's office without mentioning a "suspicion it may be the child," and nobody associated the report with that case, the area or place reported would still have been picked up by the "flag" for that so-called previously searched spot. It would be in the file and the connection made immediately.

The problems:

In Florida, a body exposed to the rain and heat deteriorates rapidly; after four additional months of exposure, the cause of death is now in question.

Television speculation shows scream that the mother could not have put the body there in or prior to August, when deputies and body-sniff dogs cleared that area and the mother was in jail. A serious timeline issue has risen from the grave, so to speak.

Private investigators were in that area a month prior to the body discovery videotaping and will testify they did not see or find anything. The laboratory reports that the body was in place for a long period, disturbed only by wildlife. They cannot pinpoint the time of death.

A psychic, Gale St. Johns, says she shot video in the same area, "feeling overwhelming …" No one can even guess what she will say. She was provided TV airtime for her "public service."

The sheriff stated that "... not searched earlier ... underwater and scheduled to go back ...;" I would not like to be present at that cross-examination.

That is enough to make the case posture clear. There are not enough aspirins... .

A case management system (CDR) to control this case was not in place; if it were, they would have discovered the pending leads or the follow-up matters not completed in the case folder. A flag system would have alerted the case manager/supervisor, detective, and department commanders. If a manual system were in use, every index item that comes into existence is checked against the file, the department records, and outside sources as deemed necessary—all routinely, all, at a minimum, daily.*

"For the want of a nail...."

Let us move on.

What does this supervisor and/or case coordinator do and how? (See Appendix F.)

He controls by:

1. Immediate Directives   &   Case Controls
   Assignments (all)   Index
   Crime scene and victim history   Leads
   Assignment (lead) sheets
   Prior incident   Periodic meetings
   Prior residence   Case updates
   Disseminates information   Team reviews
   Makes changes of assignments   Pending assignments, tickler
   And builds the case file
      In addition, he:

2. Secures all crime scene reports, including the list of entrants (see Appendix D), and places them in the report and case index. He reviews the reports for completeness and leads and makes follow-up assignments (see Appendix G).

3. Secures the dispatcher logs and time of arrival reports and has discrepancies corrected while they are still explainable.

4. Ensures that notifications of family and business partners are made either routinely or under instructions to observe and develop information. The method and details of the notification of the family of Steven E. Parent, murder victim at the Tate residence, was a

---

* *Orlando Sentinel,* December 11–20, 2008; and Orlando TV station's archives; ABC, NBC, CBS, FOX archives; Casey Anthony, defendant.

disgrace.* The case coordinator selects whether notification shall be made in person or by whatever method it takes to do it right. He ensures that the report of notification comes back to him promptly and notes the response, condition, and reactions of persons notified and any information developed or lacking for further investigation. He ensures that positive identification is made of a victim and prevents the release of identification information to the news media until the family notification has been verified.

5. Prepares, for approval, the press release information and holds back critical investigative details. What information is released should be factual and exact. Casual observations confuse everybody, but delight the press.

6. Makes sure his teams are moving rapidly, checking their progress by insisting on periodic callbacks. He ensures they complete their assignments, that there is no delay in securing information even if you must wake up the neighborhood.

7. Establishes cooperation with other agencies, assigns their personnel (if they are to be part of the investigation), and requires them to submit reports to him as per the agreement. He reminds them of the "silence to the press" rule. If they violate the news release rule, he sends them home immediately and brings their indiscretion to the attention of their (and his) superiors.

8. Sets up the case index immediately. Do not wait to see how the case is going to develop. Playing catch-up football is a tough game. If it is a case where clerical assistance is needed, a single individual should be responsible for the index. Start looking for index associations immediately. A manual index can be difficult; an automated index requires sophisticated programming. Select the automated file characteristics best suited for the department, such as Soundex, strictly alphabetical, or others, a case management file, and a flag system.

The case index (see Appendix F and Chapter 15) will identify associations for possible investigative leads. In addition, it will serve as a locator and aid retrieval of sought-after information. Further, substantial amounts of time will be saved in preparing the case for prosecution.

The supervisor/case coordinator is responsible for pursuing the investigation according to the facts of the case. He must control the tendency of presumptive theorists to inject their opinion into the case and thus attempt to steer the investigation according to their "gut level or instincts" or otherwise. The problem with theorists is their

---

* Bugliosi, *Helter Skelter*, 22–23.

attraction to direct the case and focus on the theory, disregarding other leads or avenues that if pursued may bear fruit. Use the facts, and develop factual information. Let the theorists dream or think of possibilities, but do not permit theories to be mentioned in an investigative report. **A report must be a factual account of the investigation without theory or the opinion of any investigator.** If theory is inserted into a report, there may well be some difficult moments in a courtroom, either explaining the reasoning or disproving it. If you wish written theories or opinions for reference or recall purposes, file them elsewhere if they do not specifically point to or mention the case. If they exist and do refer to the case and its facts, place them on the administrative side of the file and provide them to the prosecutor.

A few examples of why opinion and theory should be avoided will help clarify the problem and place it in perspective. A case coordinator reading the Manson investigative reports carefully would have corrected certain faults prior to trial or would have been prepared to explain them. Let us examine a few errors from the Manson murders that point to the problem.

The LAPD official report concluded that "the knife that inflicted the stab wounds was probably a bayonet." This was based upon a suggestion, not actual knowledge. Bugliosi stated that "…this not only eliminated a number of other possibilities, it also presumed that only one knife had been used."[*] The police report should have stuck to facts— i.e., describing the nature, measurement, and number of wounds—and left the written opinion as to the instrument to medical-expert testimony or other factual information in their possession. The investigation should focus on identifying weapons discovered by investigation that could be the murder weapon and permit laboratory or medical experts to tie the weapon(s) to the wound(s).

The LAPD had a number of theories on the Tate killings:

a. A drug party with one participant "freaking out"
b. The result of a drug "burn," which is an argument over money or bad drugs from a pusher or buyer
c. A variation of the second theory—the killers deciding to keep the money or drugs
d. The residential burglary theory
e. "Deaths by hire," with the killer murdering all the occupants of the house to avoid identification[†]

The drug theory seemed to make the most sense, and the investigative team initially focused on that direction. They rejected the

[*] *Ibid.*, p. 17.
[†] *Ibid.*, 19–20.

LASO attempt to give them a strong lead developed from one of their murder cases with strong similarities to the Tate killings.* The LAPD investigative team focused on a theory and rejected fact. The supervision/case coordination failed to ensure that information coming to the attention of investigators was reported into the system for appropriate evaluation; they permitted investigators to decide what leads or information were pertinent. If a lead comes to the attention of anyone, it goes into the file. The case supervisor/coordinator decides its use, priority, assignment, or rejection, notes the lead sheet, and places it appropriately in the file or things-to-do slot or clipboard. It is indexed as it is received as circumstances permit, but no less frequently than daily. It is flagged if appropriate. It is reviewed at a higher level set by the department. The supervisor/coordinator discusses and listens to advice and recommendations from his team, but then he decides.

The LAPD report on the La Bianca murders, also a Manson family pair of killings, stated, "The knife recovered from his [Leno La Bianca] throat appeared to be the weapon used in both homicides."† This was a presumption, since the pathologist did not measure the dimensions of the wounds (another case coordination failure). Bugliosi says, "The ramifications of this one presumption were immense. A single weapon indicated that there was probably a single killer."‡ The knife found in La Bianca's throat belonged to him and came from the residence. The defense could now claim the killer (singular) came to the residence unarmed (no intent to kill, at least a claim of that). This error would have affected whether the death penalty could be invoked. A review of the investigation proved that the knife found in the throat could not have caused all of the wounds. I would guess there were a few anxious moments in the courtroom that were not necessary if supervision and case coordination were better. This type of statement should have been removed from the report when it was initially submitted under the report correction methods established in the department. (Report writing, submission rules and impacts, correction methods, and corrected report retention policies are completely different subjects. **Once the original writer signs or initials a report, it is a record.** All further additions, deletions, and rewording must follow the report correction, substitution, and retention methods.)

* *Ibid.*, 33–34.
† *Ibid.*, 45.
‡ *Ibid.*, 45, 340.

The supervisor/case coordinator is responsible for keeping this type of problem to a minimum. While a single error may not be fatal, an accumulation of mistakes or omissions destroys the credibility of the investigation until one last small failure convinces one juror that the police were inept and the case is lost.

Objectivity is the rule. Subjectivity is the exception. Conclusions may be drawn through the process of deductive or inductive reasoning—i.e., inferences that conclusions follow from the examined premises (deductive); or logical progression, one step logically leading on to the next (inductive). Conclusions or inferences reached by investigating facts provide stronger evidence and case direction than mere theory or opinion. Use the facts!

9. Uses the index and the department's existing data information systems to work for him, or at least not against him. If the department has information, it should be retrievable. If the department does not have what is being sought (information, items) and subsequently does come into possession of what is being sought, the system should point to the earlier seeker and inform him or her. This is the function of a flag system. An information system that requires central filing of all index items (names; addresses; lost, found, stolen, and abandoned property; wanted and missing persons, etc.) can be made to produce sought-after information and put cases and information together as required. This is a main failure of manual systems. Retaining and rechecking all prior negatively answered inquiries is an expensive nightmare and fraught with error. Those systems require constant reinquiries of case officers, adding to lost time and increased clerical costs, but most costly is the loss of information.

For example, in a murder investigation where the murder weapon sought was a .22 caliber Buntline Special, identified as such from broken grips found at a crime scene (the same ones that "moved," according to scene photographs mentioned earlier), the case coordinator should be able to place a notice in the files that would flag attention to any such gun coming into the possession of the department. Since police departments handle tons of paperwork on all their activities, it should be able, regardless of volume, to track major or sought-after identifiable items. The LAPD was seeking exactly such a gun used in the Tate killings. On September 1, 1969, this gun was booked as "found evidence" into the LAPD Van Nuys property section. Between September 3 and 5, 1969, the first batch of confidential "flyers" seeking the gun were sent out by the Tate investigative team. The system never put the investigators together with the property clerks.

The LAPD had the gun they were looking for and did not know it.* Manual flag systems can extend the search-inquiry-reply to as far as your clerks. And automated flag systems can extend the search-inquiry-reply as far as your technology, internal, and state systems allow. I will repeat! The supervisor/case coordinator is the control key for a successful investigation. The more experienced and capable this officer is, the smoother and more effectively the investigation will progress. It is a tough but rewarding job.

The figures at the end of this chapter show a typical reporting structure for a major-case investigation team where the main thrust of a case is within one jurisdiction and other agencies are merely supportive. Illustrations at the end of this chapter portray a major-case control system where, for example, Fort Lauderdale is the controlling agency with three other cities contributing to the investigation, each with personnel assigned to duties within their own jurisdiction (this does not preclude investigators from assisting in other jurisdictions). Each team is controlled through an existing command structure. They also show an uncontrolled case—chaos. Central desk reporting improves case control. More on this term CDR in the proactive case part of this book.

Crime Scene Unit

The crime scene van is back in the garage, its equipment checked and resupplied. After coffee and a ten-minute conference/conversation to sum up all their activities to ensure that all is known to all and loose ends are tied up, they continue with the following:

Examine evidence and submit to the laboratory as directed by the case manager.

Attend the autopsy (if applicable) for additional photos, evidence from the body, jewelry, clothing, and any items found in pockets or on the body.

Report to the case manager the findings of the medical examiner with his or her protocols, if readily available. Taping the conversation is a good idea if it is not one of those joke-telling sessions.

Examine and classify control prints and eliminations.

Process any additional case-related matter.

Collect, check, correct, and complete crime scene notes where necessary.

* *Ibid.*, 54, 65, 70, 346.

Set up a case tickler to keep after the lab for their reports. It is filed in the crime scene unit tickler file along with every other case. Send copies of all index items to the case coordinator. Complete with the current evidence status.

The coordination work is not yet finished. During the investigative phase of the case, the other principal entities involved must have their activities supervised and/or coordinated and integrated into the case and report. The case coordinator is also responsible for ensuring that the crime scene unit:

1. Prepares evidence for the laboratory and obtains supervisory clearance to ship or deliver the evidence to a crime laboratory. Submit a copy of all paperwork to the case coordinator for indexing, filing, and include a copy of the case tickler. Do this each time a process is completed. Notice that this is a second tickler, and it is for the coordinator. Do this since the case coordinator will be moving on to other, more pressing, matters within a nonidentifiable period. It is insurance for the case controller as well as keeping him directly in touch with that case. If you are operating on a computer-controlled system, this is an easy matter. Others use formatted internal e-mails or hand-mail notes of status inquiries.
2. Contacts the crime laboratory with any special instructions or information. Also, forwards the identified case priorities and establishes schedules or positions on any matter with the laboratory. Then files a memo or report to all files, mostly handwritten on a formatted notepad, and informs the coordinator of any problems.
3. Takes control of the case latent prints and continues the process of elimination. The crime scene unit should report all immediate findings to the case supervisor/coordinator and follow up with a written report (administrative side of case file) that specifically locates where the prints are filed—usually in CSI pending case files. All *cases* are indexed at this point.
4. Attends the autopsy (if applicable). At least one officer (possibly one in training) and a crime scene technician that processed the crime scene should be present at the autopsy and *photograph:*
   a. The body as delivered to the morgue: bag with body, then body without bag. The bag is saved and collected for crime scene unit processing.
   b. The body nude before and after cleaning.
   c. All wounds and marks.
   d. Hands (both sides), face, and teeth.
   e. Front, rear, and both sides of the body.
   f. The autopsy as it progresses.

The investigator assigned to supervise the crime scene should be present at the autopsy. He or she will view and record all body conditions as the pathologist examines. The investigator will report back to the case coordinator the preliminary findings, and the

a. Pathologist's name
b. Cause of death
c. Evidence removed from the body
d. Type, location, number, and description of wounds, marks, etc.
e. And, if your department maintains training files, a training unit report for their file and use regarding the in-training attending officer

The investigator must be able to inform the pathologist of all known details and circumstances about the body, crime scene, and conditions at the time of discovery—temperature, weather, ground conditions, etc. Yes, I know the medical examiner on scene should have done that, but it is your case. The investigator reconstructs the crime (facts) as best as can be done at the time. Facts known about the deceased's last moments (i.e., time, place, physical condition, last meal, and activity) will aid the pathologist in determining the time of death and may explain any discovered anomalies. This is a place to note that, in a few cases, the time of death may be of sufficient import to be held secret for some period. That is one of many reasons that information is not released until after autopsy, if at all. The public information officer must be aware of that; that is part of case preparation and standard procedures.

The investigator or crime scene officer will claim and process all evidence, clothing, and property secured at the autopsy if a crime unit person is not present, along with a copy of the scene medical examiner's report or notes.

The pathologist should be instructed not to release any details of the autopsy. He may issue a statement as agreed in the interagency agreements, a general statement that the victim is dead by homicide, not murder. Homicide is not necessarily a crime, and it is usually too early to start locking that issue down. He should avoid details such as the caliber of wounds or the identification of the murder instrument. There should be no comment on the condition of the body or statements regarding sexual assaults in any detail that would cause the loss of investigative keys. The case information must be kept within the law enforcement circle.

The pathologist does:

1. Establish the cause of death and what did not cause it.
2. View the crime scene photos and sketches.
3. Have the body x-rayed for identification purposes and to locate possible evidence, such as fractures, bullets, or foreign objects.

4. Discuss the presence or absence of rigor mortis. Generally:
   a. Rigor mortis starts in the eyelids and lower jaw within two to five hours after death.
   b. It spreads from the face down to the trunk and legs; the upper body is completed in ten hours, the entire body in sixteen hours.
   c. Rigor mortis lasts thirty-six to forty-eight hours, then relaxation commences, starting in the face, working down, and is complete in eighteen hours.
   d. Poisons may start rigor immediately.
   e. Spasms at death sometimes cause a lock grip.
5. Discuss the position of the body and its meanings or possibilities.
6. Obtain, from the investigator or coroner, the room or air temperature at the crime scene and a water sample if the body was in water.
7. Retain as evidence and turn over to the police the bags that covered the victim's hands and head during transport, in addition to the body bag. Retain the cotton sheets or body wraps used for transportation for police examination for contents or evidence.
8. Conduct external examination of the body for sex, age, height, race, frame, weight, etc.
9. Permit the crime scene technician to fingerprint the body for positive identification and print elimination purposes. (Never rely on the availability of prints of the deceased).
10. Take dental impressions if necessary, particularly if identification is uncertain and/or there were signs of a combative struggle at the crime scene. The mouth should be carefully examined first, for bits of flesh, blood, fibers, hair, or other foreign matter.
11. Record the body temperature (normal is 98.6 °F). Temperature drops two to three degrees in the first hour, then one and a half degrees each hour to a maximum of eighteen hours (generally). Temperatures should be taken rectally, at least four inches up the anus.
12. Note and describe wounds, depth, and nature. Do not permit the pathologist to probe or expand a wound before it is measured. Do not permit the pathologist to remove bullets using metal-tipped forceps.
13. Inspect the hands and nails and secure fingernail scrapings or take clips of nails.

The case coordinator sees that this **is done** by controlling the work through lead assignment sheets, direct orders, or department case autopsy formats and procedures.

The reason I put a little investigative detail in at this point is to reinforce that one officer is there to be trained and another there to further the case, not go out of the room "for coffee" or tell jokes to cover up the unease people have at autopsies. Of course, if they are old-timers, they will bring lunch and tell jokes anyway, between moments of getting the job done.

The crime scene unit's complete file is copied to the coordinator as it is created, with the original filed with the case file when the case is closed.

Crime Laboratory

> Liaison
> Priorities
> Reports

The case supervisor/coordinator should establish a working relationship with the crime laboratory on each major case.

Priorities for the examination of evidence and specific results or findings obtained from the examinations should be discussed and clearly understood. Advice or leads offered by the laboratory should be directed to the case supervisor/coordinator for action.

Approval of all evidence submissions, and the associated paperwork, is the responsibility of the case supervisor/coordinator. His pending-response lead sheets ensure that the laboratory reports' due dates are tickled, oral reports are obtained when expected, and all evidence submitted is returned and stored after examination or noted as retained at the laboratory. All conversations with the laboratory are logged and noted, usually on the lead sheet or its "continued" page and eventually into the master case and report file, administrative side.

Each time a control process is mentioned, think of a method that the department can put in place to further the objective, such as preprinted formatted tickler notes, or other methods of tracking all case items. Ticklers are filed by date the reminder item is due, removed when received, or action taken when it fails to appear on the due date. The action: call the person required to perform and find the status and reason for the delay. Take appropriate action.

Medical Examiner

> Reporting
> Media cooperation

The medical examiner should attend the autopsy—a more accurate term would be necropsy (body examination), but autopsy (see for one's self) is more common—with the police crime scene unit personnel, the assigned case investigator, and of course the forensic pathologist.

Clarity, purpose, and mutual sharing of knowledge greatly enhance an investigation into the cause of death. That will minimize unexplained or confusing matters. The confusion that surrounded the autopsy of President Kennedy after his assassination was caused in part by a communication failure. Doctors at Parkland Hospital in Dallas worked on the president, but the autopsy took place at Bethesda Naval Hospital outside of Washington, DC. **The Navy pathologists, unaware of what occurred at Parkland, were misled by the appearance of the neck wounds. At Dallas, a small existing wound had been surgically enlarged to permit insertion of a breathing tube. The Navy pathologists noted the tracheotomy but were unaware it was also an exit wound.** They were confronted with an entrance wound in the back strap muscles, but no bullet or exit wound was found.* A telephone call could have cleared up this mystery. The question is, who was ultimately responsible for the investigation? The answer, the Dallas Police Department! Regardless of the confusion, or the enormity of conflict of interest, or the power and the ability of the presidential party to bring pressure, a murder had been committed in the city of Dallas. The police had simply lost control of parts of the investigation, including the corpus delicti. Moreover, efforts to coordinate the investigation with the FBI and Secret Service were inadequate to the task. There was no coordination of the principal entities, nor had a case investigator or crime scene officer been assigned, or possibly not permitted, to accompany the body to Washington, DC. Relying on the Secret Service and the FBI agents present at the autopsy was an obvious error; they had no more information than the doctors did. Congress has since given the FBI jurisdiction in murder of federal officials. Today in such situations, the Dallas police would take the response phase and early investigative phase initially, then turn control over to the FBI and assume a cooperating role.

Prosecutor

Provide information.
Provide legal guidance.

The case supervisor/coordinator should continue to keep the prosecutor informed of the investigator's progress. He should insist that the prosecutor read all material statements as soon as possible. Regarding major cases, the

---

* Warren Commission Report P. 60, appendix 8, 519, appendix 9.

usual attitude of not wishing to read statements prior to arrest is wrong. Errors, omissions, and confusing or conflicting testimony should be addressed, then make any corrections immediately. These tasks and contacts should be noted in the case log, which becomes a part of the case administrative file. The log may be one source of part of the crime timeline, which is a separate report which, when completed, is placed in the case file. In *some* discovery states, it is open to discovery; it is your option in nondiscovery states, since all time-line data can be recaptured from the case file itself. Advice from the prosecutor regarding interviews, particularly custodial or suspects, searches, and seizures should be promptly handled and logged. Discussions on evidence admissibility, proof requirements, and general case coordination procedures, should be the rule rather than the exception. This must be done by the time of arrest, earlier if possible. Do not wait.

Public Information Officer

Conduct briefings.

The function of the PIO continues to be one of keeping the media at bay from the investigation in addition to keeping them informed with factual information regarding the case. Of course, the PIO must stay within the established guidelines. One has only to read of the actions of the press corps during the Kennedy murder case and see how they turned on the Dallas police.* Beware of the true motivation and objectives of the media.

Support Services

Analysts
Records
Technical equipment

The case supervisor/coordinator is responsible for initiating and controlling all record searches, reports, and other sources of information from his or her agency, as well as from other agencies. Contacting other agencies for information about similar crimes, leads, or associations must be controlled through lead and/or assignment sheets. This is a "reminder issue" for the investigative team; see that it is observed. The coordinator will catch some of

* For detailed research, check archives (Nov 22–30) of Dallas papers, NY and LA Times, and other national papers.

this by reading every report. He or she will discover unsourced information reported, or if sourced but not indexed. Both are errors.

Analysis of information must be directed toward a stated purpose or time, and effort may well be dissipated.

The case coordinator must record and control all use of technical equipment such as surveillance cameras, trackers, and listening devices. That is in addition to the department equipment procedures, usually the checkout, check-in authority, notice, and log procedure.

The case index, filing, serializing of reports, and associating this work to the investigation in an orderly and retrievable manner can best be accomplished when you know the sequence of events, orders, and discussions (case log). When you know all of the who did what, when, and why they did it (lead and assignment sheets), then knowing what needs to be done or reported to the case file and tickler file becomes an easier task. The work of

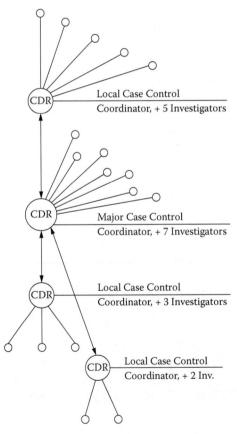

Figure 6.1 Controlled multi-team coordination.

the investigation is funneled through the case coordinator; he or she controls by using the preplanned system of logs, lead sheets, and tickler file, which can range, depending on your agency's sophistication, from a notebook and eight-by-five cards to an elaborate automated program.

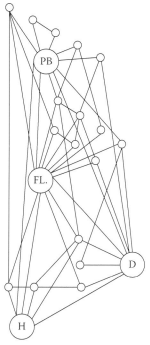

Figure 6.2 Uncontrolled multi-team investigation.

The Arrest, Trial, and Appeal

7

When an arrest(s) occurs, it slows the criminal investigation phase; there is usually euphoria among the case workers followed by a quiet satisfaction. This is as it should be, particularly after a difficult investigation. Care must be taken not to let this feeling of well-being slide into carelessness that affects the work remaining to be done. There is a tendency to move on to other cases without completing the slowing investigation's loose ends. There is also a tendency to relax the work effort since the pressure is off because of the arrest, and sometimes the remaining work gets a bit sloppy. This must not happen! Our objective is conviction, not merely arrest. It is the case supervisor's responsibility to meet the objective.

Let us continue with our theme of identifying the responsibilities of each principal entity during this phase of a major case.

Department Command
    Look important and stay out of the way.

If the department commanders have been able to keep out of the investigation up to this point, they should resist the temptation to jump in at the arrest. Officers who have worked long and hard hours on an investigation are often discouraged when department commanders intrude and take, what appears to case officers, credit based on the investigators' work. The public information officer should handle the media, preferably through a press release. If a press conference is unavoidable, let the prosecutor do the talking and answering of questions. There must be extreme care not to prejudice the defendant's right to a fair trial. The trial should take place in the court, not in the newspapers. There is no valid reason to discuss a criminal case or make remarks about the case beyond what is in the department's press guidelines. Police commanders who do so are merely seeking recognition, even if for the department. I have always felt that these media events are nothing more than "dog and pony shows" and contribute little if anything positive to the public's attitude toward the police. In fact, I believe the sight of police officials patting themselves on their own backs for performing duties is not only unprofessional, but in the eyes of the thinking public, is slightly nonsensical and makes them uncomfortable. The public understands; they see top brass when the outcome is good and the public information officer when the news is bad. That is the issue regarding public acknowledgments, not credits or praise; those are appreciated internally and usually privately among friends and fellow officers.

> Detective Command
> > Advise the prosecutor.
> > Inform other agencies.
> > Ensure proper arrest and trial preparations.
> > Inform the victim (family).

The best of circumstances regarding this notification would be to inform the family first. That gives them time to prepare for the news media onslaught if it was a high-profile case. It also allows you time to sit with the family, discuss the case, and answer their questions. Their appreciation can only add to your quiet satisfaction. It is for that family your entire department has been working so tirelessly.

If, as so often happens, the arrest comes suddenly without the opportunity to inform the family, it becomes the first priority of all notifications. I would not confirm any arrest to any non-law enforcement entity until that family is told and their needs met. They deserve the courtesy.

After the investigation identifies the person(s) responsible for the criminal act(s), there is a feeling of pressure to make an immediate arrest. We all want to see major criminal offenders removed from the street, but unless you are forced to take immediate action in order to prevent another crime, or the escape of the criminal, take a little time to review the evidence and degrees of proof with the prosecutor. There is a pervasive attitude in our business where the police feel prosecutors always want an airtight case and prosecutors feel the police are always shoe-stringing them with weak cases. A mutual review of the evidence should result in the agreement that further investigation would be fruitless. If you reach the point where you have a case, and further investigation would not produce significant results or other benefits, go for it.

If you are charging through the investigation, and circumstances require you to make an immediate arrest, abruptly and without planning, inform the prosecutor as soon as possible after the arrest and review the case to that point. Besides tying the case together, you can usually stiff him for ham and eggs at 4 a.m. It is important that the prosecutor be a part of the arrest preparation, particularly in a major criminal case. If you have the luxury of time, use it to be sure your evidence, proofs, and testimony are adequate to the task of trial and conviction.

Since we are speaking of the luxury of time, use it to your advantage. You may pick the time and place of the arrest to further the case by gaining entry to a place you were unable to access prior to this development. Consider other open cases or persons-of-interest who are in association with the soon-to-be defendant; there may be an opportunity to clear a few other matters.

The detective commanders are responsible for ensuring that the arresting officers use proper procedures and arrest techniques. This is particularly important if a "raid" situation is present or anticipated. It gets discouraging when, after all the difficult work, an important case is blown because of a faulty arrest. Usually, this is not a serious problem, but it should be on the list of considerations.

Inform all other commands within your agency and any other agency that is actively involved in the case. Do not rely on the other agency's personnel to inform their own commands; it is a proper task for the controlling agency detective command. This is not only a courtesy; it is a practical way to get the loose ends cleaned up in a hurry. Always suggest that a call between detective supervisors be made to cover all details, information swaps, and associated issues. Be sure to get your arrest information notice out very quickly to other area agencies; they also may wish to talk to your arrestee while opportunity exists.

The Public Information Officer

If possible, advise PIOs of the arrest prior to its execution. This is so they are knowledgeable in order that they can prepare the necessary case background and press release for approval by the department command before release to the media, or if something should go seriously wrong in the execution of the arrest. That is always a danger when an arrest is met with serious resistance and overwhelming force is used to end the event.

The PIO is constrained from leaking or tipping the media of the impending arrest by department rules and procedures, which provide for disciplinary action against any employee who divulges police information to unauthorized persons.

I repeat this because it is so important. The victim (or family) is often overlooked in the rush of business as a major criminal case winds up. After the arrest, the victim should be quietly informed of the situation before the media are advised and the race to the TV screens or print begins. After all, the victim is your direct client in the case.

The detective commanders should ensure that cooperation with the prosecution is smooth and trouble free. The mutual goals are the same: conviction. Arrange for the case coordinator to sit with the prosecutor during trial. The police agency should assist with witness protection, if necessary, and aid the effort to locate and transport missing witnesses. In fact, try to monitor some of the important ones—a low priority within the scheme of things and not a bad idea when you have a few minutes.

This cooperation was missing in California during the Manson murder investigation. The Los Angeles Police Department and the Los Angeles prosecutor's office differed in their views concerning the arrests of the Tate killers. The LAPD announced to the press that "warrants had been issued for three persons: Charles D. Watson, twenty-four, who was then in custody in McKinney, Texas; Patricia Krenwinkel, twenty-one, who was in custody in Mobile, Alabama; and Linda Kasabian, age and present whereabouts unknown.* Also announced was the anticipation that an additional four or five persons would be indicted. This announcement was against the wishes of the prosecutor, since he felt additional evidence was necessary for indictments and therefore that announcing the arrests would be premature. Obviously, the prosecutor felt that the main actor, Charles Manson, was not yet in the bag.† This failure to cooperate and coordinate activities certainly caused difficulties between agencies in the Manson case, but, more importantly, could cause case investigation or trial difficulties in general. Leadership should always strive to avoid this problem.

The decision on matters such as this is always the department's; personally, I believe any public announcement of pending arrests is dangerous to your officers, the case, and the public and is against common sense. The only legitimate time a department can go public when seeking a violent felon is when the public is needed to help in locating him, such as when he is "running" and when he is a serious danger to officers or the public. At times, exigent circumstances may require release of such information; or if a defendant is in hiding, this kind of information can be used as a "flushing" tool. But normally, seal court warrants and keep probable-cause arrests within the law enforcement community.

Supervisors and Investigators

Arrest and go celebrate.
Prepare for trial.

The case is at its climax when the arrest takes place. The supervisor and investigators must take care to ensure that the arrest is made legally and with proper methods. If a search warrant is called for in order to search beyond the immediate area of the arrest, get one. There have been too many incidents where valuable evidence has been suppressed by the courts when officers went beyond the scope of their authority at the time of arrest.

* Bugliosi, *Helter Skelter,* 159.
† *Ibid.,* 158–59.

Take the criminal(s) into custody and secure any evidence seized. Interrogate the prisoner(s) and take any statement made. Obviously, take care to ensure that all rights are accorded to the prisoner. Advise the prosecutor of the circumstances and details of the arrest and the criminal history of the defendant prior to any bail hearings.

Lock up the prisoner(s), bring the victim up to date, or inform them and go celebrate. As soon as possible, the case testimony and evidence presentation should be prepared for trial. The supervisor must ensure that all evidence is accounted for, witness statements are complete, and all gaps in the case are plugged with follow-up investigations or explanations prepared. One example of this problem can be identified by an LAPD Tate murder investigation error. A tape, which contained permission for a search of the Span Ranch, where .22 caliber shell casings were recovered, turned up missing. The fact that it was missing was not discovered until the issue was raised during the Manson trial.* Ouch!

The case should be reviewed with the prosecutor, anticipating any defense moves and preparing to answer any challenges to the investigation.

The case supervisor is responsible for the post-arrest case completion. The coordinator, along with the index, lead sheets, and tickler, will play a major role in the case trial preparation. It is through this system of checking the chronological case logs, leads, indexed reports, and ticklers that matters can be quickly located and addressed. **The case supervisor must collect all reports, notes, files, and any other documentation generated by the investigation.** There is one master file. Duplicate field files may be kept, but no personal or secret files should be permitted. Officers found to be keeping a personal copy of a department file should be severely disciplined. Officers found to be keeping personal files containing investigative material that was not entered into the department file should be fired.

If the department's workload is so stressed that these items *routinely* wait until "time" is available, reconsider the department priorities and capabilities. Then use overtime to get the political controllers' attention. Something has got to give or you're just spinning wheels in slush, playing catch-up, and wasting more time in the long run than the repairs take in the short run.

The case must be complete—index, statements, evidence, witnesses, exculpatory channels not investigated or checked, unfinished interviews, all leads returned, loose ends accounted for—or it remains an open case file and cannot be moved to the pending trial file draw. Waiting to see if the defendant pleads to the charge is not an option. The exception to that rule is crime laboratory examinations that were not necessary to move the investigation. Those that need to go forward regardless of the uncertainty of a trial must

---

* *Ibid.*, 348.

be monitored by the case supervisor/coordinator and timed to fit the trial preparation pace. It is a balance between wasting laboratory bench time and getting ready for trial.

Laboratory

Prepare for trial.

The case supervisor should coordinate all laboratory reports and pending examinations with the prosecutor. The laboratory should be informed of the arrest and the anticipated trial date. Direct contact should be established between the prosecutor and the laboratory supervisor in order to prepare for trial and set dates for laboratory personnel to testify at the trial. The case manager is responsible for the initial contacts; do not rely on the prosecutor's office. Do not wait until the trial date is upon you to contact the laboratory; it may be too late to avoid a date conflict.

The preceding is necessary; prosecutor's offices are notoriously inefficient, even those with "case investigators," which police departments routinely believe do the "case prep" work. If you work with one that does that well, you are indeed fortunate.

Press Officer

Prepare a press release.

The press release stays within the department guidelines, for release only after the arrests are made. No further comments from the department are in order.

Prosecutor

The police case supervisor should provide the prosecutor with a complete case summary as soon as possible. If the case coordination has been constant throughout the investigation, the summary will be easier.

From the summary, the prosecutor will able to locate and review all the evidence and prepare it for introduction into the case trial. Everything the police seized should be made available; all photographs taken of items not seized should be reviewed. Prosecutors need to build their case and prepare their trial exhibits. Early preparation permits case gaps to be closed, reduces surprises at trial, builds prosecutor confidence, and strengthens plea-bargaining positions (if that enters into the proceedings). Sometimes the investigators do not see the same significance to evidence as the prosecutor does. The LAPD evidence room contained a door with the phrase "Helter Skelter is Coming Down Fast" on it, which was seized at the Span Ranch, the Manson family home. This linked the killers with the same bloody words found at the La Bianca residence. The door had been in possession of the LAPD for five months; the prosecutor was not aware of its existence until he saw it while going through other evidence at the LAPD.* The police case coordinator and the prosecutor should be able to sit down and review the case in an orderly manner. Controlling the case with a logbook, index, assignment sheets, tickler, and report review system will produce a highly sophisticated result that will reduce the errors or complications that have been mentioned.

Prosecutors, as part of their review, should check all the laboratory reports and make sure they understand them or have any questions answered or further examinations conducted, if necessary. They should read all the case statements and cause any required corrections or follow-up investigations to be done. Follow-up matters conducted by the police require the same case control procedures as in the investigation. **If prosecutors decide to use their own staff, they must provide all of their reports and findings to the police supervisor-coordinator for review, comment, and inclusion in the police file.** Otherwise, we are back to two investigations. The case coordinator will query prosecutors about these matters, telling them to provide a laboratory evidence examination list as soon as possible so they can see that it is on a laboratory schedule. That is a memo to file-index matter, the administrative side of the case file.

The prosecutor should prepare the charges (the accusatory papers) and attend the hearings and bail proceedings. In states where the police file the charging documents in criminal cases, have those documents reviewed; prosecutors may wish to add or delete various charges or replace them with grand jury indictments. In some states, police officers prosecute their own misdemeanor and traffic cases.

During the trial preparation, prosecutors should debrief their witnesses and review their testimony to ensure complete understanding. Prosecutors also must be aware of your department's case closing process and procedures. Investigations continue after the arrest in many cases, firming up evidence, locating additional witnesses, or chasing other defendants. The defendant may also be involved in other criminal activities under investigation in different cases or other agencies. This is known due to the flag index and other agency checks. Full-disclosure states and public records cases are accessible

---

* *Ibid.*, 294.

to people you wish did not know. Depositions will be taken, some public, and most filed in open court records. Have the prosecutor attempt to get court records sealed and depositions closed if needed. One way to get the court to agree is to show continuing investigative activity. Otherwise, warn all case managers and other departments affected of the possible open records in order that they have an opportunity to adjust as best they can.

Prosecutors should request the police case coordinator to sit at the prosecutor's table during the trial and freely discuss testimony and its significance. This officer knows more about the investigation than any other individual and will be of tremendous assistance in locating information that will plug holes in the case.

Prosecutors have another important role in addition to the trial. They should coordinate their witness schedule with the police supervisor and laboratory managers, calling only the officers and examiners needed and informing them of the anticipated time of their testimony, and releasing any officers or laboratory personnel not needed so they may return to duty. There are still too many instances where law enforcement personnel sit around courtrooms waiting to appear. A little forethought can reduce this resource waste.

The prosecutor should also take the time to inform the victim of the trial results and penalty.

Defense Counsel

All police contact with defense counsel should be conducted through the prosecutor's office; there should be no exceptions to this rule. Inquiries and requests for reports made by defense counsel to the police should be referred to the prosecutor's office. Copies of all police, laboratory, or medical examiner paper that will be turned over to defense lawyers should be released through the prosecutor's office. This is a continuation of the concept that all information passes through a single point. This point now shifts to the prosecutor's case coordinator or control system. The police case supervisor should keep track and file reports on all matters involving the prosecutor and defense lawyers that relate to the police investigation or police file.

When the police and prosecutors truly cooperate, the results can be remarkable.

This is the end of the case.

To sum up, picture this: A piece of human remains is found in a remote area of wilderness; it is the only fact you know. A person is dead, and the rest of "it" may or may not be somewhere around there, or somewhere else. The cause and method of death is undetermined, the identity of this former person is unknown, how "it" got there is unknown, and who or how "it" was placed there is unknown. Where the human came from is unknown; the family also is unknown, but you know they are wondering, or at least, maybe, should be. That is all you have. However, you do have a choice; bury the remains in a pauper's grave, or make an inquiry.

Several weeks later, you put handcuffs on the killer and rapist and present him to a court where he is tried, convicted, punished, and removed from society, maybe permanently. You have just achieved something beyond the epitome of the definition of achievement. Also, you've maybe provided a little bit of rest and comfort to a family. You are entitled to your personal satisfaction and comfort. You have earned it.

Management of Resources

8

Goals/objectives
Systems
Schedules
Priorities
Evaluation
Case disposition
Budget data

This is a short chapter. Normal department management procedures deal with this issue. I do not get into the detail of overall management, just some basics.

The investigation of a major crime is a total team effort. The investigative unit must work within a department structure as a part of the greater team effort. The investigative team has the objective of convicting a criminal. The department objective, as a part of its overall responsibility, is to provide the framework and operational necessities for the investigative team. Unless the department views its work as part of a total effort toward the prioritized objectives, the individual efforts within the organization will be frustrated. One important part of a police agency's control program is the management of resources. Considering the goal of a major criminal investigation and the volumes of work for police agencies, effective management of time and human resources becomes critical. In today's world, any law enforcement agency that does not efficiently manage its time and activity is wasting tax dollars and is probably not as effective as it could be. Responsibility is shared for managing time and resources by all levels of personnel within an agency. Specific resource management responsibilities, focusing on major-case control, are as follows.

Department Command

The department commanders are responsible for the management of all functions under their jurisdiction. They should:

1. Set goals, objectives, and milestones for all functional units. These should be written and highly detailed.

2. Develop a systemic approach, which differs from systematic, to work by stating the critical-path method, identifying the tasks, and assigning the personnel to achieve the objectives.
3. Determine schedules or time estimates for the work to be accomplished.
4. Evaluate progress of the work. Decisions on continuing the work, or placing a greater or less effort, should be made from rational evaluation methods. Work that will be nonproductive should be phased out or terminated according to established priorities. Evaluation should be made from factual information as opposed to emotional, or using information derived by gut feelings or instinct.

Managers can best accomplish their major-case control goals, as stated previously, by developing or continuing to improve:

1. Case-tracking systems. This is the method of accounting for your work product and identifying the investigative status of each case. The tracking system, if organized or incorporated with a management information or database format, will track the case human resource commitments and future case goals (targets or milestones) to identify case obstacles or anticipated problems. This includes estimates of the time (hours) to complete work, expenditures of time and money (travel, per diem, etc.), as well as the progress of the case within the criminal justice system (pipeline). This is primarily used for expansive long-term investigations
2. Manpower case-reporting systems. This is the part of your statistical package that provides you with budget justification data. This information includes the types of cases, results of the investigations, hours of investigation, hours of analysis, hours of clerical support, and hours of support services. This information is then readily translated into dollar or cost figures. It can be separate or melded into the tracking format.
3. Case disposition systems. This is an add-on feature to the case-tracking system. Managers should receive more information than "case closed by conviction or dismissal." A feedback of information from the prosecutor and or court should be instituted to identify case investigative failures, evidence deficiencies, or case control failures. Procedures or techniques that caused trouble should be identified and ironed out.
4. Performance evaluation of individual investigators, supervisors, and investigative teams. Routine major-case critiques identify good and bad performance and procedural problems. Counseling and training should be recommended and implemented when improvement is

needed. Procedural problems should be assigned to a research task force or unit for problem-solving work (think tanks maybe?).

If you are a police manager and, at this point in your thinking of major-case control you can say, "I understand what I have read and agree with it, but how do I go about getting the detail work done in a manner that will work for my department," you need some help. If you are saying, "I don't understand or cannot visualize the details of the control systems discussed," you need a lot of help. If you are unable to identify professional staff people within your organization who will expertly perform your improvement program, then your first step is the instituting of a professional staff management development program. You will have to rent, train, or hire experts. You cannot afford to do nothing.

Principal Entities

Resource Management

Numerous police managers have fallen into the habit of complaining about the lack of resources to do all the work police agencies are called upon to perform. There is strong evidence to support this position in the overall sense. However, too many managers have allowed their priorities to be weakened and use the same excuse, lack of resources, for not assigning full investigative complements to major crimes. There is no justification for neglecting a high-priority investigation.

Full commitment of resources to a major criminal investigation must be made (an all-out effort) until all the critical tasks are satisfactorily completed. Examples of *some* of the critical tasks for a major reactive case are as follows:

First Twenty-four Hours

Critical Tasks	**Noncritical Tasks**
Crime scene	Standing around the scene
Witness interviews	Complete detailed statements
Suspect leads	Detailed negative statements
Neighborhood canvasses	Neighborhood follow-up
Victim's background	Crime scene history
Alarms broadcast	Area photos and sketches
Documentation of efforts	Routine terminal traffic
Keeping the coffee hot	Telling the spouse you will be late for supper

A critical task is defined as work that must be done at a particular time or else the task sought will be forever lost or its value severely diminished. It is very similar to the critical-task method of constructing a building: foundation first, roof last, everything else in a specific order of completion to permit the next step to start. The basic construction progresses and the machinery mechanics, electricians, and plumbers come and go at specified stages, four or five separate times. Contractors, of course, do it on a logical schedule and fixed plan, a luxury you will never have in a reactive criminal case. Architects and builders can dream of smooth flows with a few burps; you call yours nightmares in action with stomach cramps. It is OK though; the only person who suspects is your spouse.

Police managers are the world's foremost personnel jugglers—more than the army, because we get to do it every day. Moving people from function to higher-priority function on instant notice has become a routine. Managers, knowing the department's priorities, plan for such eventualities. Managers know where all the agency resources are working and on what priority program. When a major crime occurs and workers are needed they are in a position, since the department has preplanned, to rapidly shift resources and focus on the major case.

Some of the historic methods of effective and efficient use of resources are set forth as a reminder.

Extra help (short-term) can always be obtained by use of overtime, extended shifts, and schedule reshuffling. Changing the time of duty tours and assigning police cadets or auxiliary officers to relieve either workloads or sworn police officers from other lower-priority tasks are also possibilities.

If a crime scene has two or more locations, the two- or three-person team can be split by adding a uniform officer to each team. The crime scene work is then done "in parallel" as opposed to "in series."

Use uniform officers for extra help after their response phase duties are completed. If the initial patrol response was to flood the area, or use neighborhood patrol pattern searches or stop and checks, the continued effectiveness of this duty diminishes with time. Decide when to end that activity and use the officer for the neighborhood foot search.

Recall to duty all necessary personnel.

Use other agencies to fill in work gaps or handle other necessary work. Personnel from area law enforcement agencies can be borrowed, as preplanned. They may perform work tasks, such as area foot searches, crime scene crowd control, or, where jurisdiction permits, handle your calls.

Defer routine work. Traffic warrants, parking control, radar, or other special traffic details may be cancelled or postponed. Vice squads, criminal-warrant officers, and organized-crime investigators can usually be pulled from their work for critical tasks. The work priorities can always be reviewed in light of the immediate problem. In the Battle of the Bulge, the U.S. Army used cooks, mechanics, medics, supply, transport troops, and clerks for combat roles until the situation stabilized; the clerks were not much help. The statistical system of the department should be designed to capture all the time and effort spent (case manpower tracking, time and activity sheets) for future budget justifications. Your controllers need to see data in its raw form to understand your needs. They disburse the dollars you need, and they "feel" the ramifications in the community if the police do not succeed. The police are the entity in the community that secures its existence.

Supervisors must identify, then design on the spot, the critical path of the case and assign personnel with investigative continuity and future court testimony in mind. Random assignments of critical tasks will break case investigative continuity and cause a degree of ineffectiveness. Cases that were not coordinated with continuity and with a minimum of core investigators can be demonstrated by counting the police army in courthouse halls waiting to testify to parts of a major case.

After the first twenty-four to forty-eight hours of a major reactive criminal investigation, the case usually settles down. During this time, the supervisor/coordinator has:

1. Reviewed case progress periodically, starting at the first two-hour mark
2. Decided the critical path of investigation, with an open mind for "Plan B"
3. Assigned teams for investigative continuity
4. Conducted a nightly team review and critique
5. Evaluated the case direction and progress
6. Assigned the most appropriate case investigative team to the case critical path

The supervisor has secured or is chasing items that, if undone, will be lost forever. He or she is identifying all follow-up work to be done and making notes for future assignments, such as case documentation. In addition, the supervisor is formulating investigative priorities and designing the work to be done within the structure of the team and the resources available.

The supervisor then initiates the follow-up foot work, such as redoing the neighborhood canvass with a smaller team, in an unhurried fashion. He or she, of course, has available all statements taken during the first sweep and is in a position to note discrepancies, changes, or different slants from neighbors or witnesses.

The case is evaluated and gauged on both work and success probabilities for presentation to commanders in order that they be properly ranked in the detective unit priorities.

If the major case is a murder, never quit. Even after several months of work have elapsed and no end is in sight, always keep a specific investigator assigned. Active investigative work should be required on all capital cases, even after all original leads are exhausted, at least for one or two days every six months. People change; loyalties change; relationships change; attitudes change; information is discovered; people talk. These are all solid reasons to keep working on murder cases and other appropriate major criminal investigations.

I believe those agencies that manage and coordinate their department's functional units and their major-case investigations in an orderly climate, and systemically, will have higher productivity, greater efficiency, increased effectiveness, and one hell of a conviction percentage. That is the gauge an outsider would use to determine if competent people managed the police department.

Proactive Cases

Proactive case definition: A planned law enforcement action against known or suspected criminal activity

SA Frank Carter
Florida Department of Law Enforcement

The Preparatory Phase

9

Now the shoe is on the other foot. In proactive cases, the police select the target and initiate the investigation at a time of their choice. The targeted criminal(s) or enterprises are usually unaware, at least during the initial phase, of police interest in their criminal activity. This is the opposite situation of a reactive case, where the conduct of the criminal forces an immediate police investigation.

Reactive cases start with a sudden unannounced event requiring a rapid commitment of police resources to control or contain the situation. These cases usually gradually trail off into a more settled routine. Proactive cases start with an orderly procedure: careful examination of the targeted goals, assignment of the investigative resources, and a charted path of investigation. Some would say that reactive cases "blow up" at the beginning and proactive cases "blow up" at the end.

The point is made; the cases differ at the starting points, with the police in command of the initiative in proactive cases. Some examples of typical proactive investigations are:

- Drug smuggling
- Frauds, conspiracy schemes
- Career-criminal investigations
- Organized-crime investigations, including gangs and illegal cartels
- Computer crimes; many large-city police departments have created computer crime units. State police and state investigative departments have special computer crime units to handle the major frauds, computer theft of trade secrets, and child predator and child pornography crimes. This is a growing need, and coordination plans with other agencies is a priority.
- Robbery, burglary, auto theft rings, and other conspiracies
- Gambling, where it is still unlawful. The largest gambling organizations today are the states themselves. It is difficult to get excited about chasing the bookies—sort of suppressing the competition—unless, there is opportunity to get to a higher-priority crime or criminals.
- Public official corruption cases
- Loan sharking operations. (Brought back in anticipation of legislation being reactivated regarding bank and credit card firms' interest manipulations. Does anybody remember when charging more than 18% annual basis was a crime of usury, and *the* definitive issue of loan sharking? Knee capping was the usual investigative predicate.

Table 9.1　Proactive and Reactive Investigation Phases

Proactive	Reactive
Preparatory phase	Preparatory phase
Intelligence phase	Response phase
Investigative phase	Crime scene phase
Arrest/trial and appeal phase	Investigative phase
Intelligence phase	Arrest/trial and appeal phase

We are going to discuss the principles of managing and coordinating a major proactive investigation by using the same methodology employed for the reactive cases. The role of the principal entities during each phase of the investigation will be identified, examined, and discussed. The phases of the investigations are slightly different (Table 9.1).

The difference is the intelligence phase in the proactive investigation. This is due to the nature of the police attack. In reactive cases, the police must respond to the event, and in proactive cases, the police initiate events by selecting the investigative target. The intelligence phase provides the investigating agency with justification to investigate, points to the best method of attack, and identifies the scope of the work. Ending the proactive investigation with a second intelligence phase permits the police to identify "spin-off" cases and decide on a course of action for each case so identified.

Proactive cases are almost entirely investigated by detectives. There is little, if any, uniform officer participation. However, good investigators will recognize the potential contribution the uniform force can make. After all, they are the "eyes and ears" of the detectives and should be used to full advantage. Further, they will learn that detectives do not work a Monday through Friday, nine-to-five job.

Let us discuss the preparatory phase.

Department Command

- Priorities
- Objectives
- Structure
- Training
- Interagency agreements
- Intelligence policy
- Report system

The responsibilities of the department command are the same as in reactive cases, as discussed in Chapter 3. I will not repeat what was stated previously except to highlight the main points. The command responsibilities are to:

1. Establish investigative priorities.
2. Establish a clear chain of command.
3. Develop manpower allocation systems.
4. Develop case-tracking systems.
5. Develop a management systems approach (CDR).
6. Provide internal reviews (inspections).
7. Establish jurisdictional guidelines.

It is important to reemphasize the necessity of defining the agency goals and objectives relating to proactive case investigation. Case effort must be directed because police resources are being committed by a police command decision rather than reacting to an uncontrollable event. The public should and will hold their police commanders accountable for tax resources spent. Clear written objectives, supported by identifiable results, will provide police commanders with rational answers to often emotional questions.

Police-initiated investigations confront commanders with additional problems of greater degree than normally encountered in the traditional investigation. The very nature of most proactive investigations requires greater skills, and thus training in surveillance techniques and controls, electronic measures, informant development and control, and legal aspects of search, seizure, communication interceptions, and eavesdropping.

Surveillance, whether a fixed spot or moving, is a highly developed art. Success requires skill, innovation, situational thinking, and decision making. Developing surveillance plans and alternatives, use of long-range photography equipment, and concealment and disguise of a police presence are highly innovative and imaginative techniques requiring experience and training. Departments should require that officers be taught surveillance skills along with the best procedures and resource utilization. Surveillances should be planned and staffed with only sufficient personnel to achieve the surveillance objective. Far too many stakeouts are overstaffed and thus waste resources.

Controlling surveillance through reporting is extremely important, though often neglected. Supervisors should approve in advance all surveillances. Spontaneous surveillances, though rare, do occur and should be called in to a supervisor and reported at the first possible opportunity.

All intelligence cases carry an assigned number that is entered in the department intelligence files. The names, addresses, and other index information are in the same format as the main department and criminal case file formats to provide interchange of data. Intelligence supervisors, under strict department criteria, decide which items to flag within the department's files and how to handle out-of-agency inquiries. **When a flag is raised by an inquiry, the *intelligence office* has predecided which gets an immediate response, a delayed response, or a response with a phone call to the inquiring agency. The *department decides* which items require an auto-response**

to an inquiring street officer to protect him and inform him about what he is dealing with at that moment. Requirements of secrecy have a point where the options rapidly diminish. The problem is eased with a list of instructions readily available, such as: grab him, duck, ticket and release, or inspect his car for safety equipment until the surveillance follow car or dogs arrive. Then add, get the now suspect of something out of the car for the in-patrol-car camera to surreptitiously get a full photo; side view also, please. All this is coded with preplanned training and instructions.

Surveillance logs, recording the date, time, and event, should be required at all times. Fill the log in immediately or as soon as possible for each remarkable incident as it occurs by whomever observed the event. Organizational procedures must require strict compliance. Logs may be admissible in court and certainly portray evidence of proper control. They tend to support testimony, and they depict a professional approach to an investigation. Failure to maintain logs brings faulty testimony, unsupported by recording; defense attorneys will explore suspicion of fraud or perjury. In addition, supervisors not present at a surveillance have a greater degree of assurance that their charges are performing their assignments.

Police commanders who neglect to control all surveillances are flirting with disaster. One only has to be reminded of the debacle at the Monroe County Sheriff's Department, Rochester, New York, when a detective created a false log in a major organized-crime case.* Lack of command controls permitted this error to occur (some would say it encouraged perjury), and resulting convictions were overturned. The sheriff's department was staggered by investigations, and officers were indicted and dismissed. The morale of that department suffered through the recovery difficulties. Credibility of all law enforcement suffers through this abuse.

Electronic measures require training and control. The operation of electronic wire intercept equipment, body and room "bugs," and tracking devices require special skills. Training for use and operational control is necessary. Methods of warranted surreptitious entry of buildings are a skill most burglars would love to know; sadly, some do. The procedure and controls of this sensitive investigative approach are a command responsibility. Strict compliance with all court orders and department rules is an absolute. Recording of conversations, transcribing requirements, evidence-packaging procedures, control of original tapes and duplicates, installation and recovery of wire intercepts, tracking and "bugging" devices, all require advanced skills and dexterity. Failure of an agency to teach these skills means the agency simply cannot conduct a major proactive investigation with its own resources.

---

* *Rochester Times,* Union Gannett Publishing Co., Rochester, NY, archives.

Another agency becomes a necessity or is heavily relied upon, and probably the case control passes to them.

Control procedures for electronic measures are another critical factor. Inventory, access, accountability, use, and installation are all important department command responsibilities. This equipment must be stored under lock and key with severely limited access and strict accountability. Without control, abuse will occur. Equipment that cannot be used without a court order should not be removed from the controlling person without a court order and signed approval from a high-ranking officer. This officer is usually the agency head or an executive officer, never a line or operational commander. If your department has a legal office, that person's signature or initials should be required on all paperwork relating to the use of court-ordered equipment. The court order is just that. It's not a court approval. The difference is in the level of accountability; the order shifts it to the court, not a police supervisor. The court will be the decider of issues, including whether the police supervisor followed the department's rules as well as the courts and statutes.

Department intercept procedures need to be clearly written and address, in detail, the following:

1. Clear definition of terms
2. When court orders are required
3. When, how, and who may use equipment for training, demonstration, and maintenance
4. Department authorizations
5. Execution of order procedures
6. Termination of order procedures
7. Reports, logs, and work papers (assignments and schedules of use)
8. Recording (taping) procedures
9. Disclosure of information rules
10. Transcript duties and control
11. Notice rules regarding persons intercepted, courts, and other agencies
12. Consent to intercept procedures
13. Inventory and storage procedures
14. Inspection requirements
15. Department policy for use internally and/or with other agencies

See Appendix H for an **example** of an order, not a sample order. This order is provided to show that controls are necessary. Fit your department's order to your law and policies. Copying this example would be a mistake; it was designed for a specific agency under their then existing controls. It will not be applicable to your department or jurisdiction. It does show that a legal officer or prosecutor is necessarily involved in its development. Any formatted warrant applications, affidavits, orders, and warrant forms must match and follow the department's order.

Informant control is another critical department command responsibility. Departments that still permit officers to have personal "snitches" that are unknown to the appropriate supervisors are rare. Most agencies have set up a formal informant identification and control program defining their criminal informants (criminals and associates, including relatives), their protected sources (selected reputable citizens) and new possible sources (undetermined or not vetted), and nonreputable characters used with caution due to a specific necessity. Label these carefully to be sure interested citizens are not in a similar category as "criminal informants." They deserve protection as well. Control procedures for all classes are necessary. Department policy should address:

1. Recruitment and processing
2. Confidential symbol assignment
3. Profile sheets, name cards, and photographs
4. Criminal history and current wanted-person checks
5. Fingerprints (consider excluding reputable interested citizens after a satisfactory criminal history and internal file check)
6. Reports, status, contact control
7. Abrogation procedures
8. Transfer of informants to other officers or agencies

No investigative intelligence should ever be permitted in a case file without identifying the source; use numbers or symbols for informants. Properly structured informant identification provides for protecting the source of information, yet identifies the source to appropriate department officials. If an officer will not identify his source of information, he cannot use the information or the source; this is an absolute rule. There is a judgmental dilemma with this problem. The information may be solid and needed. Prosecutors must be informed of the problem and assist in working through it with the police. The evidentiary issues are complicated, and bad results can cause severe repercussions. The rule still applies in those agencies without a history of maladministration or corruption. The problem in departments not having controls is not the informant control program, but agency management and lack of adequate control procedures.

No police commander in his right mind would ever permit a report that read, "The following information was received from a reliable source" (confidential source) and leave it unchallenged. The source must be identified and placed in the department's files and the information attributed to that source by a symbol or code number in the report. If that is not acceptable to the parties, it cannot be used. Note: there could be an exculpatory evidence problem here also; that takes us to police ethics, another subject. One avenue for you to consider is a requirement that *any* new or unidentified source-informant must be vetted in the administration area of the department before any, emphasize *any,* contact with an investigative team is permitted. Do it as a routine in the ordinary course of department business. Contact your legal officer about this, for there are no excuses for nondisclosure of possible exculpatory evidence, legally or ethically, relative to a specific active investigation.

Other concerns of informant control are the contacts between informants and officers. Report all contacts immediately, preferably in advance, preferably witnessed by another officer, and certainly written up as soon as possible after the contact if prior notice was impossible. Department commanders are responsible for ensuring that clear procedures are in effect and enforced to protect both the agency and the investigator from the obvious evils evident without such control (such as corruption charges against the officer, whether true or false, false information, or nonexistent sources of information). Training the officers to deal with criminal informants should emphasize the controls, informant mentality and motives, as well as the best methods of interviewing and getting information.

The most repeated name in the file will be "unidentified source." List them with as many identifiers obtained: male, female, accent, stutters, says "you know" every other word, can't complete a sentence, etc., etc. Eventually some will be identified. This is for direct information regarding a case. General tipsters on a variety of matters require selectivity and judgment.

Legal aspects of search, seizure, and eavesdropping are a training problem that never ends. A typical proactive investigation usually involves a cast of characters who will be able to afford competent legal defenders. Cases of this nature will go through an appeal process and be subject to close legal scrutiny. The continuous flow of court decisions concerning search, seizure, and eavesdropping change or reaffirm the nuances of the law. Officers must be confident their actions and procedures are correct. Regular training that updates and improves the knowledge and understanding of current practice is a command responsibility. The nature of investigative techniques in proactive cases constantly engages the officer with search and seizure law. Department commanders will recognize the success of their training programs and the achievements of their experienced officers in this difficult field when attorneys call and ask for legal opinions from the investigators. Yes, that does happen. Besides that, if officers are well versed in the law of search and seizure, they might learn to enjoy the cross examination in court.

Training investigators in the aforementioned techniques can be time consuming and difficult, particularly in smaller agencies. Managers must decide whether their own agency has the capabilities to engage in the type of investigation requiring these skills. Nevertheless, even if you need help, you must have the written policy and procedure in place if you are to participate in a major criminal proactive case. In states where that is not readily available, or the training is not up to necessary standards, plead through your association for the state police or state investigative agency to provide that for you. If they cannot, you are all in trouble. It is a matter where you visit with and advise your political controllers.

The department command is responsible for interagency agreements. In proactive investigations, the managing and coordination problems require these agreements to consider, in addition to those mentioned in Chapter 3:

1. Personnel commitments
2. Specialists
3. Prosecutor/investigator teams
4. Responsibilities of the chain of command

Personnel commitments require serious consideration. A proactive investigation is long term in nature, from a month to several years. When you decide to participate in such a case, be prepared to commit personnel for the duration of the investigation. If you agree to join another agency's case, be prepared to support the case until completed. This requires planning, information, and clear case objectives in order to gauge your total contribution to the case. Management must consider, as policy, the experience of the officers, their career development, and the role or required input of the contributing department. If you are expecting to control, lead, or carry a major share of the case, you must use high-quality investigators and be prepared to leave them on the case for long-term periods. Planned reassignments or rotations are necessarily thought out in advance. Consider a case investigator's institutional knowledge along with informant use, evidence, and testimony issues as an example.

Specialists such as crime analysts provide the information sources, flows, connections, charts of gangs and drug cartels, financial fraud paths of money and paper, and trends, and all with strong collocation skills applied and much more.

Specialists such as accountants, securities examiners, real estate transaction experts, technicians, and analysts needed for specific purposes must be identified, cleared, and available for use. Often these specialists may be from outside the law enforcement agency's employ. They are special consultants under contract; this is a difficult process for some agencies and presents some unique problems. The foremost problem is the mental block law enforcement agencies have against using nonsworn people in investigative roles. Once you accept that most of their work is "desk" or research work, the problem usually goes away. More and more state and federal agencies are developing specialist capabilities within their sworn investigative staffs that are available to city and county agencies on a priority basis. Department managers must provide the resources for investigations and this, of course, requires preparation.

Prosecutor/investigator teams are the best method to attack complicated long-term high-crime investigations. When the target is identified, investigative agreements should be secured from the prosecutor to ensure his or her participation in the investigation. This provides direct legal support, gains a prosecutorial commitment, and enlists the prosecutor in the investigation on a positive note. A letter of understanding to the prosecutor should be hand delivered to him or her after reaching the agreement. More about this later.

The department command has the responsibility to set procedures, which preach and insist on a management by objectives approach for major proactive criminal investigations. The department system should provide for a pause, however slight, after the initial intelligence phase for a case review, at the appropriate command level, to ensure that objectives have been set and are attainable. This is particularly true in sensitive or volatile cases. If your targets are high government officials such as state legislators, cabinet officers, or county or city commissioners, you want to take your best shot and be sure of your case predicate. Remember the old adage "Don't wound the King;" it is an overblown statement. In police circles, "Don't wound the Court Jester" is a better descriptor. The true reason for careful consideration is that it is harmful to all public order for the police to "take a shot" and miss. The critical task is to provide a go/no-go decision. The management review of the case after the intelligence workup determines the adequacy of the preparation, justification, basis of the information available, and methodology of the information validation process.

The decision to maintain a case in an intelligence mode or to try for approval of an active investigation rests with the intelligence unit case agent supervisor. Many departments make a serious error in case management when they permit investigators to take what is essentially information and work themselves into an active investigation without command approval. The department is then committed to an investigation where objectives may not be clear, resources to conduct the work may not be available, and/or a conflict with competing priorities may arise. Proactive cases have a history of expanding in scope; this requires resources, and thus a command-level approval. Normally, supervisors are not permitted to commit resources beyond their immediate supervision. They must accomplish their tasks within their own resources or seek higher approval. Supervisors may commit their own people but not others'. When this rule is not followed, resources are overworked and underachieve. Department commanders are responsible for placing in effect an agency structure along with procedures that ensure that all supervisors, case workers, and managers understand the scope of their authority and work within it.

Department commanders are responsible for the development and implementation of clear, written intelligence policies. Agencies with an intelligence section must have an intelligence management system; it is important, but in another book, maybe. The nature of proactive investigations usually means the police will work with information supplied from a variety of sources. Unless a system for determining the validity of the information is in place, a lot of "garbage" will creep into your files. There are solid reasons, supported by experience, for police agencies to be actively engaged in the criminal-intelligence business. Lack of policy based on defined responsibility and purpose has led many police agencies into troubled times with the abuses that occur when law enforcement officers have access to unbridled information of a derogatory nature about citizens without a valid police and statutory interest. Department commanders must develop an intelligence criteria based on the lawfully defined purpose of their agency and limit their gathering of information to that lawful purpose.

Information and/or sources that have access to actual information of a nature that is not directly "statute friendly" but does have the possibility to lead to such "positive" information have a place. Receive it, look at it, and retain it in the *trash bin* for its designated period, then cascade it out to destruction … or case use, where it makes itself into the department intelligence case files. The case now has a criminal predicate, and the information may be retained under the intelligence case file procedure. The theory is that it will transform into an active investigative case; more on this later.

An intelligence policy should:

1. State the authority that permits or directs the police to gather intelligence. If such a statute does not exist in your state, use the inherent authority to investigate crimes within the state as the predicate to collect information about criminal activity. Then limit your policy to just that.
2. Define the limits of authority, statutory or internal.
3. Define the terms, such as: information, intelligence, criminal intelligence, investigative information, etc.
4. Set guidelines on the gathering of information.
5. Set information validation principles.
6. Require analysis—a little more detailed than the normal lists of recently released from prison burglars, robbers, and drug dealers with their addresses, vehicles, associates, hangouts, and parole or probation officer phone numbers; a bit more sophisticated than the burglary and robbery maps with MOs and time of crimes in neighborhoods or regions. (The new computer display boards are a great squad room addition for these.)
7. Provide for internal and external access rules.

8. Set procedures for dissemination.
9. Provide a retention policy for department records, limited records, public records, confidential records, restricted without clearance records, trash bins, prior to destruction review, reactivation of trash bin records, destruction policies, and destruction of records and witness of destruction certifications, which include the method, date, time, and place of destruction.

   The public-political arena in which we work used to be simple; that is no longer the case, due to some law enforcement abuses, congressional overkill, and state legislative posturing via statutes. It is sad commentary that the 9/11 Commission failed to seriously address but only noted that the "failure of the FBI and CIA" to communicate was because of a congressional act (FISA), which included statutory restrictions on manner of and material collected! Even in a terrorist-driven climate our "political controllers" failed; they condemned the FBI-CIA for their *failure* to break the law. Imagine that oddity, the FBI actually obeying congressional law. What's the world coming to?

10. Provide a destruction procedure (cascade is this book's method).
11. Provide for periodic internal review and inspections of intelligence operations.

As an adjunct to the intelligence policy, but no less important, is the command responsibility to set procedures for the purchase of information and detail the procedures for money transfer. The internal audit trail of "buy money" and informant funds is of critical importance if you are to maintain your integrity as well as reduce the possibility of theft and/or embezzlement—along with, as you well know, checks to ensure you are not buying false information. Those are mostly various federal bureau issues, but watch for it anyway.

Department intelligence procedures should provide for identifying and setting policy on spin-off cases developed during the investigation. We all know from experience that when a major investigation is initiated, many other criminal activities are discovered, or old dormant cases emerge in a new light. The structure of command control of a major case should provide for a review and decision on whether to expand the original objectives to include the newly discovered criminal activity, shelve it for future action, or pass it on to another investigative unit or agency. The decision to change objectives of an active investigation must be the responsibility of the appropriate command level (predetermined by policy), not an investigator or first-line supervisor. Changes in objectives usually require additional resources or the abandonment of the original objective. Without policy and procedure to control major-case objectives, managers will lose control of priorities and department resources. Here is another point: In reactive major cases, the police usually have an opportunity to "shake the bad-apple tree," so to speak, for other matters of interest, as in proactive cases. Be careful you do not get too distracted from the main goal.

As stated in Chapter 3, department commanders are responsible for developing and implementing a reporting system. Whether the reporting system is manual, electronic, or a combination of both, good control practices dictate that agencies have at least:

1. Investigative reports: event reports for immediate street-closed matters with specified department-indexed content. Then gradually scale up the detailed report content to fit the various reporting issues by class of misdemeanor and felony, high misdemeanors and violent felonies. It is not your fault that in some places a tow truck driver can be charged as a third-degree felon for not having his address on the side of his truck, while a guy who beats his wife or kids half to death can be referred to a family court dispute resolution class. Therefore, your report design system needs to consider these matters.
2. Administrative data sheets
3. Investigative summaries or synopsis
4. Prosecutor's summary
5. Statements of subjects, witnesses
6. Examination reports (laboratory, medical, evidence)
7. Surveillance logs
8. Investigative forms (waiver of rights, consent to search, electronic intercept logs, surveillance logs, lead sheets, interview sheets, etc.)
9. Memoranda
10. Profile and index cards
11. Assignment and tickler cards
12. Evidence and property forms
13. And more, yadda, yadda

Remember, all of this must be designed as part of an integrated system with indexing in mind.

Detective Command

Priority shuffling
Grasp of all other activities
Work flows
Prosecutor liaison

Fix responsibility on one person for all cases. Remember that individual responsibility for any defined unit always rests with the unit leader. Overall responsibility for all designated detective units also rests in one higher-ranked leader, and so it goes all the way up to the top. Responsibility cannot be delegated away, only work matter designated to an individual. The chief is responsible for everything; the patrol officer is responsible for his or her assigned and regular duties.

Commanders of investigating units also have a responsibility to prepare their commands for proactive case investigation. It is the commander's task to fix supervisory responsibility with an individual for major-case control, reactive and proactive. Investigatory unit commanders coordinate all activities within their jurisdiction. They assign resources and coordinate intersquad activities. Detective leaders are always ready to shuffle resources according to department and unit priorities. They set the criteria and policy of the unit work schedules and work commitments. Part of the commanders' responsibility is to evaluate the effectiveness of their working supervisors.

Unit commanders must have a system of inspection within their unit to ensure that cases are properly administered and investigated. Merely ordering that cases be indexed, reported, filed, and prepared for presentation to prosecutors, without checking for compliance, is a sign of a slack manager. Smooth clerical flow and readiness of equipment are part of commanders' responsibilities. Theirs is the task of continuously improving the workers' capabilities.

Detective commanders must have an accurate grasp of all investigative activities within their unit and their rate of progress. They continuously evaluate case progress against resource commitments by a system of report review, conferences, briefings, and interviews. Detective leaders make recommendations or decisions (which depend on the department's structure) on opening or closing cases by evaluation and knowledge of the unit's priorities and the resources available. Sometimes these are hard choices and difficult to make. Decisions are particularly difficult with a crew of energetic and aggressive investigators; they will give a leader no peace for treading on their cases. Reality requires choices, priorities, evaluation, and systematic review to produce the rationale for the decisions. The investigators may not like it, but they will respect the decision. At least your more experienced personnel will understand the problem.

In order for commanders to accomplish their tasks, they must know their personnel and their various skills and expertise. They must nurture and use the skills to their best productive ability. When personnel whose capabilities and skills need development are identified, assign them to a specific case for appropriate training and instruction, or to squads that are currently exercising those skills. Specialized needs are always in short supply, so develop those special skills in a number of officers. This creates depth to a unit. If a football team needs a kicker they get one, and if possible a backup, usually not the right guard. If the owner tells the coach the right guard is more cost effective, the coach tells the owner how many extra points and field goals he will have to do without. This knowledge and preparation is what commanders use when they assign investigators to a major criminal investigation team. The team does not just materialize from whatever resources happen to be available (exceptions temporarily arise in reactive cases); that is inefficient and wastes precious investigative time. Commanders select the major proactive cases and the working teams. That is their job.

In the beginning of this book, I listed a few professions or trades where commanders should have a working knowledge. Well here comes another one (again, not in detail but at least consider it)—money laundering. How is it done; how do you find it, chase it, seize it, and be able to keep it or return it to the victims? As a detective commander, you need to be ahead of your troops; if they need to know they will ask you. This is where you use your contacts in the Bahamas, Cayman Islands, or where is that bank … ? Marianas or somewhere out there, you know, the island with all the bird turds. "Yeah, the place where you can open your own bank in the morning, be registered and certified and moving dollars all over the world after lunch." "That's right … I remember, you can leave the next day with all the transfers made to your private places and with all of the bank's records." "Right, you even to get to name your bank … like T. T. E. H. Bank of Nevis." "What's that mean?" "The Trail Ends Here. Let's go ask the Captain."

Everyone is aware that varieties of organized crime, conspirators, and co-conspirators have been with us for centuries; they did the condo bustouts, land frauds, and cash-skimming deals along with the gambling, liquor, and the prostitution business, with a lot of truck hijacking and warehouse thefts. In addition, they ran the off-load thefts at all ports and controlled the unions in construction, transport, hotels, and operating engineers. Most of that is now under reasonable levels of control. Today it is money laundering, both drug and frauds. We don't do tax evasion.

It is a big business; it is the concealing of the origin, possession, and distribution of multimillions of dollars. Drug importation, distribution, and selling requires huge amounts of cash to flow in both directions. It is Florida's third largest commercial activity.

You need an analyst(s) well versed in banking, finance, and communications as well as the street investigators. The game is called "follow the money," from suitcase to cartel to distributor. The crime of selling the illegal drug on a street corner starts the collection, which flows upward to cartel control. All along the way cash is consolidated into large but manageable amounts, like a million. Cash cutouts are made along the way as payments in amounts that also need to be hidden. It flows into businesses to "tax it" and out to legitimate possession with visible wealth to spend and avoid an IRS net worth tax investigation.

How? They buy racetrack winning tickets at par plus 10 percent cash and redeem dollars at window cash-outs and similar methods. This is washing.

Bundle it into $10,000 or under for wire transfers to avoid currency reporting. The IRS will lower that someday.

Run money through businesses; buy shopping malls and apartment complexes that are sold and resold until the origin becomes murky; or two or three charities.

Today, they have moved into diamonds, gold, and financial paper, market trading for cash losses of derivatives, and such.

The thug in a hurry finds the rare homeless man from under an interstate bridge that actually has paper identification, cleans him up, gets him to a storefront lawyer, and has him make a will. He tosses him into the intracoastal waterway and inherits a bunch of money, coincidentally just under the tax level. "Gee," the thug says, "he must have been the poor soul I took home once and fed. God ... that's awful, where did they find him? ... You said what? Aw ... gee."

Which means we switch gears and move into financial fraud. I recommend to you Howard Silverstone's *Forensic Accounting & Fraud Investigations* (John Wiley & Sons, Hoboken, NJ, 2007) as one source.

Commanders and detectives need to understand terms and systems. Due diligence is part analysis of transactions prior to the transaction and part investigation of the parties, sources, and the transaction itself. Financial fraud occurs in the absence of due diligence. Ask Mr. Madoff's former customers. Financial examiners know the transaction, customers, costs, both visible and underlying, products, markets and market risk, factories, and asset maintenance, and they visit the seller. When you see "aggressive accounting" in business reports or audits, it is a flag in itself. That is the due diligence matter; then the police do the who, what, where, when, and how. In addition, the police do the what was specifically signed, certified, and produced, then they identify the keeper of the record.

Then throw in liquidity, analysis ratios, capital and its ratios, and market to book accounting (values set at different levels).

The launderers hide the audit trail via check-to-cash-to-check and reverse through multiple businesses going in complete disorder into separate banking systems until the cash is spaghetti through comingling of various assets.

Smaller operators use smart cards or cash with no identification, like most politician cash contributions under $200 and sent in via the Internet. Why not? Congress and state legislatures allow that as well as the nonfiduciary class of laws for Wall Street. Throw in electronic fund transfers in and out of the country and back in through our "island bank." Remember, the ones the banker gets to take all records home from.

The cash or loans from the offshore shell bank comes back. It's less "overhead" to multiple corporations—cash-heavy businesses like casinos, bars, and vending machine operators—which is "repaid" to himself, less purchases he makes in value items and property, which is now clean as tax-paid profit from the shell or real business. They pay politicians with overvalued purchases from a mutual owner source, which equals more spaghetti, with a difficult-to-reach investigative predicate necessary to start a criminal investigation. Alternatively, they use undervalued sales of assets to politicians that are readily sold at a higher true market value resulting in a huge profit. This is why police agencies like to start with an IRS fraud unit transaction review.

Commanders should understand those terms as well as financial statements, margins, and ratio analysis.

Do you think this one example is enough? You can always use my sheriff's fallback position: "Call the State Police." I guess I will continue with the norm. You get my point.

Detective unit leaders are responsible for maintaining contacts and liaison with prosecutors, courts, and other agency counterparts to be assured of good working relationships. The department policy and procedure will provide the manner of recording those contacts and the results of agreements or understandings, usually some form of memorandum for distribution within the command structure of the agency. **All command-level agreements and understandings within and outside the agency must be known and understood by all command-level personnel and distributed as needed.**

Investigative unit commanders control case expenditures by policy, procedure, and their best judgment. They do this by being good at their jobs, being well experienced, and having solid information for decision making. Again, not like reactive cases where you fly by the seat of your experience. If commanders pay attention to the preceding paragraphs and develop a unit system based on the thoughts stated, they will do a good job.

Finally, detective unit commanders must be ready to give advice and suggest investigative paths to their supervisors when they need help. However, detective commanders, as in reactive cases, must not become actively involved in investigations for all the same reasons mentioned in Part I of this book.

Supervisors/Investigators

Ready to roll
Future plans
Sources of information
Training

Supervisors and investigators prepare for proactive case investigation the same as they would for reactive investigations. There are some additional thoughts for consideration that are necessary due to the long-term nature of proactive investigations. If a case is going to take six months to a year to investigate, supervisors must consider and plan for such things as:

1. Vacations
2. Sick leave or hospitalization
3. Resignations, retirements, and promotions
4. Moonlighting problems
5. Changes of case investigative personnel

Consider the future career plans of your officers and their career development when assigned to cases that may take years to complete. It is like special details in uniform and detective units: two-year maximum assignment, then back to uniform or regular detective work. Weigh trucks for two years, work narcotic details for two years, then back. To do otherwise is to kill career advancement, possibly lose a good future manager, and risk the "evils" of permanent assignments, which occur to both officers and the department. Agencies that do otherwise are usually run "politically," either elected and/or by internal "politics," such as in "good old boy." Please try to avoid that situation.

Supervisors must be aware of and be familiar with the department's management systems. When people know what is expected of them, and the standard of performance is outlined or stated, the objective identified, and the methods of work charted, they will perform much more effectively.

Now the mundane, slow time: There are always slow periods where an active investigation stalls due to the nature of the case or uncontrollable situations. If the personnel cannot be assigned to temporarily assist on other cases or other units' temporary needs, consider in-service training, firearms requalification, time off, catching up on reports, cleaning the coffeepot, taking the annual inventory, early or late. Essentially, **use upcoming events to fit the operational unit's schedule, not administrative timetables.**

Analysts

Research and report.

Analysts are an important factor in proactive major criminal investigations. There is much research needed on targeted criminals and/or their business enterprises. If you do not have "civilian" analysts, someone, usually an investigator, will have to do the yeoman's work. Sometimes you can borrow a uniform officer from the light-duty list. Some years back the New York State Police did that. They sent a healing trooper to the Department of Motor Vehicles record center to scan vehicle reregistration and title documents;

after the DMV had finished their review, they passed through the trooper before filing. It turned into a full-time job because he was pulling so much fraudulent paper: the man was uncanny in his ability to spot telltales while scanning. In New York City, there was enough work to assign a tow truck to the detective assigned to chase their vehicle recovery leads.

Some of the typical proactive major-case work requiring research and analytical skills to link together pieces of information for investigative follow-up are (keep index and flag systems in your head while reading the list; uniforms and administration also use the service):

1. Criminal histories
2. Property and title searchers
3. Telephone toll sorts, numbers and linkage
4. Business and associate relationships
5. Corporate license and ownership research
6. License and tag checks, owned vehicles and transfers/purchases
7. Money audits and bank transfer research
8. Intelligence file search
9. Public and other departments' records research
10. And much more that need not be mentioned here

The analyst(s) will be constantly checking all department files; working with a flag system helps, depending on your agency size and operations. Consider the analyst the "flag" watcher, flag waver, reporter, and ensurer. They will call whoever should have been notified in whatever plan you set; they catch the off-hour communications traffic activity to ensure all is working well. They check other agency files and public files via phone, computer, or communication net message. They can work many regular cases or several major cases simultaneously.

Analysts, whether they be sworn officers or civilian specialists, must be trained in their work (there are analyst training courses, averaging about forty hours, available). In addition, the department must have information source material available or advise the researchers where and what they seek is available. Analysts must also be very familiar with the department administrative systems.

Other Agencies

Secure agreements and commitments.
Define responsibilities.
Share costs.
Share information.

Very few law enforcement agencies will conduct a major proactive investigation without working with or using other agencies' resources. Agreements between agencies are more critical than the reactive case agreements. The long-term nature of proactive cases means other agencies' resources will be tied up and therefore not available to the "mother" agency. The case-controlling agency has the responsibility for making the agreements and being sure each participating agency fully understands its commitments. A memorandum of agreement is the preferred method; memory is faulty and perceptions always change with time.

Secure clear case investigation agreements and, once made, honor them. It takes a mutual agreement to change or drop an understanding. When agreements are broken, so is faith. In addition to the general interagency agreements mentioned in Part I of this book, it is particularly important in proactive investigations to agree on:

1. Case supervision and who controls the case. Control procedures must be clear and firm. There can be only one leader; cases are not investigated by committee. There is ample evidence of failure, squabbling, and recriminations where joint investigations and/or task forces worked without a strong leader or had split case supervision.

2. Where the decision-making responsibility rests. Clearly define which agency is the managing agency and who decides the issues.

3. Cost sharing and financial responsibility. The case intelligence workup should attempt to identify and estimate the case costs (travel, per diem, equipment purchases, rentals, source or buy money, etc.). Agree on who pays what costs, and set aside the money. Where new or unanticipated costs arise, quickly decide and agree on who pays. The case-controlling department's system should handle the payments and maintain confidentiality. Does the other agency you are working with have a system that will protect the confidentiality of the case? Find out, and make the decisions necessary to ensure the investigation is protected. There is more of a problem with public disclosure of spent or designated funds than penetration or in-agency leaks.

4. Where appropriate, a coordinated investigative/prosecutor team approach should be agreed upon. The prosecutor should be able to schedule a set amount of attorney time to the investigation. In jurisdictions where this has been accomplished, the case success rate increased remarkably. Remember that the objective is to convict.

5. A review to determine the scope of the case (during the intelligence phase). Agree on who participates and identify their roles. Once an agreement is made to enter a case investigation, stay involved until the original objectives are met or another review cancels the

effort. If additional objectives are identified or the scope of the case is expanded beyond the original estimate, secure new agreements or release agencies who cannot commit their resources beyond the original agreement.

6. Press statements at the arrest or conclusion of the case. Obviously, no news releases are made while the case is in progress. If statements must be made, the case-controlling agency is the only agency permitted to speak and then only within established guidelines. Secure firm agreements on this. If there are no press guidelines in place within the controlling agency, develop them for the specific case being investigated. The case prosecutor is always the best place for press statement responsibility to rest. That should be your goal on press agreements.

7. What specialists are needed, costs, and who will supply them. Determine their availability prior to initiating a case.

8. Information-sharing and -reporting methods. No holding back of information or case paperwork can be tolerated in interagency investigations. If you will not share information and reports, do not participate in the case.

Prosecutor's Office Investigator/Prosecutor Teams

Prosecution policy

Secure from your prosecutor his or her priorities in relation to your case. There is no sense in conducting an investigation if your district attorney is not interested in prosecuting. There have been instances where long investigations have targeted criminal enterprises such as common organized-crime enterprises, made several good prosecutable cases, only to have them laid aside due to prosecutorial disinterest or higher priorities. This is a total waste of investigative resources. The way to deal with or correct such a problem is beyond the scope of this book.

Where agreements to pursue an investigation are made, identify the legal personnel who will work with you. Try to secure a commitment to have an attorney observe parts of the actual investigation in a role that does not inject him or her into the case. A lawyer should be made available, preferably the one who will appear in court, and not subjected to other office duties or catching street crimes to prosecute while engaged with you on some specific aspect of the case. If you cannot secure a full-time commitment, agree on a number of weekly hours and try to get the prosecutor to stick to the agreement.

Usually a prosecutor intake attorney (the case review and charge filing attorney) can squeeze out a few hours to review your case and provide legal advice. A few misdemeanor cases and borderline felonies may be dumped, but then, those would have been pled out quickly anyhow with time-served, catch-and-release results—particularly if your department just did a "street sweep" to clean up a complaining neighborhood.

All prospective policy matters should be settled. Understand the evidence, testimony, and proof standard the prosecutor desires.

The interagency agreements secured prior to resource commitment will go a long way toward smoothing a difficult project. Without them, you are almost guaranteed disruptions.

Pro-Active Case Development Cycle

	Preliminary Phase	Intelligence Phase	Investigative Phase	Arrest Trial Appeal Phase	Intelligence Phase
Resource Growth					
Major Activities	Planning				
		Analysis-Associations			Analysis
		Background			
		Resource, I.D.			
			Surveillance - Visual - Electronics		
			Subpoena-Tolls		
			Investigations		
			Prosecution Summaries		
				Arrests	
				Prosecute	
					Spin Offs

Figure 9.1 Proactive case development cycle.

Intelligence Phase 10

All proactive major criminal investigations must be preceded by an intelligence workup and assessment. Normally this is a careful gathering of information, analysis, resource identification, and commitment to the case. There may be instances in proactive cases where immediate decisions must be made, but I cannot think of one. We must react to major events as discussed in Part I, but we need not react in a proactive case. Sudden political pressure to arrest a class of people too quickly is not acceptable, can never be acceptable, and will end only with disastrous results, mostly internal within the unit assigned. The other side of that is you cannot accept direction via political pressure not to arrest criminals because of classifications or status. You cannot lead police officers with a political rope around your neck.

If a series of robberies are occurring in a geographical area, we must respond to each individual case, but we need not create a "team" to chase them as a proactive case without an assessment. If a trawler is seized with thirty tons of marijuana and three smugglers, we must react to the immediate seizure but need not start an immediate major proactive smuggling investigation without an assessment. Indeed, just the opposite is true; if we do charge in to form robbery task forces or smuggling investigations without thought and assessment, we will inevitably waste valuable time and personnel. Such a reaction is usually a response to a panicked political leader from the "Somebody do something" school of government.

The intelligence phase is important, and each entity has specific responsibilities. Let us continue.

Department Command

All cases that are politically sensitive, such as investigating the local prosecutor, high-ranking police officials, or political officeholders, require a command-level decision. All the processes that are used and considered by the detective command for "routine cases" are then presented to the department head.

Command-level decisions are also required whenever resources beyond the control of the detective unit are required (you cannot commit resources you do not own). Additionally, command-level approval is necessary if your agency's personnel are to be loaned to another controlling agency in a major criminal investigation.

Detective Command Review

Get the case agent information.
Be familiar with scope of proposal.
Identify resources.
Estimate time frames (milestones).
Decide on **central desk reporting (CDR).**

Detective commanders will review all case intelligence work for the go/no-go decision. This requires a presentation of facts and their sources. Commanders must judge the reliability of the information and demand verification or validation data. This keeps the department from being led down an unknown or inadequately prepared path. The intelligence presentation should identify the other agencies needed, which agreements to put in place, and what commitments are in the making or expected. Determine if the other agencies have reviewed the intelligence and if they concur. Whether the agencies will be able to work together is another question to be answered. Especially, decide the intelligence data classifications, dissemination issues, and a common label language for formatting. Keep terrorism in mind with the database structure of the Fusion Centers to ease data integration.

As an example, to retain a secrecy position in a major-case investigation, the department may wish to classify some items as on a "need to know" basis for outside-of-case queries or direct contacts. If your department "hits on" another department's file, in which they have an interest in your query subject, each party knowing a query was made on the specific subject or matter covers that issue. **That means pick up the phone, talk, and release information or deal with the issue.**

Investigative unit commanders must be entirely familiar with the scope of the proposed investigation. They must grasp the entire case proposal and integrate the new case possibilities with other existing work, priorities, and available resources. The intelligence review requires that all information submitted meet the department intelligence policy criteria. The reliability and identification of all sources of information is a critical factor and can never be adequately stressed or emphasized.

The case objectives must be clearly identified. The targets and the anticipated statutory violations must be stated. If the trawler with the thirty tons of marijuana seized and three smugglers arrested constitutes a part of a major drug-smuggling ring, and intelligence from the persons and documents seized, boat ownership, cell telephone toll sorts, navigational charts, and criminal associations identify some of that specific operation's backers, then they and their activities are the objective—with an eye toward whom they work for, the necessary chain from which the drug was produced, to whom the proceeds were distributed, and the location of the fruit of the crime, property or cash you can seize. Commanders then must assure themselves that the proposed resource commitment and investigative time estimates are based on valid assumptions—or present this to the DEA for their control. Your decision.

Estimates of the time frames (milestones) needed to reach the objectives must be presented to the unit commander for evaluation. If you know the objectives (for example, the three drug smugglers' operation), you evaluate the information on hand relative to the evidentiary proofs needed. Decide on the most probable method of investigation and identify the case critical path. You may select:

- Surveillance
- Penetration/informant
- Electronic intercept or eavesdropping
- Subpoena/records search
- Interviews/statements
- All of the above
- In addition, investigative probes

Let us run two quick relevant situations.

In the aforementioned trawler matter, the scene was a lone trawler coming up an isolated river in the middle of the night, fortuitously discovered by the Coast Guard and quickly seized by the police. If the three arrested crew members were quickly removed from the scene and replaced by three police officers who then waited, what would occur? The area sweep produced no people or vehicles capable of removing the cargo or signs that anyone but the police knew of the seizure. Let your imagination run. If the police, instead, made a show of the seizure, called the TV people, lit up the area, and started the removal of the cargo, you can picture a different result.

In the second scenario, let's say the narcotics squad lets you know that night that they intended another corner sales bust of three street dealers based on warrants or previous probable-cause cases produced by "undercover buys;" a supervisor decides to send two intelligence squad members to observe. Let us call them the proactive team. They watch the "narcs" grab and arrest two of the three dealers along with one customer who unfortunately lived a life of bad timing. The third dealer, thinking he was lucky, poor soul, would do something. The hullabaloo is over and he is left alone, but in the normal crowd around such places. What do you think he will do, where will he go, and whom will he call on his cell phone? The intelligence investigation of "follow the suitcase" has just started. They will watch and observe, disregarding low-level crimes (nonvictim) to see what, where, and to whom it leads. Addresses, associations, additional phone numbers, and vehicles are identified, and eventually, after a lot of patience and false starts, one guy carrying the "suitcase" appears and a long-distance surveillance commences. The scope of a new case is now being determined. Picture where this is going.

Prior to execution of warrants, the index should be searched to trip any flags, particularly as to all regional agencies and jurisdictions to alert supervision of other police interest in any of the soon-to-be-disturbed subjects. Agencies that have not placed any flags in their or the statewide system will not be alerted. It is axiomatic that for any planned interviews on any case, especially intelligence cases, where the identity of the interviewee is known, an index flag trip search is made. This is an absolute rule when working violent felony, terrorism, and warrant cases. **There are too many multiagency and overlapping jurisdiction cases with task forces, special investigations, and lone agency contacts running around and occasionally brushing one another to not let left-right hands in on any foreseen contact of any similarly situated person.**

The index control system will ensure that all such notices and responses will be sent to preapproved supervisors or general responses will be given to inquiries under a developed code and classification system.

The "bust 'em, book 'em, and let's go get a beer" arrests can continue as normal even if they are a totally ineffective numbers game, relative to the ultimate objective. This does not become serious until you are dealing with methamphetamine distributors. Today the police need the information as to where the required precursors come from with more than just a label to work with. The stakes have increased exponentially since Hezbollah has become a principal distributor of the precursors in Canada and the United States.

Identify the work to be done, estimate the time it will take, and give it a go. I once had an investigator ask, "How do you estimate how long an investigation will take if you never did that before?" I told him to use the SWAG system (scientific wild ass guess), but estimate. Base it on experience with investigative tasks. You must get a handle on your resource commitments. They rarely will be exact and you may not achieve your objectives, but it gives you a gauge to work by, and further experience will improve your time estimate to a surprising degree of accuracy. After you experience a few major proactive cases, with clearly identified objectives and honest evaluation of the intelligence available, you will be able to accurately estimate a three-month investigation to within plus or minus a week or two. Further, adapting to the exceptions and unanticipated issues becomes easier.

Consider having your warrant squads, including violent felony and traffic, assigned to the intelligence unit. Its work is a great source of information and has the additional advantage of being able to hold a minor warrant or two in your pockets—a form of multitasking.

Try a focus on the gangs, mobs, and rings.

Check with the parole and probation departments; these are major sources of intelligence, and depending on what you are seeking, add the DARE officers and school protection officers. Last, do not forget your uniform officers and regular detectives for their input.

Experienced commanders will be able to judge the progress of the case work to determine honest effort as opposed to the union rule of slowing the work to meet an artificially extended deadline.

Next, detective commanders must obtain the resources, initiate and execute all interagency agreements necessary to the case, secure agreement from the prosecutor, and ask for and receive the initial case work schedule.

A decision is necessary about the central desk reporting (CDR) point. This is critical if your agency is still using manual indices and case control procedures. If you use data processing to index, flag, and track cases, the appropriate codes and programming must be checked and any changes implemented. As in a reactive case, all reports and assignments must be reported through the case central point. Picture if you will five agencies, geographically separated, all performing pieces of investigative work without a central point of case control. (See Figure 10.1.) If you do not, most data winds up in the individual department's files and is not connected, except by inquiries. Ideally, all information, requests, reports, leads, etc., go to agency number five (CDR), but if information should pass between agency one and two, which is certainly possible, even practical, the agreement must be that both agency one and two report the action and results to the CDR at number

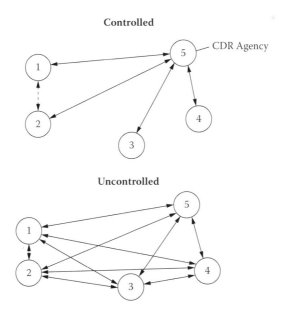

Figure 10.1 Controlled—uncontrolled.

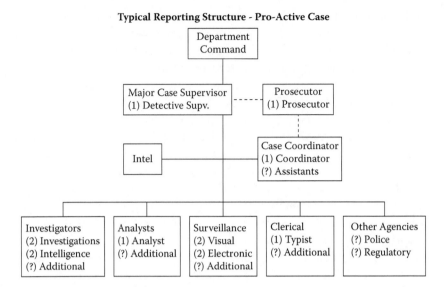

Figure 10.2 Typical reporting structure—proactive.

5 for review and index checking. The control agent inspects all points from time to time to manage this. An automated and coordinated system within all five agencies is the ideal.

The critical path of the investigation has been decided; noncritical matters may be identified to fill in case downtime. For example, you may decide to conduct a surveillance of some "'dopers'" and they take a two-week vacation. Plan to fill in with:

1. Noncritical case matters
2. Reports
3. Statements, supplements to clean up, transcribing, etc.
4. Maintenance of equipment
5. Training
6. Use on other cases (mule work only)
7. Time off

The data is in and evaluated. The decision is made to go or not go based on the intelligence investigation. If the decision is to go for it, implement and stress all management policies and agreements and give your full support. Assign the resources and commence the investigation. The intelligence case now becomes a criminal investigation, and the file is transferred to active.

Finally, the department system must have a check valve. All intelligence cases that have received supervisory approval are presented to the specified command level for final decision. You must have a report review system that reviews all intelligence cases or reported information. This brings to command-level attention those cases that were disapproved for investigation by lower-level supervisory personnel. A first-line supervisor should have the authority to reject an incomplete intelligence case, but that decision should be reviewed at the command level. With this procedure in place, the first-line supervisors must first make their go/no-go decision, but their rejections and the reasoning are reviewed as well. This process ensures that commanders get better work from supervisors, develop supervisory decision-making skills, and still not miss any investigations of interest.

Investigator/Analysts/Surveillance

Identify a major case.
Do the intelligence workup.
Present it to the supervisor.
Start the index and analysis.
Document actions.

Major proactive criminal investigations usually start as a result of investigators developing information. When an investigator has potential proactive case information, a complete intelligence workup should be considered. Communication with a first-line supervisor usually results in a quick evaluation of the worthiness of the information. An intelligence case usually covers such items as:

1. Target identification
2. Criminal activity (suspected or known)
3. Scope of activity (suspected or known)
4. Background information and current status of targets
5. Validation of sources of information insofar as possible
6. Identification of associates and the scope of their activity
7. Identification of victim(s)/customer, if any
8. Identification of victim(s)/customers' associates or possible witnesses
9. Toll analysis (may be feasible in some cases at this stage; make sure the target is not notified by the telephone company—see the state statutes regarding this)
10. Linking analysis, and criminal-activity flowcharts

The intelligence workup should be presented to a supervisor with an outline of the proposed investigation. Identify as well as you can resource requirements, specialists, time frames, objectives, and anticipated milestones.

Before going to active case investigation, the intelligence unit provides a list of all names, addresses, properties, vehicles, aircraft, vessels, hangouts, associates, victims, phone numbers, and businesses, etc., and starts a *case index*. Selected items may be placed in the *department master index* at this time. Flags are optional at this stage.

Intelligence workups may use some of the usual probes:

- Place a bet.
- Buy a piece of crack.
- Take a few pictures of the prostitutes, particularly if you need a few more informants in that neighborhood.
- Conduct a few quick surveillances to identify players, habits, hangouts, associates, vehicles, phones, employment, addresses, and unusual or infrequent contacts.
- Check public records. If you are doing a possible financial fraud case or public scams, check the ads and similar ads by what appear to be competitors; often they are the same. You locate additional victims and tie-ins to other associates. As to the ads, if it looks too good to be true … etc. Call them and see what they offer you.
- Identify group associations.
- Do discreet informant checks.

Submit information to analysis for any links that can be identified, criminal histories, or other investigations under way involving the same people (both internally and with other agencies).

Investigators can and will provide:

1. Systematic planning of case concentration
2. Opportunities to communicate opinions, observations, and problems to management
3. Documentation of all intelligence case development actions. They become part of the case file, whether retained as an intelligence case or transferred to the active criminal case process. If the case is rejected, the file remains an intelligence file and is handled as a normal department intelligence matter.

The time involved completing an intelligence workup varies with each case. Sometimes it is possible to complete work after several hours of intense review. More often, several days' work is required, and, on occasion, intelligence work-ups may take several weeks.

First-Line Supervisors

Make operational decisions.
Assign resources.
Fix case responsibility (do not delegate supervision).
Make decisions on operational methods.

First-line supervisors have the responsibility to identify a case lead investigator or reporting officer during the intelligence phase of an investigation
workup when the department does not have an intelligence unit—or, if one
exists, circumstances require independent action. This fixes the responsibility of investigation and reporting (this is not delegation of supervision). The
supervisor ensures that the department's intelligence section is advised if the
case was not received from the intel unit, and the records section is advised
of the case. File check "flags" are established for target and priority subjects
at this time.

The supervisor assists the investigators in preparing the case for command-level presentation, projecting resources and time frames and identifying case investigation problems. When ready, supervisors bring the case to
their commander for review and decision.

First-line supervisors are responsible for being aware of their team's
strengths and weaknesses in order to best utilize their talents. They assign
investigators to the case and identify their roles. They bring the team
together for the case-opening conference and outline the path of investigation and expectations for all to know. Supervisors must not overcommit their
resources to unrealistic work standards and must be fair in the distribution
of workloads. There is no time to play games of cronyism or favoritism in
a long-term investigation. Particularly important is the process of integrating personnel from other agencies into an investigative team. They must be
assigned to work to the best of their abilities. The good jobs must be shared
along with the dog work for long-term cases. If the controlling agency dis-
criminates against personnel from other agencies by abusing them, they will
not be around long. Certainly, you will have a discontented work crew.

Supervisors must ensure that the agreed-upon administrative paper flow
is understood by all and that the central desk reporting (CDR) concept is
accepted and implemented.

The control and decision-making responsibility is established at this
point. Supervisors make the operational decisions on resource commitments allocation and distribution, not the investigator in charge (case agent).
For example, if surveillance is required, supervisors decide the number and
names of officers who will be assigned. If a wire intercept location (plant) is
established, it is the supervisor's responsibility to approve the monitoring

post assignment and schedule. This is true even if the monitoring is inside a special place in the department itself, meaning technology and phone company cooperation is at work. Supervisors must control these matters to perform their responsibility of fair and equitable work distribution

First-line supervisors must establish their authority at the beginning of the case, emphasizing the point that they make all decisions on the investigative methodology. They should encourage advice from the investigators, but they have the decision-making responsibility.

As you can see, this is an abbreviated form of an intelligence unit workup. The reason this appears is to show the efficiency advantage of having intelligence units. Case workups by detective units divert resources on "maybes" rather than concentrating on active investigations.

Prosecutor

Evaluate.
Anticipate legal issues and problems.
Assist in case attack methods.

The prosecutor, as part of the investigative team, evaluates the intelligence workup. He or she reviews the sources of information and the validity of that information from a legal standpoint. The prosecutor should identify and anticipate legal problems that may arise and suggest what is necessary to overcome, go around, or go through such problems.

During the intelligence phase, the prosecutor should identify the trial lawyers, if possible, and assign them to the case, as agreed upon, for the duration of the case. The trial lawyer and/or the prosecutor should enter the discussions of the case investigative attack methods and discuss the operational critical paths.

Department Intelligence Section Flag System

Files and information

If your department does not have a formal and full-time intelligence section, the responsibility for information and intelligence, implementation, and working control of your intelligence policy should be vested with one individual. Intelligence responsibility should be fixed.

The intelligence unit must provide all available information and leads to a case investigator during an intelligence workup. This unit must prepare for receiving information during the investigation, identifying possible spin-off cases, and feeding back information to the case management. The intelligence unit must actively participate in the case file review to identify new links or associations as the case progresses.

The intelligence section will search file documents and reports, initiate a flag system to provide intelligence information from other sources, and report all such information to the case supervisor. All outside inquiries regarding the cast of characters under investigation must be reported to the case manager. There should never be an instance where intelligence is withheld from the case managers. Intelligence units may also do leads from the coordinator of a reactive case. **The precase agreements set up the auto-flag responses to all queries and supervisors.**

You have a decision to go for it; let's move on to the investigative phase. All of the intelligence unit's (if any) and the investigators' workup suggestions are melded and completed.

This is the place where I digress for another moment. Intelligence units or officers assigned intelligence duties in addition to their normal work need to take advantage of the people on probation or paroled within their jurisdictions. This is an area the police neglected for a long period due to the era we struggled through; remember the old chants "Stop harassing the poor souls; they have paid the price to society; give them a chance; they need assistance to emerge; they are more victims of society than criminals." Most of those criminal advocates have learned the lesson; when a failed social program resulted in a criminal, and his arrest, he became a police problem.

The police are not a social service; they are a protective and a corrective service. The twains do not meet. One works toward rehabilitation or prevention to reach the goal of helping a person toward community acceptance and involvement. We praise and appreciate any successes they may have achieved. The police serve to protect the community from a failed social attempt to create a civilized person. That is a vast and significant divide. People who did not believe that the results of such "melding of services" would be detrimental to both and not helpful to either clouded the issue. The police "collect the failures" and introduce them to "forced corrective institutions" for placement to prevent their criminal activities while incarcerated along with reprogramming, if possible.

Part of the reprogramming is to release some prisoners early to determine if they will abide by the rules. They have required responsibilities to report and stay away from criminal associates, among others. You and I know the recidivism rate is very high and has nothing to do with police harassment. They are a wealth of information with a leverage bar in the hands of the police. Use it wisely; let them show they are ready to be good citizens by aiding the police. Consider it an offer of help.

Police departments know when an imprisoned felon is released; if you do not receive notice in your state, get it in law or rule from your controllers.

If you are part of a criminal justice information system, that is a part you should use. Contact should be made; part of the parole rules should include cooperating with the police, parole officers, and *society*.

You will quickly determine who is "going straight" and who is not. The intelligence unit can use the eyes and ears in the criminal's and associates' "community" with good results. That should be one more addition to intelligence unit duties; contact, interview, and report to file for indexing on a regular basis. A *complete* file of any criminal includes and starts from the time of the original investigation into his activities. After his arrest, the file should include his jail contacts and visitor lists, including who posted bail, his state prison contacts, mail lists, visitors, and inside associates who are identified by the correctional facility. When the felon is released on parole, probation, or completed sentence, those items should be included with the release notice and added to the criminal file and indexed. Knowledge is power. However, be selective in this arena; we do not need the poor tow truck driver with the unpainted door if he was not stealing cars.

A note of caution regarding contacts with probationers or parolees; the original intent of police-convict contact rules or law (depends on your state) was to require the convict control people to be aware of their charge's activities, their involvement or contacts with other criminals, or their involvement in renewed criminal conduct. The rule cuts both ways; when police attempt to use the controlled convict as a direct probe or participant in criminal activity to further an investigation, the convict cannot do so without permission of the parole or probation officer in control and, in some instances, the case-controlling judge. Personally, I do not recommend such overt use; keep the issue to information, known or "heard," unless it is a very serious matter and no other path is available. That will be rare, and discussion with the parole and probation controllers is a necessity.

The Investigation · 11

The intricacies of a major proactive criminal investigation require careful managing and coordinating. We have seen how important control systems are for reactive cases. The importance of good control increases to critical levels for long-term, complex investigations. Let us take just a moment to picture a major proactive case in our minds. Whether the case is a safe-cracking group, prostitution racket investigation, or a multistate fraud or drug-smuggling operation, political boundary lines delineating police jurisdictions will be crossed. Not only will the case move from city to city but probably will also be of interest to county, state, and federal authorities. Local drug sale investigations are merely harassing tactics if one officer buys cocaine and arrests the dealer. They become major proactive investigations when the objective is to identify the scope of the dealing, the payoff and transport systems, the protectors and who is corrupted, the ill-gotten financial gains, and other criminal associates and activities. Multiple agencies and interests will be involved in proactive cases. It then follows that managing by objective, full disclosure, and central desk reporting become absolutes or both administrative and operational failures will occur. Law enforcement is now so expensive we can no longer tolerate "good ole boy" approaches to case management. Officers' time is precious and must be productive.

One method of improving effectiveness, efficiency, and productivity is by managing the investigation.

Department Command

Look important and stay out of the way.

The main function of command-level officers during the investigation is to monitor the case progress and see that the objectives are being adhered to and met.

Detective Command—Monitor Progress

Decide whether to alter or broaden objectives.
Control spin-off cases.
Provide advice and direction.

Establish the CDR and flag system.

Monitor critical-path investigation.

The primary function of detective commanders during the investigation is to monitor the case progress and see that the objectives are being adhered to and met. Their responsibility must be emphasized. Failure to stick to the objectives can be disastrous. Cases deteriorate and effort becomes diffused when investigations change course without restating new objectives.

Let us discuss an example. A case has the original objectives of convicting three dope smugglers on smuggling and conspiracy charges in a state court. The objectives include the targets, the charges expected, the prosecution vehicle, the investigative path, and resources. The expected time frame of the investigation was figured based on those objectives. Then, during the investigation, as so often happens, a discovery is made that the targets are involved with additional persons of the same or higher-level criminal activity and/or information is discovered that the targets are responsible for other crimes, for example, murder. The investigators, if not monitored and controlled, will broaden the original objectives to include the new discoveries on the basis that the new information is of higher priority than the original objectives. This must not be allowed. There are a multitude of reasons; some are:

1. Additional resources will be required, and investigators do not have authority to commit department resources. Only managers do.
2. The original objectives may be abandoned while managers of many agencies believe they are being addressed.
3. There may be other agencies working on the same information unknown to the investigative team and thus duplicative investigations are taking place. This should be determined prior to case opening, during the case on occasions, and through routine interagency contacts. Every new index item that is identified during the investigation must be entered into the index and checked for flags. Every principal or person of investigative interest must be flagged. Every such name or address must be checked prior to any contact with that person or place. This is always a problem; while an investigation or intelligence case is being worked, new names and places continuously pop up. Check to see if anybody else is interested in them before you make contact. If a contact is routinely made with people in the ordinary course of things, not much damage will result; if you are investigating a major case, or major intelligence case, where investigative inquiries are necessary, severe damage may result—particularly if a federal organization is involved and you are unaware of that.

4. Investigators do not change work assignments or priorities; department managers do.
5. The ability to work at a preestablished pace is threatened by adding workloads and attempting to accomplish all the new work with what are now insufficient resources. Effort is dissipated, the progress rate slows, and slow-moving investigations soon stop.

When investigators discover new targets, higher priorities, or additional criminal activity (and they will), there is a method of dealing with this information. The system should handle the new intelligence as it handled the original case intelligence: process it through the steps taken in the intelligence phase by the intelligence unit. The information is evaluated and validated. Estimates are made on the time frames and resources it will take to investigate. Objectives are stated and priorities assigned. The "new case" can then be reviewed and a decision handed down. You may decide to:

1. Handle the matter as a spin-off case and shelve it for future investigation.
2. Assign additional resources to the original team and add the new objectives.
3. Abandon the original objectives (for later pursuit) and attack the higher priorities with the original team.
4. Pass the information on to another agency for their action and continue your original investigation.

The decision on the course of action to be taken is made at the department or detective command level, not at the supervisor or investigative level. Decisions to broaden objectives after a resource review or change objectives for greater targets of opportunity involve all the agencies that were committed to the original case. This means they must be made aware of, and approve, the new investigative commitments. After all, their officers are working for the "home" agency, not yours.

Failure to adhere to original objectives, or changing them without defining the new resource commitments, is the single most prevalent cause of investigative slowdowns and failures to produce expected results.

Detective commanders control the case and monitor progress and milestone achievements. They must have complete awareness of progress toward the objectives and accomplish this through report review and frequent conferences with case supervisors. Commanders may give advice and/or orders to expedite the case.

Unit commanders must be aware of all their resource commitments and their investigative team's actions at all times. If they know what is happening, they have the flexibility to commit resources to other incidents on a priority basis based on rational rather than panic decisions.

Detective commanders maintain contact with other agency commanders and prosecutors to keep them apprised of the case progress, problems, and schedule.

Detective commanders check to see that the central desk reporting (CDR) system is well established and working. The same principles as stated in Chapter 6 of this book apply to the central control point concept. All contacts and reports from investigators, intelligence units, analysts, and other agencies are controlled through this desk. This is the funnel for all case information. The CDR point maintains and controls:

1. The case index
2. Location of case activities
3. Responses from various agencies' "flag" systems from record rooms, intelligence sections, motor vehicle and licensing agencies, the National Crime Information Center (NCIC), etc.

The CDR point should make frequent routine checks with all agencies and/or geographical locations involved in the case to ensure control compliance and to keep informed of activity and progress. The size and area of activity decide the location and number of CDR reporting points, but all terminate in the single and controlling desk. This can be decided only by judgment and the progress of the case. The whole process can be packed in a briefcase.

Here is a final word about the critical-path investigation method. I will try an analysis to set the picture of what this entails. Picture a building project: Someone needs a new office building. They select from the architects available, who then decide its appearance and structure based on its proposed function; they look for a location and conduct land studies, studies on traffic and neighborhood issues and determine what site preparation is needed prior to construction. They will perform some tests, probes if you will, on the land itself, determining what weight it will hold or surcharge issues, undersurface material, water, drainage routes, and utility services available. They decide based upon the *intelligence* reported.

Next, they develop a cost chart, determine the time span needed for construction, arrange for the contractors for the work, and arrange for the purchase and delivery schedule of the materials. This results in many subcontractors for each of the four main trades: the overall manager who *constructs* the structure, the *plumber,* the *electrician,* and the *heating-air conditioning man* sit and meet.

Those people all talk over the job and decide to coordinate their schedules so that at each stage of the building, each arrives at a scheduled time with their appropriate labor and material to put in place within the structure, which is to be ready at that time and date to receive each trade. In order to do that, each step from each trade must coincide with the construction progress and not interfere with another trade. How they do that is called the critical path. This is the go/no-go decision point. The intelligence phase is over, almost; they must be ready to deal with changes and unforeseen situations.

The detective command must do the same thing, which is relative to the work. First, the target is identified, and what you hope to achieve, the scope of the investigation, and what you intend to do with spin-off crimes are identified along the way. We have discussed those. Take, as an example, a drug ring in your jurisdiction that is the target. The decision is whether you start by identifying where the profits go, who gets them, the value, and its seizure status. Alternatively, start from the bottom and work up, which will be the critical path; each is radically different as to investigative issues. That is the case critical path. An investigative path for each approach is necessary, for each trade involved, and they must all coordinate and mesh. Try it as a mental exercise with a drug operation you are familiar with and see what comes up.

Some months later, the detective commander and case lead investigator walk up to a beach cabana on the French Riviera with all paper and service notices in hand, bringing drinks, and sit down next to "Boss man" and his girlfriend. His bodyguards are restless. The commander makes a point to look at his watch, nods, and sees Boss man nervously looking at them and the gendarmes in the background. You say, "Here, you're going to need this." You hand them their martinis, give him his papers, bring out the cuffs, and dangle them. At that moment, he knows his entire empire is crashing down with the sound of splintering doors and yells of surprise. And ... his cell phone remains silent.

Supervisor/Coordinator (One, Two, Three ... People)

Manage the case.
Allocate assigned resources.
Schedule and coordinate.
Participate (limited).
Direct, guide, and order.
Watch objectives.
Take action on spin-offs.
Control central desk reporting.
Design the surveillances and the teams.

The supervisor manages and coordinates the case. If the investigation involves a small three- or four-person team, the supervisor acts as a case coordinator. If the investigative team consists of twenty or thirty agencies, the supervisor must have an adequate working staff of coordinators and clerical help.

The intelligence phase identifies this need. If the original objectives and scope broaden, part of the secondary intelligence review identifies and provides for adequate case control as well as investigative resources. Trying to accomplish too much with too little is a historical police fault and one of the reasons we are all great study subjects for stress problems, ulcers, heart attacks, and dog kicking.

A typical proactive major-case structure appears in Figure 10.2, with the main investigative thrust within one agency. Illustrations at the end of this chapter represent a typical interagency major-case control with four agencies participating. If this hypothetical investigation were to expand by five or seven additional jurisdictions, a state agency should be used to coordinate, if possible, since most are structured to perform in this manner. The expanded case control would look like the figure with the hypothetical control vested in the state's regional office at Miami. Please note that the second figure at the end of this chapter does not extend out of the state. In reality, they can and do, in fact to several states on occasion. This requires a higher degree or level of coordination.

Supervisors allocate the resources provided to conduct the case. They assign work fairly by talent, experience, priority toward the objective, and the most critical path of investigation. They schedule and assign surveillance teams, stakeouts, and personnel for electronic intercept plant sites with an equitable division of work and time off.

The case coordinator interfaces with other department supervisors on the mutual use of resources and settles disputes on agency priority matters with the next-higher level of supervision.

The supervisor ensures that all critical reports are submitted daily and the noncritical, weekly. It is extremely important in long-term investigations to keep the paper flow up to date. Once you fall behind, you can never catch up. Use whatever it takes to get the work done, dictation, hand written, or typed. The supervisor or coordinator must read all the reports, challenge, and have corrected all errors and incomplete or inadequate work. All language confusion must be eliminated as it is spotted. Opinions and misleading statements must be removed from operational reports. As in reactive case reporting, theory and opinion belong on memoranda and should not be a part of the investigation side of the file. Supervisors control the case by:

1. Reviewing work
2. Checking quality of work
3. Checking for completeness
4. Directing the work
5. Questioning investigative activity and investigator's statements. Supervisors must challenge the authenticity and validation methods until they are thoroughly satisfied. If they do not, it is their credibility that will suffer.

6. Not satisfying themselves with oral reports

Case *supervisors* must assist the investigators with their work. They accomplish this by working with them and participating in selected phases of the investigation. They are involved in the case but not tied up. They can be the "extra body" that is so often needed to fill in gaps that routinely occur. They check case progress, hold conferences, and guide the investigative path by issuing instructions. Supervisors arrange schedules and check surveillances and "plant" site teams for compliance with the department rules. They lead and direct the case by suggestion and orders to the lead agent (case agent/investigator in charge).

Supervisors and/or their case coordinators must review all evidence to ensure it has been properly obtained, secured, and accounted for, and is complete. They ensure that it is properly identified (examined, if necessary) and stored. They maintain contact with the assigned prosecutor's attorney(s), review progress and evidence, and discuss case development.

Case supervisors are responsible for keeping the investigation on the path toward the objectives. They avoid getting involved in side issues and ensure that case investigators do not change objectives without approval of the detective commander. Case supervisors are responsible for identifying and taking an action on all spin-off cases. They either direct other in-department resources toward the developed lead or receive command approval to send the lead to another agency for investigation and determine conditions under which the case is transferred. They must protect their case. They may also elect to request permission to broaden their case, where warranted, by identifying the new objectives and the additional resources required, and seek command approval. Supervisors control the investigation and always plan ahead. They prepare for downtime or slack time by using such "filler" work as:

1. Intelligence gathering
2. Report writing
3. Noncritical-case development
4. Case and evidence reviews with the investigative team (conferences)
5. Training and maintenance
6. Time off

Case supervisors will attend frequent meetings with their staff supervisor, keeping that person informed of the case progress, problems, and development. They coordinate and cooperate with other department supervisors, sharing resource needs according to orders or priorities. The word is cooperate.

The case supervisor informs the prosecutor of the case progress, providing up-to-date information and anticipated milestones on a timely basis. The prosecutor needs some advance notice of when he or she may expect arrests and trials.

Case supervisors keep the intelligence work going collaterally with the investigation and ensure that all participating agencies share in both the intelligence learned and investigative facts developed. They do this in a timely fashion with meetings, contacts, and always in writing. **The coordinator tracks all information dissemination; copies of the information distribution lists are filed on the administrative side of the case folder.**

Case supervisors frequently check the CDR system for bottlenecks, late reporting, lack of compliance, and proper dissemination of case activity and progress. **They ensure that all participating agencies are coordinating their work.** Their case index will be a part of your file, and pieces of it, if not all of it, may be discoverable to the defense. I will mention here that prosecutions may be separate in separate jurisdictions, or consolidated where appropriate, or moved to a federal court on occasion where it becomes one case, maybe. Sometimes this changes as the case proceeds. Many of these cases will get the interest of the DEA; command-level people would have made them aware of the investigation to avoid clashing with and disturbing their activities. Pieces of your case may involve coordination with a piece of a DEA investigation. Sometimes a joined-at-the-hip case proceeds for a while until it is satisfactorily transferred or received back to the original path. Unbelievably, that can be done smoothly. It also results in one of three selective prosecution options—federal, state, or combined federal and state by splitting charges, whichever way works best to your advantage.

Supervisors/coordinators are responsible for managing and coordinating all leads and assignments as in the reactive cases. They do this with:

1. Assignment sheets
2. Lead sheets
3. Tickler files
4. Index
5. Logbook, which is a chronological log of all pertinent occurrences and orders issued; that is, a case-oriented timeline as opposed to the event timeline of a reactive case.

Case supervisors must keep their supervisor aware of progress and resource commitment and discuss any adjustments necessary. Understaffed supervisors have never been bashful about requesting additional help. By the same standard, when they are overstaffed, they should surrender unnecessary help.

Frequent team conferences are held where the facts of the case are discussed to be sure all investigators are aware of the entire scope of the investigation and its progress. When the investigative team consists of eight officers,

all may attend the meeting. When the investigation involves thirty departments, each with its own investigative team, then the meetings are limited
to key supervisors with the leading agencies, who will in turn disseminate
appropriate information to their own people. A ten-person meeting is about
the limit; any number above that and you have a convention. Minutes are
kept in the case administrative side of the file. Major geographical spreads
create additional coordination problems. One supervisor is designated as
overall case supervisor with identified resources allocated to him or her (as
per agreement) even if part-time. The overall case supervisor must coordinate all the work at the appropriate level in each jurisdiction. This is difficult,
particularly when crossing command lines. (See figures at the end of Chapter
6.) The supervisor (and his or her coordinators) have been selected because
of their ability, skill, and experience, not because of their rank or title. The
preinvestigation work identifies, and the control agency designates, the case
supervisor, who leads the team regardless of any rank or title assigned to the
investigative teams. When interagency teams are put together, a leader has
been designated and is acting at the express orders of the controlling agency
leader (the chief, sheriff, superintendent, or commissioner).

The case index is a critical and integral part of the management of any
major case. The proactive case index is even more important than the reactive type. There are usually thousands more items collected over a longer
period of time. The investigation will suffer without the index. The index
must be kept current. The index points the way to documentation location.
The index provides investigators and analysts with the capability of identifying leads, associations, and other investigative information on a timely
basis. The index must be fed to the central department files (and other agencies' files) as soon as possible to make the flag system(s) work and therefore
of value. The task is enormous and works on the same criteria as stated in
Chapter 6. (See Appendix F.)

Failures to maintain the case index result in:

1. Nonavailability of investigative information for the investigators,
   prosecutors, or case monitors
2. The lack of information sharing, particularly in large, complex cases
   spread over a geographical area with information flows originating
   from several sources (agencies)
3. The left hand not knowing what the right hand is doing
4. Duplication of effort
5. Lost investigative opportunities

Obviously, a major proactive case needs a competent supervisor/coordi-
nator and adequate and trained clerical help (full-time, part-time, or pools)

Investigators/Analysts

Investigate.
Record and report.
Feed the index.
Coordinate surveillance and plant site.
Stick to the objectives.
Use minimum personnel.
Be flexible.

As in all criminal investigations, the actual case workers make or break the effort. Most police investigators normally work alone and hook up with a partner for selective matters. All case information developed is within their grasp. There was no real need for elaborate case index systems, controls, or going to supervisors for permission to perform investigative acts. The investigators usually decided their own method of case development, chased leads in any order they deemed appropriate, and generally acted independently of close supervision. What a shock it must be to the fiercely independent investigators to become involved in a major criminal investigation, either reactive or proactive, for the first time. Their wings are clipped, their egos may be bruised, and they may feel they have been reduced to a "go-fer" or errand boy. Those investigators must learn to adapt. Major-case investigation is a team effort, and every move, act, or fact learned by an investigator must be known, directed, and controlled by a team leader. Without rigid controls, the case will be more chaotic than our normal world of chaos.

The investigators must investigate and inform the case controller of all pertinent information. They must consult with all other case investigators and share all information. There can be no secrets or information held back. There is no room for individual case isolation. If an egomaniac is identified on a major-case team, he or she should be removed. Assign the nonteam player to watch the local jail walls to make sure no one escapes that night.

Investigators must record all information accurately, validate and confirm it, and report it in a timely fashion. They must feed the case index promptly and check the case index frequently to identify information they are interested in obtaining. Each investigator should maintain his or her own investigative log (notebook). The major-case team has decided on the reporting system index that all agencies will use (usually the controlling agencies), and each investigator should use that system. It saves time. It is up to the controlling agency to forward copies of reports to each participating agency if requested or needed.

The issue of integrating differing forms from other agencies is worked out in your mutual aid agreements. Index information is the important factor to get right.

The controlling investigator or case supervisor/coordinator assigns leads and/or investigative work to the team workers. The investigators must complete and report each assignment and never go beyond the assigned work without the case supervisor's approval. When situations require immediate field decisions, judgment must be used and accepted, but any nonassigned work that was done must be reported (called in) to the case supervisor/coordinator as soon as possible. The supervisor then makes the decision on any further investigative action. This rule permits controlled initiative.

Surveillance reports and logs contain hard information. This must be fed to the index promptly. Other case investigators must be informed of all pertinent information. This may be done by direct contact, but the case supervisor/coordinator definitely must be informed within the selected time frames for the case. Those vary, depending on the nature of the investigation.

The supervisor schedules wire intercept or listening post work. The investigator in charge provides for fair distribution of site work and relief. Less-experienced officers can be trained and utilized at plant locations. Minimize the personnel used on listening posts or surveillances.

Investigators must stick to the objectives. Report all spin-off case opportunities to the supervisor with recommendations to incorporate them into the investigation or broaden the scope of the case. They are either case leads or intelligence leads, which means in writing.

Investigators/analysts should chart the case, using link analysis, and keep the chart up to date, probably on a wall chart. You can post it across the room from the critical-path chart. Report all index items to the CDR person. Just as a corporate organization can be charted, so can criminal enterprises. A chart has great value in assisting agents, supervisors, commanders, and prosecutors in picturing the case. As personnel change on the investigation team (as they will over a period of time), the chart is a great visual aid in bringing new investigative blood up to speed.

The case investigators must feed the system routinely. The case coordinator will see that reports are fed into the agency's file system (central files).

The investigation must be conducted aggressively and with flexibility. Changes in duty assignments occur regularly on major long-term cases, and investigators must quickly adapt to different work and work schedules.

When temporary work must be done in different geographical areas, outside the jurisdictions involved in the case, use a competent local or state agency to perform the specific work for you. Avoid travel for minor work. Travel only for critical work or matters that will require court testimony.

Sometimes sudden or unanticipated events occur and bursts of additional resources are needed. As in reactive cases, they can be obtained from:

1. Other agencies
2. Other department units
3. Uniform forces
4. Overtime (this can kill your budget)

Use the uniform forces for residence, business, vehicle checks, and random observations with a loose surveillance patrol technique. While they are on patrol, they can cruise by selected locations and report license numbers, activity, etc. The system should be designed so the results and information learned are promptly reported. That is a patrol post assignment that goes into the post patrol book where it is controlled. The officer does a lead sheet return, and you get it through the internal-routing mail system. The post assignments should have instructions for immediate information you want "called in."

Prosecutor

Be aware of case objectives.
Define statutes.
Define requirements for each element of proof the statute demands.
Provide legal assistance.
Review evidence .
Deal with discovery problems.
Share in benefits and failures.
Participate in the team effort.

Prosecutors are a key element in any major proactive investigation. They must be made aware of the case objectives. Prosecutors will define the appropriate statutes and their requirements of proof. They must receive timely investigative information and be invited to assist in charting the investigative path. They will be crucial in deciding:

1. Probable-cause sufficiency
2. Subpoena methods and the timing of service
3. Eavesdropping coordination and preparation
4. Development of strategies
5. Establishment and confirmation of proof requirements

The prosecutor should remind the investigators of exclusionary rules and the civil liabilities for abusive acts.

The prosecutor should have access to and review the complete evidence package.

The prosecutor will:

1. Provide legal advice on searches, seizures, and criminal charges.
2. Prepare legal papers, indictments, search warrants, arrest warrants (capiases), and intercept orders. This saves a lot of time. However, the department or specified persons within the department must have the experience and capability to perform each of those tasks when a prosecutor is not available and "paper" is needed on short notice.

The case manager should tell the prosecutor of all anticipated use of criminal informants prior to their use. Discuss discovery problems and protection of the informant and under what circumstances the informant will be identified or not identified. Too many cases have been built with informers, only to have disagreement and/or loss of valuable evidence because prosecutors and police often cannot agree on informant status or use.

The prosecutor will define his or her priorities and come to agreement on the case as it develops.

Prosecutors should be committed to the case. They will share in the responsibility, benefits, successes, and failures. Cooperative work often negates any "finger-pointing" when mistakes happen.

All meetings, decisions, and suggestions are reported by memorandum to the case administrative file for maintaining a case history.

The investigation is best conducted by using the investigative plan developed during the intelligence phase. The objectives are defined, resources estimated, and the critical path and investigative methodology designed. The case is controlled by assigning an experienced coordinator/supervisor, who directs and monitors the work through a central point (CDR). An index, tickler, assignment sheets, and case logs are the tools of the tracking effort. Investigations that are planned, coordinated, and conducted by teamwork will be successful.

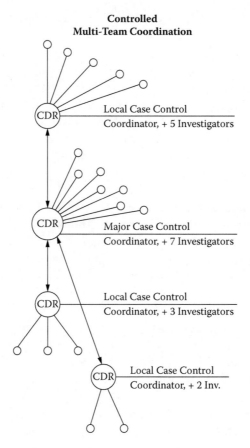

Figure 11.1 Controlled multi-team coordination.

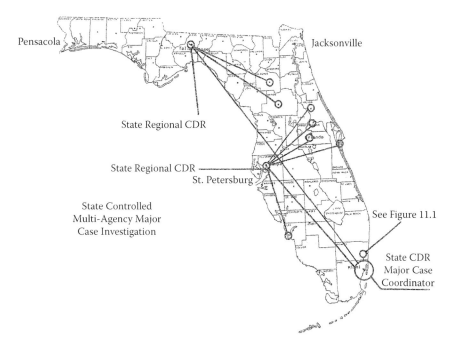

Figure 11.2 State-controlled multi-team major-case investigation.

Arrest and Trial

12

After a successful investigation, there comes a time when the plug is pulled and the arrests take place. During this phase, as in the previous phases, there are responsibilities for several of the case principal entities.

Department Command

Look important and stay out of the way.

Detective Command

Set the final evidence review meeting where the case against each defendant is given a thorough check and discussion to determine the evidence availability, value, and weight. The prosecutor has usually reviewed the "prosecution status" during the case, but a final check is necessary, particularly as to admissibility problems. It is good to invite him or her.

The witness review, including officer and support personnel, other agency, civilian, informant, and laboratory examiner personnel, is conducted at this meeting for basically the same reasons—availability, status, weight and credibility issues. This includes appropriate rechecks of criminal histories and a records search. Notes or memoranda are filed on the administrative side of the case file and indexed with each participant's name, organization, and comments. This is nondiscoverable work product, especially if a prosecutor is present.

This meeting is usually nearing the date of the anticipated arrests, so it is a good place to decide the contingency plans if the arrest process is disrupted for any reason or anything must be changed. This is also an administrative side report.

This is also the place to be sure the police-to-prosecutor final case report is properly structured and complete. The case coordinator prepares the report prior to this meeting. Every witness has his own package, which includes every statement he made, by page where he appears in the report, and his index data. It also includes copies of criminal-history checks and any other paper you have as to the witness. The same thing occurs for every piece of evidence. Included is the source of each piece of information received for every package and item in it. You not only succeed in putting your case together, you have completed half of the prosecutor's trial brief.

The police department decides the report structure; usually it is the progression of the case in chronological order with attached statements, evidence sheets, logs, and miscellaneous data attached. The prosecutor's trial brief is subject matter-oriented, consisting of witnesses, evidence, order of trial, court case law and statutes, elements of proof needed, and each piece of evidence and the witness that will be used in the order of proof. Included also in the trial brief will be the complete police report.

I suggest it be done this way and at this point because the case is about finished. It needs to be checked for each item mentioned, so it naturally is the place to put it into an orderly submission package. Have a copy machine handy. This is where duplicates bloom; a single witness may be a factor for three or more pieces of evidence. One evidence package may have more than one officer and witness statements in the package, and one or more officers and witnesses may have one or more evidence items in their packages. Ask the prosecutor; they each have their own system for that. Or submit it in a general order for them to rearrange in their personal preference. Then, include the administrative package of the case file; it provides the names and addresses of all witnesses, officers, and laboratory personnel, locations of evidence, the rest of the case flotsam, and the index data for each. A well-kept case index relieves most of that work and simplifies the process. The package can be like a bank statement that is one or two cents off, hell to find, while a thousand-dollar error is a piece of cake. The pain level goes up or down based on the thoroughness of the case coordinator and his or her insistence on correct detail as the case progressed. If you do not do this, it will take hours upon hours of time at your office and days and days at a prosecutor's office. If the defense fails to waive speedy trial, the pressure is on. And it is time to:

Coordinate the arrest.
Decide when and how to make the arrest.

Inform the press only after all principals are in custody and all other agencies involved clear it for public consumption. Avoid any inferences or disclosures of work efforts under way that may have come up after the original clearances or while the arrests were under way. The responsibility of coordinating the arrest is the detective commander's, particularly if arrests are to take place in several jurisdictions. Agencies that participated in the investigation will of course be assigned to arrest the criminals within their borders. Criminals may be arrested in jurisdictions whose agencies did not participate in the investigation: the decision whether to inform and use these agencies is made by the case-controlling department. They must be notified as you approach the arrest time; any reason you did not notify them has ceased to exist as your officers approach the doors. This is an extremely rare occurrence but still happens.

The detective commander must decide the method of arrest and the timing. He or she, along with a prosecutor, should decide if the arrest will:

1. Be made during the commission of the criminal activity
2. Be made by indictment and/or warrants, generally executed by a police raid, or private-counsel turn-in
3. Be by arrest warrants with selected sequential pickups. Using the domino effect arrest theory is sometimes productive, particularly when wire intercepts are still in place. When the word of the arrests spreads, criminals tend to use the phones with less than normal discretion.
4. Be by summons/subpoena
5. Be selective arrests by the "pick 'em off" method. The case may be such that you can arrest a cell or individuals while continuing with the main investigation. You decide if the method will further the case or warn off people not arrested. Sometimes you need to make lower-level arrests to try to turn a defendant into an informant. The arrest may be the lever you need. These issues are discussed and worked out to make sure the arrest(s) do not hinder further case activities.

After a long investigation, investigators usually must relocate many of the defendants prior to the arrests and initiate loose surveillances. If you have not worked on a subject for several months and are now going to arrest him, you must be sure of his availability if the arrest is going to be made by the raid method. All case principals should be located and watched and their patterns of movement reestablished. Once the word is out, you know how fast they can leave town.

The timing of the arrest must be set. The only valid motives to consider in timing the arrest are:

1. Safety of the officers and public
2. Furthering the case

News media deadlines and TV coverage are the worst criteria for timing an arrest. Commanders who consider media coverage in the arrest timing, for whatever reason, are bordering on shameful negligence and are certainly guilty of maladministration. If an officer should ever be hurt during an arrest, timed not for safety or case furtherance purposes but for press coverage, it turns the event into a public issue with all appropriate condemnations. Never bring the press with you, or prewarn them, as in a tip-off—not a peep or hint. It is unprofessional, dangerous, unnecessary, and a discredit to your profession. Never time an arrest to meet a "news cycle." Arresting people for major criminal offenses is a deadly serious business requiring total concentration of thought and effort.

If you receive media inquiries prior to the arrest, it means an internal leak exists. That raises the issue that the defendants also may have been alerted. You may choose to move faster, cancel, or proceed as planned; that is a decision based on conditions. Decide beforehand the possible varieties of responses, warnings, threats, misdirection, etc., you will give the media and be prepared to deal with them.

The arrest, coordinated with other law enforcement agencies, must also be coordinated with the prosecutor (or prosecutors, if judicial circuit boundaries are crossed).

Consider the crime victim, if there is one. That notification should be done by a police officer, in person if there was a death or serious injury to a family involved in the case, as soon as confirmation of the arrest is received, and always prior to the press.

A press release should be prepared using the department's public information officer and coordinated with the prosecutor. I suggest that the prosecutor is the most appropriate person to deal with the media.

Supervisor

Prepare the arrest plans.
Line up personnel.
Issue equipment and orders.
Consider safety and case objectives.

The case supervisor is responsible for developing and initiating the detailed arrest plans, assignments, and prearrest surveillances.

Raid personnel are identified and assigned to specific locations or targets. Uniform officers should be used and placed in the forefront to ensure that the criminals, or possibly innocents if an error is made, recognize it is the police coming through the door. Too many police raids look like a band of armed revolutionaries or pirates, and this is dangerous to the police, public, and criminals. The arresting team should wear department-marked police jackets or wear some kind of identification, such as armbands or single-color hats, if they are not uniformed. Each officer must be informed of his or her tasks, assignment, responsibilities, and details of the arrest technique to be employed. All members of this team should be introduced to each other and be able to recognize each other, time permitting. Officers must know what they can expect in the way of arrest site layout, resistance, and who may be present who is not a defendant. Prior knowledge of any weapons, destructive devices, guards, attack dogs, and special steel door barricades are relatively easy matters to deal with; it is the surprise of finding such things that you must be prepared for.

The supervisor should:

1. Assign teams.
2. Ensure all are properly equipped.
3. Brief everyone, including on the rules of conduct. The officers must act lawfully, with restraint, and not unnecessarily destroy or disarray property.
4. Always remind the officers to be careful of the unknown.
5. Keep undercover agents off site and out of sight. No "hooded" agents can be permitted at the site. Keep any within cell phone contact if you think you will need to speak with them about some matter or item.
6. Use only sufficient personnel to achieve success. Passengers or "rubbernecks" should be kept away if possible; if you cannot, they must remain away until the place is secured and the evidence located and secured. If the arrests(s) involve narcotics, departmental orders or procedures, including use of evidence "contamination" sheets, should be invoked to keep unnecessary personnel off site. **Do not let the narcotics squad people on the site; their clothes are often contaminated from their work.** If you do use them, put them in uniform, clean and shaved. I have always preferred uniform officers be the arresting officers with follow-up crime scene people for evidence collection. Further, the psychology behind any thoughts of resistance is greatly reduced, if not eliminated, by the up-front appearance of uniformed officers. The squad detective-in-charge will be present for details that he or she wants addressed or looked for. Any case investigators needed may appear after the scene is secured and defendants removed from the site. Be sure to consider any possibilities of press photos or TV videos of undercover personnel.

Investigators

Arrest

Investigators must carry out their assignments by arresting with proper methods. Try to further the case, but do not go beyond legal parameters. Secure all evidence properly, and act with restraint. The case is already made; do not make foolish mistakes.

Go over each report submitted. ensure that all index items have reached the index, and fix any errors, prior to the prearrest conference. If additional matters come to mind and a supplemental report is required, file one. This is the time to make all corrections with supplemental reports, not changes in the originals. Under no circumstance can a "new" original be substituted for the one already on file. Use supplements or the department error correction procedure.

Prosecutors Prepare for Court

The prosecutor may hold a press conference (if appropriate) at his or her office. Normally the detective commander is present and generally silent, responding only to unimportant questions. The case supervisor and investigators should be kept away from the news media. Investigators do not make statements, and certainly no quotes by investigators should appear in the media. This allows deniability to press inaccuracies and out-of context statements and prevents ill-considered statements made without thinking.

Coordinate with the law enforcement agencies for court appearances, schedules, other case commitments, witnesses, evidence submission, and laboratory coordination through the case supervisor.

Prosecutors prepare all court paper and arrange for appearances, hearings, etc.

Secure a case summary as soon as possible. Review all evidence and testimony, and prepare for trial. During this review, all parties should be alert for additional spin-off cases.

Complete cooperation at this phase is most important. A lot of hard work has accomplished some arrests. The whole investigation was conducted to reach this point. The objective, conviction, is within grasp.

Some final and loose thoughts.

Some cases take long periods of time before trial or disposition. Consider rechecking your index files or spin-off case files, including intelligence files, for any activity that involved your current case defendant for relevant or exculpatory evidence at least a month prior to trial or other disposition. Your index flag system should have alerted the case manager. Recheck; then inform your prosecutor that you did that, and place a note in your file of that contact.

Some of your defendants will be out on bail. Have a routine for checking upon them as the responsibility of the intelligence unit or the original case supervisor. A tickler, which has the pending court date appearances, can be used to check up on them. It will not surprise the experienced officers reading this that checking can be fruitful. Lying under oath often has its foundation created after arrest by the defendants' contacts and movements. Knowledge of those by the police can be the explosive device used by the cross-examiner. Just be sure the officers do not speak to the defendant about the case for which he is under arrest. Further, it is another way to use downtime without boring your investigators.

Intelligence/Critique

13

After a major criminal investigation, it is normal to hold a case critique. After a proactive investigation, this critique should be expanded into a new intelligence review.

The critique determines personnel achievements and flaws, management problems, investigation deficiencies, or lost time. Training needs identified result in in-service class outline improvements, administrative changes, or corrections to put in place. Equipment failures are noted and dealt with, as are special problems that arose and caused difficulties in the case involving other agencies, trades, lawyers, the public, and victims. Discussions resolve these matters; they are assigned to someone for study or to look further into any problems that need fixing.

The intelligence review is an entirely different matter. It is done in two or more steps.

The purpose is to:

1. Identify criminal information and intelligence. The best way to start this is to have the case supervisor meet with an intelligence officer and an analyst. If your agency is too small to have those positions as specialties, use the case supervisor, an investigator who did not participate in the investigation, and a clerk/stenographer. They will review the entire case file along with the case administrative file prior to the full case review. That team will prepare a report or outline of the case, splitting those who were arrested from the criminal activities of others identified during the investigation and not arrested. In addition, they will identify anyone involved who provided information that may be of further use in a neighborhood or specific criminal trade. Other crimes identified will be listed.

   This is a job for experienced officers. The case supervisor will pick up any items missing from his or her case and fix those; the non-case investigator will pick out new leads for any criminal activities and take an intelligent look at them to decide which should be explored by the department, shunted to another agency, or just placed in a pending development of intelligence file for future reference. The clerk/stenographer will identify administrative snags, index errors, file issues, clear those up, and list them for discussion. Then the department review will take place after the assigned team reads the preliminary report and reviews the entire file.

2. Identify other targets for investigation. This is the main purpose of the review. When the review team meets, it will consist of the preliminary team and selected department managers and supervisors. The decisions to be made include further intelligence and/or analysis probes. Targets are selected on a priority basis. The decision as to who investigates is made within the department, and other agencies are notified of the potential case in their jurisdiction, including federal issues for the FBI, DEA, Treasury, or Homeland Security. The prereview team presents this to the review panel for questions and decisions.

3. Determine if the criminal activity just investigated has ended by the arrests or is continuing and worthy of additional police attack. This is usually a quick check within a short time period to determine if the criminal activity was broken, was seriously disrupted, or whether the arrested players are back to work (on bail) or replaced by new criminals. Again, decisions.

Do not wait for the trial. Set up a case review as soon as convenient. The case review should include the detective commander, the case supervisor, an intelligence officer, the principal case investigator(s), a stenographer, and any other command personnel selected by the chief.

Also, consider training, equipment/administrative affairs, and personnel development issues discovered.

The case review should consist of the ordinary case critique, the precase intelligence workup, and the case just completed, for:

1. Investigative problems encountered
2. Techniques used and their effectiveness
3. System blocks or bottlenecks
4. Suggestions
5. Personnel evaluations and problems
6. Intelligence review, which:
   a. Identifies and reviews all spin-off cases. This includes identifying career criminals and setting them up for continuous observation and investigation. This is the very purpose of intelligence units: identifying criminal activity, who is committing the crimes, and then selecting a path for the purpose of ending the criminal activity.
   b. Identifies new criminal intelligence and/or intelligence opportunities, including new informants, concerned citizens of interest to the department, and street people to be exploited.

      c. Results in preliminary decisions on the status and/or direction the department will take with regard to each identified case.

      d. Sends intelligence to the analysis people for a final report or dissemination to appropriate commands and other agencies.

4. The decision as to whether the department will track the defendants through the criminal justice process, from court to jail to parole or probation where the intelligence unit puts them back up on the radar screen. This is done by opening an intelligence case on each selected defendant. Sometimes you may wish the court deputies to identify any persons contacting the defendant in the courtroom (i.e., family, friends, or associates). Obtain the date of release from prison, inmate visitor lists, correspondence return addresses, or mailed-to lists, if available. On parolees or probationers, set up a contact or loose surveillance. This is based on your information, whether the defendant has information or knowledge regarding current activities or whether he will immediately return to his old trade upon release. This is an intelligence unit function, done according to the value-priority-workload scale. Do this for selected reactive case defendants as well.

My point is that if you have a management system in place for this, it will be used and produce results. Career criminals fit this category as a high priority. The theory is to chase the communities' criminals as a dedicated task in itself, not just on a case-by-case, as they come along, basis.

Have the aforementioned meeting agenda distributed prior to the meeting to be sure it is constructive. The stenographer is ready to insert her notes in the proper category and prepare the report. Attached to the report are the instructions to each affected unit to supply the information mentioned and forward that to the detective commander for distribution and actions.

Some of the most valuable criminal intelligence comes from the police investigation. It is worth a few hours of time to review major criminal investigations for just such intelligence. There is usually an abundance of information, mostly validated and available for future or immediate use.

In the index chapter (Chapter 15), you see where those arrested and sentenced receive further attention at the case closing time, after all appeals and/or sentencing are over. It is here that jailed persons or new probationers have an intelligence file opened, or continued if opened, by the item four procedure stated previously for further investigative actions based on the review recommendations. There is no good reason to wait until that time if during the intelligence critique interesting or special circumstances arise. The department has a form for this further activity, a lead sheet or other dedicated purpose form.

The first time a department does one of these reviews, the case workforce is presented with factors they have not faced before with such precision. They are informed of their work product impact on the commanders, good and bad. They see the interest of the department in their work. The results are improved case activity and details collected, improved communication up and down, and better work on "the next" case knowing a detailed review will be held. Commanders will notice more interest in street observations among the workforce than just the case at hand and under investigation. The troops will look for new case opportunities coincidental to the main case and introduce those into the system rather than "pocket" them for local use or personal street information. This is a now productive force at work and they love it. Take advantage of it. When they see the results, they might stop bitching about the paperwork … well, maybe … we cannot expect miracles. Departments may even recover some of the burnouts in the bracket of fifteen- to twenty-year veterans starting to look forward to retirement and a small private detective agency to occupy their time.

Resource Management 14

This book was written for application to any size police agency. You must determine, from the size, capabilities, and jurisdictional limitations of your agency, where you would fit in a major criminal investigation. You may lead or participate under another agency's direction. The principles of major-case control, and how entities interrelate, have been stated; it is up to you to apply those principles to your situation.

This chapter will briefly discuss some generalities of management and case control. Some of the statements are reminders of what has already been said. They are worth repeating.

Resource Control

Case-tracking system
Manpower reporting system
Goals and objectives
Systems approach
Schedule and phasing
Evaluation
Performance
Critical-path method
Index

Determining the level of supervision is always difficult. Let your mind be flexible. Escalate supervisory control to be comfortable with the span of geographical jurisdiction and agencies participating. If you have one team of ten men, use one appropriate-level supervisor. When you have multiple agencies, for example, fifteen departments, each with its own investigative team working, one agency and one person, appropriately ranked (by experience), should be responsible for case management. The organizational structure of the controlling agency should be designed to absorb this type of case. (See figures in Chapters 10 and 11.) Local police agencies should learn to rely on state or federal law enforcement departments in multijurisdictional situations. Most states have investigative units designed to cope with this very issue, coordinating multiple jurisdictions in a single investigation (actually, numerous investigative cases compiled into one due to a common link). This way the resource control is identified and the units become responsive to the higher command (regardless of the individual's rank). A supervisor is designated as the investigation leader and is in charge of all other resources assigned, including other unit supervisors. **Be flexible; design and fit the structure to the case control problem, not the other way around.**

Always fix responsibility within a single agency and a single individual within that agency, and give him or her the authority needed to operate. Identify the agency responsible for case control, agree on the participants, and stick to the agreement. **The case responsibility may shift to another agency after reexamining objectives and the realities encountered in the actual investigation;** even then, keep your original, sometimes adjusted, commitments. The supervisor in charge must have the promised resources at his or her disposal for the agreed-upon time period. The supervisor in turn must provide all participating agencies with progress reports and anticipated time frames to complete work.

Cooperating agencies are always responsible for their own supervision of the greater goal, their department, and their personnel. The major-case manager is responsible for supervision of all case personnel, internal or other agency, as to the case work, including whether they stay or are asked to bow out, for whatever purpose.

Resources are wasted in overkilling a case. Delaying arrests in order to secure additional counts on an indictment is usually nonproductive work. Jail sentences are usually the same for multiple counts of the same offense. Waiting to catch a few minor functionaries identified during the investigation is not always productive or worth the additional resource investment. Some investigators will try to make a career out of a proactive case if you permit them to do so. When the objectives are met and proof is sufficient, move the case. Bring it "down." When objectives change for higher goals, go through the preliminary steps again:

1. Set new objectives.
2. Identify resources needed.
3. Identify the case control point.

If you have sufficient evidence to indict on the original case objectives, consider obtaining sealed indictments, pocket them (if the court will allow it), and wait for the proper moment of timing in relation to the new objectives. For example, if you learn that your smuggler targets have committed murder, you may want to consider using smuggling warrants to further a murder case. Or, you may want to charge the defendants on smuggling, as though your investigation were over, and lead them to believe they are "home free" on the killing.

Departments also use the pick-off method while the case is ongoing; arresting a few lower-level people along the way appears, to them, as a normal loss of their resources in the ordinary course of their business. Wait and watch for the replacements, do what you will with them, but use the opportunity to determine their recruiter or leader. They tend to return to the area of their predecessors to be shown the "turf" by the recruiter. It all depends on your priorities and resources. The police are never out of business or lack something to do.

People Wasters

Surveillance teams can be people wasters.

Use minimal resources on surveillances. Needs should dictate the number of personnel assigned; shorting yourself rather than trying to prepare for every contingency probably will not hurt your case. Remember, if you miss your target once, you will have another chance. Versatility and aggressiveness in personnel can solve most surveillance problems.

Too often investigators want to "get in on the action," particularly when a case is about to culminate. Many officers volunteer for surveillance teams. Supervisors must resist the temptation to overstaff a surveillance team because of worker enthusiasm. Too many surveillances go beyond expected time frames, and all your officers "burn out" and sufficient replacements are no longer available. How many dope transactions ever go off on schedule?

Fear of criticism is a waster of resources. There is a tendency among inexperienced supervisors to try to do everything one can think of rather than prioritize. If you fear criticism or making a mistake, you are in the wrong business. **We do not make right or wrong decisions; we make decisions that work or do not work.**

Electronic-intercept plant sites are people wasters. The hours of listening should be established. Schedule time for listening to intercepts only to the extent necessary to achieve your objective. The first three days of interception should set a pattern. The nature of the information sought helps scheduling judgment. If it is a gambling wire, you record only during peak traffic. If it is a dope-smuggling wire, you record based on the call pattern. If it is a murder-for-hire wire, you listen twenty-four hours around the clock. You get the idea.

Use the following methods to control wire intercepts:

1. Schedule for peak times.
2. Assign minimal personnel.
3. Disallow stragglers or visitors (not much work is done when visiting). Use slow times to work on other matters, such as marking your tapes for later transcription. Preserve the original, for the prosecutor, and a single copy for the department records. Use a third for marking for

any future transcription. Your records must always identify the total number of tapes copied. Keep them to a minimum and always know who has them, the purpose for which they have them, and the location. This is part of your case management procedures.

The marking for future transcription of tapes should be done as soon as possible. The best place is at the point of interception during slow times. In addition, the marking for transcription should have a secondary purpose; that is, marking for intelligence transcription for forwarding to appropriate department people at the appropriate time, all within your agency's case control records and procedures. Good defense attorneys will ask, among other things, how many copies of the tape were made, what for, and where they are, then demand they be produced for their examination. Protect your intelligence information from this possible screening by selecting specific information from the case file tape and reducing it to writing for the intelligence unit. That same information remains available in the original raw form to the defense and prosecutor; let them decide for themselves what is relevant to their case. This does not violate the "exculpatory evidence" or discovery rules. **It is important, very important, that you track an intelligence lead and determine if its content *discovers or points* to additional unknown matters that are exculpatory or relevant to the original case.** Index material noted on that tape is indexed in the case index file. You do that by checking the intelligence file periodically, especially at least a month prior to trial. A properly designed index flag will do that for you once that material is indexed. Do that at the plant site for every tape.

The data you are identifying and taking notes on from the tape for intelligence purposes need not be revealed. Each state handles discovery or production of evidence slightly differently; check with your legal counsel. The tape(s) remain intact for anyone with authority to listen to; what you do with them is the department's business.

4. Permit only legitimate case investigative or supervisory personnel at a plant site. Each time a person appears at an intercept site, record the time in and out, the date, and a few words describing the purpose.
5. Inspect and review the operation periodically for efficiency, pattern changes, and rule compliance. Conduct some unannounced spot checks.
6. Review the work rate.

Two-person teams on routine interviews can be people wasters: one person is adequate, unless safety or a critical statement requires verification. Taping the interview can often serve as validation.

Personnel work assignments are covered in many other books regarding case investigations. I will not go deeply into those in this book. However, it is appropriate to point out that investigative officers should work alone as often as possible, "partnering up" only in specific situations, such as when needing a second witness to a statement or event, or when a probable dangerous situation is logically suspected.

Officers should not "partner up" for long periods; use any available detective or uniform when needed. Use the time-tested formula of not locking two-, or in some agencies three-, person teams on any long-term basis. The same rule goes for major cases.

Agencies have long recognized the need to avoid long-term "special assignments." The best example to point to are "drug units"—one-year assignments, two at most, and then out. Major-case assignments are similar. Meet the immediate needs, and then split the teams up.

Let us play with a "suppose" or "what if." What if you find yourself investigating a cocaine drug sales problem at a local school or college and you wish to end that specific problem, at least for a while. The department does not wish to do a major investigation, just end the dealer and user issue. Consider contacting the state police agency, not to join the case, but to pick up the trail to the source. They can assign a case investigator to supplement the local case by trailing back to the source of the school drug distribution. The department coordinates arrests with the state's investigation. Once the source link is identified and sufficient evidence and direction are in hand, both entities can decide on an arrest date for the problem. Chances are the state or department officers will find that the dealer's distributor does business with more than one dealer in the community; then locally follow that lead while the state backtracks to the distributor's source. All are then informed when a new delivery is arriving and when to join the state police surveillance, or just watch the local dealer until the source arrives and you are ready for another arrest. Probable cause is obtained by either watching the new transaction with immediate arrest and following up with a premises search warrant, or having a house search warrant based on the totality of the investigation in your pocket awaiting its execution upon arrival of the drugs. The decision is based upon the local agreement with the state. Sometimes it includes the distributor or waits until after the distributor leaves, depending upon the state's wishes; they may be at the point of determining the distributor's route or source. They need that to further escalate their case back up the chain, eventually turning it over to the DEA for the Colombian or Mexican connection investigation.

Sometimes the local dealer has to go to the source at a special meet. The process is reversed. The locals call the state and meet along the way, where the state picks up, for trailing purposes, the source players; the locals follow their guy back home and pick a time and place for arrest or further investigation. This way the department is part of the major investigation without the full officer participation that would be required if bound to an agreement. This is often used by smaller agencies with very limited resources. It accomplishes the same thing, even if fragmented. This avoids the usual loss of opportunity when the larger agency is not notified until after the local arrest. **Always make contact with associated agencies, especially the state investigative department, long before you close a case that has implications and activities that extend beyond your jurisdiction.** It saves everyone a lot of time and resources. It is called police coordination. It leads to faster and greater results that actually have a deeper impact on local origin problems than working the same issue repeatedly.

Some General Comments

Institute and continuously inspect, not just check:

1. Case-tracking system
2. Manpower reporting system
3. Budget estimates of future needs
4. Case controls and expended time, money, and equipment
5. Effectiveness measures
6. Goals and objectives
7. Systems approach to case management (CDR)
8. Schedules and time phasing
9. Feedback from the prosecutor
10. Personnel evaluation, both team and individual
11. Critical and noncritical paths of investigation

The secret to major-case control, both reactive and proactive, is simply put:

1. Control and inspections
2. Coordination and organization
3. Systems and objectives

The Index

15

The index—we have been talking about it throughout this book. I placed this chapter next to last because the *case index* is used or put in use at the beginning of each major case and continues to the end of each case. It is integrated with the *department master index* simultaneously or shortly after the entry into the working case file. The case file becomes part of a larger process. The case index itself is the easiest part of the whole system; it is alphabetized, by categories of your choice, in a book, folders, tabbed files, or on a laptop. It includes names, addresses, etc., etc., with a referenced report page number(s). The case control is best designed to meld into the department index, which is married to state and federal information systems and databases through the law enforcement communication network. It works when the case entries are reported through the case manager at the CDR point, which in turn accesses all data files. The trick is to have the case manager's selected entries file-checked for matches (hits) or similarities reported back to him or her. The case manager sets the timing of repetition inquiries. In addition, it searches files to whatever extent or scope the manager sets in place for past queries of similar data made by any prior inquirer. Further, it is flagged to capture all future similar data entries or queries, starting, as an example, with the patrol post book data that shows the past sixty days of activity, incidents, and suspicious people and vehicles that were noted and indexed. The post book is usually brought to the crime scene by the first responder working that post and is available for case manager review on site. The process can be carried to and through the entire law enforcement file record system; that is the goal.

Those patrol post index items are already entered into the department files as a daily routine, as should the department detectives' work data from their daily activity reports be as well. Since the case manager has complete control over the case CDR, he receives notice of all file data, past and present, from the department as he enters the case index items. Future entries or queries are reported to the case manager as they are received at the database. That takes care of the in-house issue; **the case manager is tapped into all files and department feeds, as is every other case manager or uniform supervisor in the department when hits occur regarding their work entries.**

All other police agencies or other support entities such as laboratories involved in the case submit their reports to the CDR for entry as prearranged by agreement. This is where more critical precase agreement thinking comes back up. We spoke of sharing files and reports of similarities with compatible systems within a county, region, or state. This is where it pays off for case investigation and intelligence files. This is why you must consider and cooperate with state or regional Fusion Centers and the state law enforcement communication system. **We are in the business where every agency in the same business should know about everyone else's business by a simple query.** The more automated we are, the easier this is to accomplish. The more information we obtain and then enter into the system, the better it will produce results.

If the patrol in Loner City observes a vehicle with three known burglars pass through, he notes that. If he stops them and finds nothing suspicious, he notes that. If the burglars did not see the patrol observation, they may continue to a planned work site in Loner City or elsewhere; if stopped they will probably just go get a beer. However, within a day or so, they will go to the planned but delayed work site to commit their burglary. If the information is entered into the Loner City department's index, there is a better chance that information will get to a detective, burglary or not. He then knows who is out running around. If a burglary occurs, the detective has at least some information to work with. If not, the detective gets the chance to shake them for information or at least raise the known burglars' concern about the attention they are receiving. This is the sixty-day trash bin information, in some cases picked up by an intelligence unit. If a police dispatcher gets a call from a meter reader about a suspicious bag on a piece of property, the CDR and case manager get to know about that since the piece of property was entered in the index. So do the dispatch supervisor and uniform and detective supervision at a predetermined level. That depends on the sophistication of the system. If departments all collect the trash and investigative information in the same or similar manner, they could all toss it into a regionally-connected trash bin, in addition to the case information files in the main department indexes. Look at your regional law enforcement structure and develop the system to fit your needs.

Some issues need discussion.

Let us get the department's master index out of the way first. It contains every criminal case file, including the case-specific index, management files, noncriminal investigations and their indexes, administrative data, personnel data, inventory data, fiscal data, budget data, traffic accident and ticket data, event investigations data, communications data, and a list that would carry this page on for two more. Let us not go there. The data must be subdivided into public records data, privacy records data, and limited internal-access and special-access data.

Closed criminal case file data is divided into public and nonpublic, pending awaiting public status and never public as directed by controlling laws. It includes among the regular data collection of specified categories (the case input) items like officers assigned, intelligence matter separations, open, and closed. In addition, it includes review and destruction data, destruction via public notice requirements, etc., etc. Let us not go there, but become aware of the impact upon criminal cases. If you need a file, you get it or "Records" sends it to you. What you need to know is who else is looking at that subject matter and why. A flag system tells you.

The index will be discussed in that light.

Everyone reading this has been fashioning the details of the index in their minds by associating it to the subject being discussed in relationship to their own department's record system.

The index ought to be called the nightmare: The police want everything retained; the civil libertarians do not want anything retained. Administrators want as little as possible retained, and that, in the simplest of formats. The budget controllers want the cost reduced at every annual meeting; the legislative staffs want all retention ended upon statutorily defined dates, such as the statute of limitations, as an example. Then there are the politicians; they want everything either retained or not retained, depending on whose ox is being gored, then instantly available or not available when they need it to support their position or slam the opposition. Then, they want nothing in the police files when any citizen complains about police files and its content regarding the issues of invasion of privacy, spying, embarrassment by circumstance, or the general "it just isn't right."

Remember that everything that comes into an active case file is there because it was picked up during the criminal case investigation or a criminal intelligence case file, the case preinvestigation. It is at the close of a case where the decisions are made as to what is retained or started on its path to destruction according to the controlling statutes and/or records policies. Recall that a closed-by-arrest case is after all appeals are completed. (FBI crime statistics have shortened that, for their purposes only, to the date of arrest.) **This is the final check to see that the indexed case files match the department's master files index before the detective's copy of the case file is stored in the closed-case section of the records room. This is also the time you notify the intelligence officer via department process of case closing and final dispositions.** In some states this file is about to become public; remove the nonpublic parts and prepare a redaction memo or instructions for the nonpublic information that cannot be removed due to its case nature. That would include information that is in use in another open investigation or open intelligence file that would be harmful to that case if made public. The nightmare has just gone up to three-aspirin status.

The intelligence office opens a new file when appropriate or supplements a prior file with the case disposition material, including jail time with expected release date, probation information, and any other pertinent information. They may choose to interview the prisoner in jail, or probationers at a convenient time and place. The information machine moves on. The selection criteria are a judgment issue. Never put a case and therefore its information to rest without the future in mind.

I adopt the position that we keep it if we know from our experience it is useful, or if the law requires it kept. It is processed as quickly as possible; use it, store it, recover it, inspect it periodically, then after its estimated useful life, dump it out of the index into a pending-destruction bin with "notice of query" flags directed to the destruction bin supervisor. This bin is a retainer, which requires a supervisor to approve searching around in the destruction bin to retrieve a flag hit item and reinstall it in a file and the accessible department index or continue its path to destruction. Then pick a deadline, say ninety days, just to be different from the sixty-day intake trash bin: if no one asks or no flag hits occur within that deadline, it is destroyed. (Please remember that those time frames are arbitrary for book purposes only; they can be whatever fits best to your requirements or statutes.) I call it a cascade destruction formula. Essentially, when the useful life is over it gets a several-step cascade to flow out of the system with a capability of retrieval until it is finally destroyed. (See illustration at the end of this chapter.)

The key to a successful system is the interpretation of "if we know from experience it is useful." The information collection must be based on a good-faith effort to avoid retention of "privacy material," which if leaked or lawfully released causes unnecessary harm to a private person. The retention must be for a legitimate and realistic law enforcement purpose. That retention standard is written in the department order format, defended with clear explanations to our political controllers, when asked, and periodically inspected and updated. Simply put, keep the crap out.

The first cascade is just a timeline or marker for a *department master index* item during which no activity has demanded attention, or was hit on, for that set time period. (Note that we are still speaking of the department master file, not the case-specific index within the "murder book"/folder, which retains all case-associated data intact with that case file until the entire case file is destroyed at the end of its normal retention period and after the closing date, usually set by state law.) For example, misdemeanors have a normal retention period of five or ten years, felonies twenty-five years, major closed violent felonies fifty years; open murders, on the other hand, require a case-by-case decision after fifty years. As an aside, all pending/inactive felonies should require an active investigative action at a minimum of once a year. Those are closed, after review for legal exceptions, by the statute of limitations as unsolved; they are not destroyed at that point.

A typical cascade destruction system starts at the input. Police departments keep all kinds of files with set retention periods set by policy or law. We are interested only in criminal cases and any matters where there is police contact with the public for untold varieties of reasons—citizen reports, complaints from crimes to annoyance, traffic tickets, and accidents by air-craft, truck, train, vessel, persons, cars, and events, which may be of use. All go into the index; let us call it the Big Pond. From Big Pond, one stream cascades to the Trash Bin Pond and one stream to the Retention Pond. The trash bin has a sixty-day capacity, then spills to the Destruction Pond. The Retention Pond has various outlets, all set by policy date or statutory date, then cascades to the Destruction Pond, which has a ninety-day capacity. If any queries are made with hits in the Destruction Pond, they are piped back to the inquirer and re-stored in either the Retention Pond for a new fixed date or the Trash Pond for another sixty days. If there are no queries, the matter goes back to the Destruction Pond for ninety days, then to the incinerator pond of fire.

The trash bin cascade is where you dump the *unused* trash, such as the sixty-day patrol post sheets, thus starting them on the ninety-day destruc-tion path, retrievable by a hit after a supervisor's review.

Each type or category of retained files has its set *retention* period suit-able to the nature of the file, as in intelligence files or statutes. At the desig-nated end date, it is then dumped over the first cascade into a shallow pool, the Destruction Pond, where it slowly sinks to the bottom of the continuous incoming trash; it sits outside of the normal active flags, trash, and retention files: except a **supervisor-only** flag rings on any hit during that ninety-day period. It requires a supervisor's approval for release, but only after notice to the inquirer, discussion, then a decision as to whether it goes back into the mainstream-flagged index. The retention pond has a statutory fixed time for all files so dumped. It continues on its merry way to destruction, with an extra-added ninety-day pool time. If the destruction item sits in the destruc-tion pool for that additional ninety-day time frame without any inquiries, it is allowed to cascade into the incinerate pile. That period usually has a required (fixed date) or maximum shelf period (allowed date) set by a state records library statute. If not, set a reasonable time period for a regular peri-odical destruction of files, and burn, erase, but never put it in the public domain or sell or give away the material. It must disappear from life by a rule-set process. If you get to choose allowable dates, select what is best for the department. It is a privacy matter, and we should not invade it more than is justifiably reasonable.

In a manual file system, it is better to keep the intake trash bin separate from the destruction file. In a computer database, your programmer may wish to mix them, with a split in hit responses with intake, auto-response to the inquirer; the destruction bin hits flagged to supervisor-only for custom construction. Nonhit files travel the same path to destruction.

By cascading, we get the most out of the life of the item under the political umbrella within which we must work. The civil liberties people, while never happy, will see a removal of information under controlled supervision with accountability. The item is tracked for any abuse that is identified by identifying who inquired and the purpose of every master index inquiry. The query is best controlled by the receiving department. Demanding agencies are identified, and preauthorizations with procedures are normal, using file or agency control numbers. If the inquiry comes via the state police information communication net, a copy to file of the inquiry and your response is all the control needed. Internal, routine "off the street inquiries" can be identified and tracked by badge numbers. This type of inquiry also serves as a record retention extension tool if a hit or match is found, responded to, acted upon, and conducted in the normal course of business. Credibility and control are accomplished by periodic inspection; every item can be traced to a department file or to another agency and to the person making the inquiry.

Politicians love a simple but appealing compromise that satisfies their needs. The trick to success is to present it to the police department political controllers, who set the rules, as a difficult compromise for the police to accept, because it is. The police accept the responsibility for the law or rule. That makes any politician happy and the police get to set a reasonable rule to meet their needs. In addition, the police get to set the method and technology of how the index is set up and operated, essentially defining the mechanics of the process rather than responding to some vague political direction with deliberately unclear restrictions, which can change with the legislative wind. Further, since we live in a bureaucratic society, we get to keep selected reports of what we had in the files and when we destroyed it. That has to be identified, but the "information" is not present, just the item identification, which would include the original case file number, usually a name with date of birth and address, plus general data to validate the case content generic identity. This should be quite sketchy or of outline format; however, that may be useful in some matters.

Police case files are retained under state law by state records retention statutes, usually set at a designated term of twenty-five to fifty years, depending on the nature of the file. Open murder files are retained forever or until all reasonable expectations of life of all parties identified within the file are exhausted. Thus a hit on the master index, which now includes the destruction-consolidated index names and data, leads you back to a closed case that is in storage, eventually for destruction under the state's direction. Many states have file destruction centers where you can warehouse old, dated files that are space wasters. Send them over; if a rare index hit occurs, access is available until the final state-mandated destruction date arrives.

This is particularly useful in today's charged atmosphere regarding shared information and intelligence with other agencies, particularly the federal ones. We can forward copies of our files and intelligence under instructions to the receiver, which ensures that the sender retains control over use, as defined in statutory public records or freedom of information rules. The department can also send a copy of the files being destroyed with a notice of removal and destruction per the state rules to other law enforcement agencies for their "shared" information indicating they must deal with those files under their own statutes or rules. If they desire, they can trash the file or handle it under their own rules. You are out and they have a decision. The plus side is that however one decides to share or move information, it is always under a politically generated controlling rule or law.

Let us see if I can make some sense out of what appears to be a very complicated file system. It is not. It just has room doors, some one-way, some two or more ways, some with no doors, just a window where things are passed back and forth to special customers. Some are windowless chambers where you need a special key to enter. See, that is not complicated. The index system keeps it all tied together.

Now is the time to add a third word to the information/intelligence labels we have been dealing with: evidence. Admissible evidence is one natural result of a successful process of information, turned into intelligence and then, some of it, into evidence for prosecution and trial. The reason will be clear as we discuss public records laws. In addition, now is the time to bring up the Patriot Act* and the Congressional Research Service (CRS) Report for Congress: *Fusion Centers: Issues and Options for Congress,* July 6, 2007.† Familiarize yourselves with these matters before you develop or update a system. The counterterrorism efforts will result in more and more information sharing between agencies, federal, state, or local. I suspect there will be some period of confusion in the development, operations, and handling of this issue. Work to coordinate your records to further that effort while continuing toward your own objectives. It can be done.

Public records rules are the first hurdle to identify and properly sort out. They vary from state to state. The media regularly publish 911 tapes and deposition statements; witnesses go on television and respond in unbelievable varieties of ways, most very badly. The states that keep police records outside the public realm until all issues are settled are politically sane. Those that do not are destructive to individual privacy rights by exposing citizens to danger, criminal acts, embarrassment, humiliation, and media exploitation for public entertainment. It is good government to open public records in order for citizens to observe all government actions for their review, but only within a proper time frame and with respect to the greater rights of the individuals who created the government, control the government, direct the government, and limit the government to its proper role and duties.

---

* Public Law 107-56.
† See http//epic.org/privacy/fusion/crs_fusionrpt.pdf—Order Code RL34070.

Public Records Law Issues

Rather than continue with the main flow of this text with a matter that many are familiar with, I have highlighted the aforementioned issue (boldface). At the end of these few pages, it is noted by another highlight. Feel free to skip it. However, my thoughts on the matter appear in the following.

Those states without serious police record intrusions will have political pressure on them to create public access. Police agencies within those states should be prepared to define reasonable methods of accommodating that pressure by presenting reasonable responses to avoid the error of those states that made "overbroad" rules in political haste to feed a political base without thinking of the individual citizen's right of privacy (a subright of liberty). Pay particular attention to the ability to destroy records of matters that were kept for short-term use to see if they are of value to the police. These are the trash bin items. It is ironic that in some states the police are required to keep what they wish to destroy, while the government restricts use of the information, sharing of information, in attempts to limit invasions of privacy, then opens it to the public for nothing more than its entertainment value.

Many states have made 911 audio-tapes public records and require that they be released to the public. Try your best to get that changed. The voice, tone of voice, reported information, background sounds, and dispatcher instructions are investigative in nature and must not be public record during the investigation. As a compromise, you could agree that the name, place, time, and nature of the crime be released by a spokesperson, after review by a case manager to ensure that it would not interfere with the case or safety of any person—such as kidnappings, some hostage matters, criminals at large while in the escape phase, or in matters where a criminal's location is unknown but his vehicle is under police surveillance near an apartment complex. Then throw into this mix certain residential burglaries, major thefts from financial organizations, and a continuing list that is endless. Not a single item in an active police criminal investigation should be public, not even data that is public outside of the case, unless the police wish to release it for purposes of furthering the investigation, or for public safety. The fact that the police are collecting public data for the case under investigation is an investigative issue, and that is not open to the public; if known, it is informative to the target of the case. I repeat, try to get your controllers to understand and change those laws in jurisdictions where it is a problem.

Police agencies within states that have overly broad intrusions ought to rethink some of their provisions. So let us take note of the main points about them for a few pages.

In addition, a few notes about discovery are included since they are of a similar nature, police files that are released to the defendant or his counsel.

First, there is a difference among states. Some have broad discovery, some limited, and some with no discovery rules but do have court-mandated obligations, usually set by case law and rules of evidence. The police and local prosecutor are responsible for ensuring compliance and that all such rules are followed. That requires complete openness to the prosecutor of your entire case file and sometimes the department's master files. This is most troublesome when you find yourself involved with an active investigation of a defendant with a matter not specific to the trial case at hand. Discuss this with the prosecutor identified by your precase agreements or with his or her office. This can get complicated, particularly with impeachment evidence; more complicated if you should obtain a search, intercept, or arrest warrant just before or during a trial on another issue; disastrous if another unit in the department is unaware of the trial and possesses exculpatory evidence. A proper department and case index with flags will eliminate this possibility. Further, you must consider other agency investigations with which you have routine contacts and know or should have known of their case operations. Think area and regional information-sharing systems, or metro police. Think other agency agreements as noted earlier in this book. Your general daily arrest notice to police in your state will alert their automated files, as their daily arrest notice will inform your department. Think of the specific office and how that office is charged to check the index, as a daily routine and its specified scope. Then think about what to do with hits, a case preparation phase matter to be set by procedure, perhaps.

Note that a routine check of the incoming message traffic backs up the normal distribution of that same material, previously mentioned, which is distributed to the appropriate "desks," where it often goes unread. It is a simple check, with balance, to keep the engine humming. If by this point you do not know what I am talking about, check with your state police agency responsible for all police intra- and interstate communications. If your state does not, as a matter of routine, provide a daily summary of crime and arrests, they have the capability but maybe not the capacity; talk with them. It is a relatively simple matter and can be broadened to include analysis, regional trends, specific data for street use, and myriads of other information.

Those are the preliminaries; now we get specific. There is no constitutional right to discovery, but trials by ambush are fast disappearing, if not gone in most places. In discovery states, all case matters are normally turned over to the defendant after a plea of not guilty and the prosecution begins in earnest. This means that all your files must be completed and in the prosecutor's possession by that time, not just the probable-cause report forwarded to the court to secure this one defendant at initial appearance, the going to trial or "plea" ruling. You may get a few days' leeway in routine cases since no one is in a hurry, but do not rely on that in a well financed and defended major case. It puts the state in the position of having to continue the court case while the defendant can allow his or her "speedy trial" date to remain intact, thereby squeezing the state's preparation requirements. The case at hand may be a high priority, but lesser cases may get dumped into the plea bargain pile.

In both discovery and nondiscovery states, *any* evidence favorable to the defendant that is material and relevant to the case, while not under a discovery rule but appears in case law due-process decisions, amounts to exculpatory evidence. The police are bound to turn that material over. The prosecutor must comply and must know of all your information relating to the defendant. The prosecutor decides what is exculpatory, not the police. The court is the final decider. If the court finds that evidence was exculpatory and was denied to the defendant, it amounts to a "case buster." The defendant is released; you may get to do it all over again, or not, based on the nature of the failure to disclose. Was it knowingly or a simple error along with the timing?

Inform the prosecutor of all impeachment evidence regarding the defendant. This is usually the criminal history of the defendant. It could include past similar crimes and contradictory statements, especially if within the case. The normal routine in major cases is to forward to the prosecutor criminal histories of all witnesses, both sides, and all witness impeachment material known to the police. This requires a department index search for every witness as well every defendant arrested. Unarrested codefendants or unindicted coconspirators raise case investigative issues too numerous to detail here that must be settled. Call your prosecutor.

The work product of the prosecutor is not normally discoverable; in some places evidence that is easily discovered by the defendant and can be reasonably obtained by him or her can be excluded from the discovery rule. Inadmissible evidence, unless exculpable, can sometimes be omitted; it depends on your state's rules. These decisions should be made by the prosecutor's office designated person, not just the trial attorney, which was discussed and decided in the precase agreement with that office.

More states and courts are finding e-mails to or from any government entity to be a *public record*. Many detectives and supervisors use internal and outside-of-department e-mail in criminal cases. Those e-mails must be clearly identified as case specific and part of the open investigation or an intelligence open case to be excluded. Beware of your structure; secure and protect all case investigative material from this intrusion. Format your e-mails as you do a report. Many citizens now send inquiries, tips, criminal case information, and personal matters to the police seeking information and help. They do not realize the e-mail may be public. If they did, the mail would not be sent in many of those instances. Moreover, some places are having public records difficulty with arrest reports. In those states, limit the arrest report to defendant personal identification data only, along with the charge and disposition information. Known unarrested associates, relatives, past addresses, past employment, vehicles, and other such matters that could be considered intelligence may be listed on a second form for intelligence profiles and filing. Agencies that use the arrest form with a probable-cause paragraph for the initial court appearance and minor-case pleas may want to review that practice. This is using flexibility where necessary. I place that here as a reminder of the constant form and system updates that are an ongoing process. That sheet could be the normal vehicle for the opening of an intelligence case; again, your choice.

Requests by the police for a public record from any government agency that contains such record are exempt from disclosure (in most states) of that request and response to the police from the public records holding agency. The rule exempt request must be a part of an active investigation, and the police must advise the agency holding the record when the case changes to inactive or closed. The reason is obvious, but many politicians do not understand the problem. The statute must be checked to be sure that the "closed" definition does not mean inactive. Make sure that department surveillance procedures are exempt, along with police resources, inventories, plans, policies regarding mobilization, deployment, activation of tactical operations, response to emergencies, and major crimes if you can get it. Continuing, include identities of all informants (confidential, criminal, interested citizen, etc.) Watch for special exemptions such as rape victims and juveniles. Try to exempt death, obscene, or other disturbing photographs. Insist that photographs of any child be exempted, as well as victims' personal assets and locations, particularly victim and witness residences. Try to exclude documents or complaint forms identifying the calling citizens' names, addresses, and employment. Add research items, academy curricula regarding investigative process and procedures, and any other matter you can reasonably define that would interfere with your responsibilities or disclose information that would be detrimental to the public by hindering or exposing police investigative operations, procedures, or individual privacy.

Frankly, that is almost everything of what the police do: invade privacy, every day, in almost every matter about which they interact with a person, place, or thing. Departments should bring this issue up every time a legislature goes into session and when they close a session, every year until it is corrected. Approach the political controllers from the correct perspective. Police represent the harmed person when their individual rights and privileges are violated, the general public when their lawful permissions and privileges are infringed upon, and are the force behind the government's ability to operate a civilized society. The military defends us from outside forces, the police from within. When a police officer violates those same rights of an individual, the best and quickest solution is most often from the police department itself, followed by the prosecutor, courts, government, and finally, when appropriate, the public and media. None of those "fix a problem" issues should be at the expense of any harmed individual or group, or adverse to good government.

The department Web site should have a general public "info" capability and "crime line" addresses as well, and secure it from the public open-records law. On major criminal reactive cases, you may wish to provide a case-specific crime public information phone number. Check with legal counsel and prosecutors; there are ways to protect this information from public access. Protect or at least warn citizens if you can. If you cannot protect e-mail crime lines, shut them down and go back to the phones until you can correct the problem. Once again, the political arena is building walls between individuals, the public, and their police.

More. Be sure information received by the department from out of state or any federal agency is handled in accordance with that jurisdiction's records or freedom of information laws and directions. It can be argued that they do not become subject to the receiving jurisdiction's public records laws as long as the department separates them from their own files as "on loan" or "private material" owned by "whomever." They are not the department's records; the sender retains the ownership and his or her rules apply, hopefully. Check with department counsel; it remains "fuzzy" in the law. If it is a serious issue in any department's jurisdiction, have it legally briefed, not just an off-the-cuff lawyer remark. Consider the wording of your department's directions notice that you send to other agencies to fill their requests for records from you, such as "classified nonpublic per Statutes (number and state)."

It is not good government to expose citizens to calamity or embarrassment by releasing police records into the pubic domain, for several legitimate reasons:

The public created and hired the police to protect them. This includes their person, privacy, property, families, and neighborhoods from a variety of criminals and other abusive activities.

There is a "moral agency" connection created that requires confidentiality that must be protected by law. Many criminal acts go unreported to the police because of fear of exposure to the public of the victim's private troubles or activities, the legal ones.

In addition, some will not report intrusions into their homes with a possibility of exposing the legitimate content within the home to predators who may watch television, see pictures of entrances, windows, security measures, and valuables, and video of where they are located, a map if you will. One example of an "innocent" exposure to harm, nongovernment, is an obituary column where the media directly informs the burglar of when and where a residence will be empty, along with sufficient data to let them know if the travel is worth their time. The wise burglar knows the police also read the obits; the unwary wind up in prison. A daily patrol post notice is quite common. Information in police files is a hundred times more dangerous to innocent citizens' privacy rights than an obituary.

There is no constitutional right of the media or public to access police records, thus overriding a privacy right (**a subright of liberty**) of an individual, especially since the government co-opted the issue of who controls the criminal case. Courts have infringed upon that privacy right. Governments have declared that crimes are against the public interest and good order and not a private matter, with courts that have ruled that the "public interest" is "greater" than an individual right. I cannot think of a single valid reason why such thinking is correct, particularly since the police have a responsibility to warn of any danger and a duty to protect individual privacy. The issue of public access to "see and monitor" the police is negated by the fact that information will shortly be public for inspection and review, after the danger and matter is fully settled, including relocations or protections implemented. Media exploitation for entertainment, sensationalism, and speculation is hardly a calm, quiet, or intensive review for promoting good government. I always thought, to a person who is raped, that it was quite a personal matter. Have you ever heard a media show state, "We have photos, but will not show the face of the individual, Mary Jones, of 123 Main Street to respect her privacy"? You and I both can think of several Web site warning notices to the public that should get their attention to raise a protest with their legislatures. Consider putting them up.

The bottom line is to read and comprehend the jurisdiction's public records law, very carefully and in depth. That means study it. Question: If you purchase information from an informant, which is an expenditure of public funds, is it a public record?

Before we get into the case files and how they are set up, keep in mind that I will discuss either index files that are manual, semiautomated, or fully automated, as the book index system fits all. In fact, a good way to build an automated index from a manual index file can be done with a box of three-by-five cards with titles and some notes on them. The computer people will label them to fit their terminology, folder, trays in folders, flag methodologies, etc. (Think, think tank session.) I repeat, this file index is for major cases or others you deem necessary, like the day-to-day routine cases. Using the same forms for both situations need not be tasked with the burden of a full index or administrative file, other than the department's routine. The department sets the scope.

Manual department index file location and control probably exist only in small agencies; most have a combination of both, and large agencies should all be fully automated by now. Further, outside-of-agency inquiries are usually done via the state's law enforcement and data information networks. The process and construction outline follow the same principles in all types of files. **Cards or high-speed computers are just the mechanics; we deal with the content.**

Police Sources of Information

I hope I have selected the best way to present this; if not both you and I will be muddled before the end of the chapter. Let us start with the police sources of information and activities. From them all information originates. While obtaining, during possession and after use, information is dealt with by the department; information is placed in various files and worked with on cases. Intelligence is produced, much of which is turned into evidence. Noninvestigative activities are addressed and then stored as reference information. To see what we have in hand, let us identify the general categories whence it came. We will use broad categories, generalize the sources, and limit them to the regular norms. Departments may add or delete any to fit circumstances.

Citizens

Contacts with citizens is a primary information source. This includes informants, responses to complaints, and day-to-day meetings of a general nature, such as assisting motorists or ticketing them. This type of information is subjected to the first filter. The officer is the first decider of raw or street information gathering, then selects and reports information as directed by the department. Records start for all complaints, traffic tickets, accidents or events, and for informants, confidential and street. The officer's judgment prevails, whether routine street stop and talk, frisks, aided by asking probing questions, or discussing the local fishing and weather. Data is observed and noted at hockshops, gang locations, bars, motels, hospitals, trouble spots, and vendors, just to begin the list. First-level supervisors know which officers produce and which collect a paycheck for minimal work. Performance ratings inform management. This is the daily ebb and flow of police activity.

Officer Observations and Probes

Officers report what they see that is of interest to the department. I will not discuss the methods and manner of inquiry; those are treated in patrol tactics, investigative queries, and interview technique courses. We are interested in what those activities produce. Street stops, observations, and inquiries produce names, addresses, vehicle numbers, locations, dates and time, associations with people, places, and activities. This is of particular interest with the new terrorist threat to the nation, and the main reason the methods of the intelligence gathering will not be discussed, whether it is directed, randomly obtained by an unending variety of methods, or event associated. The data is collected on the patrol post sheet used by succeeding shifts for a period and then stored for early destruction. The system has a method of capturing the data obtained by indexing those items. **Random data is directed to the index trash bin awaiting an inquiry or final disposal. Specific data from instructed collections or valued data innocently found is indexed and routed to the appropriate department office.** Any data the patrol officer finds as a matter of observation with heightened interest is indexed direct to the trash bin for future inquiries or hits on existing files, kept on the patrol sheet for sixty days, then processed into local files or the destruction cascade.

The collection methods, usefulness, and purpose of matters mentioned in the preceding paragraph set in a police academy course curricula would run more than forty pages, the class hours would be numbered in days, and the assigned road probation/recruit supervisor, months. Departments spend many dollars on this and ought to capture the proceeds of the efforts made.

Investigations

During a case investigation, the same things mentioned in the aforementioned paragraph occur in addition to the case itself. Remind your officers that, when dealing with a specific case, its information is relatively easy to capture; after all, it will be in the report and indexed. The sidebar issues and noncase information items that arise need investigator judgment and capture. When detectives are walking the streets and probing, turning over rocks and such, all sorts of interesting things appear. Use those by putting them into a selected department file system for direction and further exploitation, but separate from the case file unless they are relevant.

Do not forget the department communication coded responses to inquiries from street officers, uniform and detective, when they are in direct contact or confrontation with the subject of the request. Those codes will be placed by the major-case manager, inserted by him on the index entry form, and have supervisor approval and acceptance of the code class before going into the index. Most agencies entering index items accept a noncoded entry as neutral, which is "we do not know to whom you are talking, you are on your own." Today agencies, which work for good political controllers, at least have in-car computers that give patrol officers vehicle registration data, open warrants, wanted, or stolen vehicle, before the vehicle is stopped. The investigation data sometimes lacks codes; they should be added. Some examples are:

Code-Danger: wanted, warrant, stolen car, etc.

Code-No information: Clear, go about your business.

Code-Party of interest: submit contact report, identify all parties.

Code-Delay: contact communications for instructions, call for the dogs, conduct safety check, loose surveillance after release, wait for unmarked surveillance car.

And so on.

Intelligence Operations

Intelligence operations are direct probes or information-gathering techniques, whether it is the traditional sources of gamblers, prostitutes, informants, magazine or newspaper articles, parolees and probationers, or down to neighborhood "chats" with interested citizens and citizens in whom the police are interested. Sometimes the work is to develop a proactive case predicate or scope of a case, identifying the players and locations before the actual case investigations begin. Sometimes a source miraculously appears right out of the sky. Sometimes it is a result of electronic or modern technology. The intelligence files are secret and are not revealed except under department control. The same system we are developing will also handle that issue.

Our problem is, of course, the content and usefulness; the difficulty is volume. If you have a camera over tollbooths or at appropriate highway choke points checking each license plate for stolen vehicles, wanted persons (warrants issued, pending issue, or PC arrests) associated with that plate, or visible violations, you collect a lot of junk and a number of criminals. The question becomes whether there are sufficient violations to make the program worthwhile. I believe it is safe to say that this requires scanner and computer capacity, not three-by-five cards.

Other Agencies

I like the idea, regardless of department size, that an intelligence bureau, unit, or person be designated to specific intelligence tasks: constant checking, cross-checking, informant development, parole-probationer and school officer contacts, and other avenues of information such as directed probes of suspected criminal activity to build an information base and investigative sources that are invaluable and productive. It identifies the who, what, how, and sometimes the when and where. Talking to surrounding and associated agencies should not be just a random or specific case-oriented matter. That is important but not sufficient to catch the "fall through the cracks" of the routine message information transfer the statewide police communications system provides. Further, that is developed at different levels and capacities as well as content. Share and coordinate information and indexes.

Electronic Measures

These run the gamut of street cameras, "red light" runners, toll barriers, and store cameras (nongovernment) all the way to court-ordered intercepts. Most departments have the "normal" programs under control if not at full utilization. This is where I repeat the recommendation of getting a strong legal grip on the Patriot Act.* It discusses detention times of illegal border entries, defines domestic terrorism, and discusses the rules of indefinite detention, surreptitious entry, and no-notice issues. It also addresses searches of e-mail, telephone, and financial records with or without court orders, hidden subpoenas, national security letters, warrantless "taps," scope, and circumstance. Please remember the act changed the Foreign Intelligence Surveillance Act (FISA). Mostly bringing federal capabilities back up to allowed state and constitutional levels, it was the FISA act that denied federal law enforcement some methods and erected the antisharing wall between the FBI and the CIA prior to 9/11. Legal issues arise here with your data collection, retention, and distribution capabilities.

I think the book, in totality, has set the arena and parameters in which we must work. So let us cut to the chase. This is worth repeating: Information collection, retention and analysis is expensive, burdensome, and, frankly, a pain in the butt. Cascade it out, retrievably in all cases until the final destruction is as remote from intake as you can get it. Computers permit you to do that. Paper files never permitted that; take advantage.

Central desk reporting (CDR) has been discussed enough for you to see the advantages of control. That procedure is a stacked management task:

1. The "control room" case file is as discussed, so far.
2. The supervisory level is for completeness, operational issues, missed leads, corrections, new leads, other-case similarities, gangs, area patterns, and other regional routine connections or contacts.
3. Detective command gets briefs to any detail they wish, quick looks at area connections, deals with policy issues, and provides case supervision from the management perspective.
4. Department command: for all of the above (briefly), deals with wider applications to surrounding agencies, communication resolutions, information sharing, and index improvement.

Written policy tends to control management itself at times; they need to move from "what shall we do today" to "is this issue resolved yet." The backside of this is management's response with the following:

---

* Public Law 107-56.

1. Policy and procedure improvement
2. Education improvements
3. In-service training implemented and conducted
4. Training course review for detective and uniform procedures and methods
5. Planning and discussion on any range of matters such as unusual or new developments for crime escape methods, surveillance improvements, witness identification procedures, and all in-between items, down to identification of lame, lazy, and stupid errors
6. Finally, the most important, information system consolidation and automated-sharing issues

Still hoping I am on the right track here, we will move on to the specific case file index and get to the relationship with the department's main and other files, then to the outside-of-department files and sources.

Once again, the presentation will be in generalities that will fit all situations, which permits adaptation to any department size and capabilities. We deal with content.

Case Index (See Illustration at the End of the Chapter)

A criminal case file will have an index that captures the items listed and checks that against other data within the case and searches outside the case for contacts and similarities. The coordinator keeps the case file, sometimes called a "murder book;" it contains an index as well. It locates every matching item within the case and points to all similar hits outside the case file when checked against the department index and outside sources.* Automated files do this automatically; manual files do not. It's really kind of simple. In the case of "automated" formats, you must understand the scope of the automation; those that are recent may not have the department's complete files entered. That is also true when checking any other outside-the-department indexes. **A consideration that should never be forgotten is the scope and time reference of the automated files.** The old manual file index should be available, but some are in storage somewhere. The new recruits coming on the job are usually not aware anyone ever relied on paper. "Good grief, you mean someone has to read all this stuff?" The reply: "Yup and you damn

---

* Index figure. Note: all authorized inquiries received at department index files (located in Trash and Retention Ponds) are sent direct replies. Hits on files in the destruction pool require a supervisor review and decision. Queries with index hits on any destroyed files (main department index) are responded to with a notice of destruction, original date of file, supplementals, and destroyed dates. Other files, which are active, on the same subject of inquiry receive the appropriate response as normal hits.

well better comprehend and associate exactly what you are reading and its scope."

The **in-case index** locates each match to a specific numbered report page within the case file, sometimes called the index reference. The case manager/coordinator sees every item that enters the case and the case file, checks and/or enters the item into the case index, and notes the page number and other reference data in use. If he is not familiar with prior matches, he looks and decides actions, notes lead sheets or original complaint forms, and sends out new leads or inquiries to obtain whatever he is searching for. He informs persons with the need to know, adds or deletes items for meeting agendas, or takes an action as a result of seeing the new entry. He directs the case so he needs to know what is in it. This is central desk reporting (CDR). This is what detects and corrects errors early in the case. This is what prevents, or at least significantly reduces, the chance of the case errors used as examples in this book. This is what moves the case forward with specific directions and paths of investigation with the knowledge, information, and judgment of the case manager. No automated system in existence will work until the data is entered in the correct manner. **The case index data is also inserted into the department's master index insofar as it is compatible. That is needed for setting of flags to identify and capture internal or external inquiries for matches. The withheld indexable items, if any, to within-the-case data predetermined to protect selected case issues are entered in the case file immediately and the department's master index as soon as the case manager sees fit. That decision is based on the manager's best judgment and/or department procedure. The nonentered case-indexed items must be checked, marked, and easily identified as "to be entered" into the main department index. Use something as easy as a checkmark, highlighting in a different color, crossing off in manual case indexing or whatever computer control you use.** Do not make it complicated.

The file consists of various categories; they are formatted to department index specifications, and/or additional categories may be created within the scope and nature of the case but limited to the case file index. That takes care of the oddities. The greater your department capabilities and computer power, the more formatted you become.

The file has at a minimum:

- **Name and date of birth (DOB):** Every name, nickname, alias, maiden, partial name, or initial that appears in the investigation is listed. Whether exact spelling, phonetic, and/or Soundex is used is the department's choice. In a manual file, this is easy but cumbersome. In an automated file, this is easy and quick but subject to the system's capabilities and limitations. This is why the file control and input must be with an experienced case manager; he catches the case nuances, the similarities but not quite exact comparisons, the unaddressed open property issues, the shopping mall address issues, and much more. He has the sense and an independent judgment of all issues at hand. He has value and priorities in mind. He knows the case and the usefulness of the information. He is totally aware of the surroundings of the case, its contradictions, the people involved, and all issue relevancies.

The report page, lead or return sheets, and memos are included and listed. The report page number is always listed on the lead returns, including the hits. With each repeat of the name and/or DOB or other selected categories, the new report page number is added. Consider listing, using tabs or checkmarks, items such as witnesses, neighbors, associates, employers, etc., all suited to department system capabilities. That allows you to have a hit when an inquiry is made regarding an associated name; page numbers of both the principal case name and associates appear at once by the flag mechanism. That holds true for property, etc. Unidentified persons are listed as such with any identifiers you may have obtained, such as description, addresses, associates, vehicles, locations of contact, etc. Think street contact forms for an idea of what is included. Think category assignment of an index tab fit to suit the case and integration with the department's files. The case manager knows which items will be checked by the automated index, which will not, and which of those need further investigation via leads and other methods of file checking. That is his job; he will reduce the "we walked all over this guy during the investigation but did not see him" laments in the after-case review. Do not forget phone numbers, a great source of information through toll sorts and connection analysis, especially in proactive cases. The file is numeric, crossed with a name and address, and in some cases a tower location for cell calls.

Also, think of your public records laws regarding the impact of what information may become public, such as associates with criminal histories, family criminal histories, or other privacy issues. Think, think tank sessions. They will disclose whether information is to be split into differing categories and filed in different places, such as intelligence files. I prefer that the first split be within the case itself. Divide your case as you please, but consider a chronological investigative report file and an administrative report file. The investigative side indicates every investigative step, inquiry, and lead by the case timeline, crime scene, response, and investigative activity with names, places, etc., and the date, time, and location order. The administrative side contains all other issues: the witness list, every name and associate of every person involved in the case and selected histories, memoranda, schedules, and pending files, all *case indexed*. The size, scope, and sophistication determine whether you have a stand-alone case index or subindexes within the case master index for administrative, evidence, witnesses, and other specific matters. The *case file* format must be compatible with the *department's master files*. You can keep it simple or build a monster. I like simple, relevant, and complete; you can always split them if needed, such as a trial list. A quality-driven index will handle that problem.

The police problem is changing from a scarcity of information and limited retrieval capacity to information overload.

Case File Index

Administrative	Investigative
Criminal histories	Dispatcher report
Investigative assignments	Chronological investigator reports
Personnel on the case	(by date, time and place)
Briefings: date, time and place with attendees	Lead sheet returns, checked
	Pending files, leads, reports
Property, criminal, family, associates, and histories	(currently working)
	Synopsis and case summation
Businesses histories, company officers	Evidence, tests, reports
	Maps (marked) with search reports
Pending files, leads, reports (to do)	
Evidence lists, associated receipts	
Pending matters	

Orders, such as neighborhood searches and memoranda of the assignments, area maps with areas marked by scope, time, place, and team identifications

Some of the data kept on the administrative side of the report will move to the investigative side when completed. Be flexible in how you structure the file and use judgment as you would for the case direction itself. The critical task of this file is to make each entry complete with the core information as stated previously. **The coordinator will decide when each item, and which items, will be entered into the *department's master files and index.*** All items are dated by time and initialed by all connected to the process.

The department at their periodic think tank sessions has thought through these problems. A new case file system in your department will undergo some changes as improvements are made. Older systems ought to be rethought on occasion to determine if improvements will ease the burden/efficiency/cost issues.

Continuing.

- **Addresses/locations:** Postal, street addresses, rural addresses, neighborhood, and areas that are identified by a local name or county plat number. "Plunket's Woods," a kid's name for a play area; or "Markam Woods," a gated community; Times Square or Dealy Plaza. All are listed, for that is what people will refer to when asked or describing a place. As in names, all become subject to hits and associated with page numbers upon an inquiry. The department designs the list and fits it to the local, county, or regional community. If an area of interest has numerous identifiers, all are listed. Addresses of major players in the case include present, past, military, prison, college, employment, other properties, and more. Names are cross-index referenced to addresses or other locations. The coordinator decides which items identified that gratuitously turn up from out-of-case files will be indexed into the case file; relevance and judgment prevail. If the department is fully automated, all matters are indexed in the appropriate categories. It is easier to delete than add after finding an error or useless information.
- **Property** other than real property, which is covered under addresses. Most break this down by genre, such as firearms, vehicles, and electronic/household. Washers, dryers, and such things are usually excluded unless someone steals a truckload. Bicycles, tires, and auto parts are a fielders' choice. Those items are generally entered in the department's stolen-property list index, but most of it is useless without identifiers for recovery and prosecution purposes. Nevertheless, sometimes it is of value to the investigation itself. A paper index format will do for the *case oddities* or nonindexable items. A book, binder, or folders with alphabetical index by name and place, plus tabbed files for other matters for case indexing that might not fit formulated computer files/indexes works to cover all situations. Additional notes and observations dealing with unexpected case realities require flexibility and an ability to easily connect matters that all the thinking in the world could not have foreseen. **The entire success of this method is the simple point that all flows through a single controlled, flexible, and organized system that any experienced investigator can pick up, get a grip on all issues from in a short period, and find in the paper**. Departments without automated files combine this with case logbooks.

  Further, you do not have to be computer literate to operate it; it will improve with each case as it is used, by prior experience, reviews pointing out improvements or errors, and ease of setting up. It works in all weather and wherever you find yourself; and it has no batteries.

Some specific items peculiar to your case may not be easily indexed, general files may not respond to queries, but the case investigation may from within its own index checked by CDR succeed in that task. The CDR duties include reading all surrounding other-agency message traffic; viewing all photographs, evidence collection lists, and more; and setting flags for indexed items for all in-department contacts with indexed items and outside inquiries. Set flags with all outside agencies that have the capability to notify you automatically of every matching inquiry they have or receive, then set up a list of routine checks with those places that do not.

If your state still does not have regional and/or statewide continuous or hourly broadcasts by written transmissions of all burglaries, robberies, murders, major thefts, and selected other crimes and arrests, you live in a Third World country. If your department still does not distribute such notices to selected commands within your department, your procedures need a facelift. There is no reason on earth why a detective in Dream City does not know what crimes have been committed or who has been arrested in Neighbor City on his desk morning, noon, and night. He should not have to "call around" unless it is to check to see if there is a connection with one of his cases, new, pending, old, or closed. This information has been routinely available in some states and regions since the early 1930s.

Property of interest is always listed by genre and sublisted as to serialized, nonserialized, or serial number unknown. Details of identifiers are noted and listed in the report by the nature of the property in case the item is mentioned or found during the case investigation.

As new information materializes, it is added and the index checked.

Vehicles and license plates are usually listed separately due to the frequency of case involvement and the highly identifiable characteristics, specific VIN numbers, plate assignment, and subprime information of year, make, model, and color. All vehicles in the case are cross-referenced with all associated names, owner's or not, and addresses and placed in the case administrative file until it becomes appropriate to enter the information into the investigative file due to relevancy, all indexed. Other matters or items that are specific to the case may be on this list. That is the case manager/case coordinator decision; their problems and workloads guide them. Some of it may be tasked out via the lead sheets. They remove the wheat from the chaff, but not the index.

The administrative side, in addition to the witness list and all other persons associated with the case, contains criminal histories of specified subjects, and associates (entered by name and DOB) and family names of specified subjects, all cross-referenced. The list of automatic flags for the case is listed, together with other agency inquiries or responses, and other hits, including *every prior department contact* with anyone involved with the case down to the parking tickets. The case manager, who smartly says to his coordinator "handle it," decides the scope of this effort. As an aside matter of note, officer queries through the department's communication systems of any nature to internal or outside sources are listed in the department's communications files and indexed, for any case, major or normal. It automatically notifies every supervisor and case officer of the match for open, inactive, and closed cases, regardless of the closing class, by arrest, investigation, statute of limitations, or policy. It also monitors officer activity and goes a long way to ensuring that requests for information are not personal. Routine inquiries that have no direct case response/hit, such as vehicle checks while on patrol, go to the trash bin and the patrol post in-car sheet, indexed, and start their indexed cascade out of the system. Failure to note such activity in some appropriate department file is a rule violation subject to disciplinary action.

The administrative side also keeps the record of meetings, coordination decisions with other agencies, prosecutors, memos, equipment use, along with the rest of normal case flotsam and wreckage. This is all part of the central desk reporting (CDR).

The dispatcher desk is a good starting place to expand on this issue a bit. That leads to the following reports:

1. Dispatcher desk report and call tapes
2. Investigation/case report
   a. Lead sheets
   b. Lead return sheet
   c. Arrest reports
   d. Evidence control reports
   e. Lab reports
   f. Medical examiner reports
   g. Case memoranda
   h. Statements
3. Notes, tapes, photographs, and other items of indescribable variety, all of which will be marked, indexed, and filed, shipped, or stored
4. Officer time and activity reports, which must match the other reports submitted with time, place, and case number, although they are not filed with the case. Good defense lawyers dig for discrepancies, and good management collects accurate data for administrative reasons.

You see where this is going; all the sources of information listed earlier are already indexed within the department's files. Major-case investigation demands that all be checked, automatically, part automatically and part manually, or manually, depending upon the department's system in place. The case manager decides the scope based upon the nature and direction of the case. Simply put, there is no one set of rules for any police investigation.

Closing Procedures

This process is usually done after the arrest in the trial report preparation for the prosecutor's office in both proactive and reactive cases, or after a case that has been kept open after arrest for further investigation is going to be closed. Major cases require this final recheck of the index, recoding of the report from active investigation to closed in compliance with your public records laws. It is an accuracy check, with a possibility of opening a new intelligence case, which is nonpublic. The case file is sent to storage, with the administrative side and case investigation side together, less new information or newly opened criminal case information from that file, or intelligence information that was nonrelevant to the filed case itself. This is where you send disposition orders for evidence stored in evidence lockers and note which evidence is in a specific court case file under the courts control or receipted and returned to owners. Unclaimed evidence is disposed of according to your property rules or retained for some other specific purpose. Identify each page removed from the report and note in the file where it or they went, especially in cases about to go public. The removed page is going to another open investigation or open intelligence file, and you do not want to expose the information on that page to the public. Tickler dates for remaining actions and inspections are created for ease of continued control of the remaining flotsam. One purpose of this is to send *all* criminal division files, including arrest files without an associated investigation report, through an intel supervisor-controlled check to review and decide through a central desk destruction (CDD) point. He may wish to keep a name or two, locate some new sources of information, or open a new intel file.

The preceding is a tedious matter. If it cannot be done in conjunction with other after-arrest procedures, be very selective in how and when you use it. Limit it to very important matters and have it approved by the appropriate-level supervisor prior to expending the time. It is work for officers on light-duty status.

Building a formatted index to fit a case index, as well as department, regional, state, and federal indexes, is another very tedious matter. Think, think tanks.

Flag Systems

Let us delve into some of the features of index/flag systems. It is central to the department and checks for, on demand or inquiry to those permitted access, every file within the department for a mate or match of the item asked for and reports all matches to the inquirer and to the department or unit that placed that item in the file. In addition, it captures all inquiries

received from outside authorized agencies and reports to those agencies any matches along with all other prior inquiries received (if that is built into the system; that is the end goal). For example, if an investigator searches the state criminal-history records for Charlie Mugger and the return says "no record," the response informs the investigator that a similar inquiry was made by the Blissful County Sheriff's Office on such and such date and time by Officer Hopeful. This can be done with automated files through the law enforcement communication system, or by a phone call or e-mail to the state department, which then conducts an automated (or manual) search of its files. The degree of success or failure all depends upon the sophistication, design structure, and capabilities of all structures in all agencies searching and responding. *This is why the case manager must be experienced; he knows who has what, what it contains, and how reliable it is.* For personnel-strapped agencies, this may be a "call the state police" issue. We sometimes forget that "no record" means the specific item, as spelled, was checked against a specific file without finding a match. That means not one thing more in an automated system.

The index/flag process also saves every inquiry and source of that inquiry for the set period. It informs inquirers of past inquiries and vice versa, hits or no hits. It further informs all past inquirers of any future inquiries when received. Further, it reports any *case* entries specific to the *case* to any other control point operating in an extended *department case* to all participants in the investigation, thus ensuring that the left hand is aware of the right-hand activities with the same indexed matter. Think carefully in order to open up your *case files* to law enforcement agencies as much as possible. Think more carefully when opening up *intelligence files* to law enforcement organizations; stricter scrutiny is the norm. This also could be a forum or process that can be used to identify a "file leak" in the system, depending on how the sharing of information and openness is structured. Security of files issues is another subject. Access and level of access can be touchy; open it to law enforcement as much as possible, but that is another subject.

Inside-the-department inquiries are selective as to who is authorized to review that file, requiring identity verification for preapproved law enforcement members and usually requiring review and approval by the record unit supervisor for administrative files. And, it is always followed by a notice to the "ownership" unit responsible for the placement of the file.

This is where the department sets the access rules for which doors to the files are open, shut, one-way or two-way, windows only for looking at certain materials, and who possesses the keys for locked doors and what parameters are set to open them. This is think tank-driven by the top administrative policy makers with form designers, computer system designers, and programmers. Every department sets its own internal criteria, guided or directed by the state rules for use of the state law enforcement communications network and associated records laws. Some departments have constructed or joined regional systems; some have not. The introduction of Fusion Centers has expanded the intelligence- and information-sharing responsibilities and capabilities. It is a work in progress. If any departments are reconstructing or melding their systems with state or federal organizations, it is natural to work with them and construct a major-case control process that uses the added power to control, forward, and receive data.

A major *criminal-case management* system is independent of the multiagency intelligence organizations but should have an ease of contributing to it and allowing access to the department's main index file under agreed-upon conditions. The CDR process and the associated *case index* controls the investigative information gathered. The case manager, following policy and law, decides what and when any index item is entered into the *department's index* file. Assuming the department's index is available, under terms of agreement with the state and federals, to Fusion Center matters and other police agency routine matters, the CDR and case index becomes an integration issue of timing the input due to case control issues; usually it is a short delay.

If the major case is involved with methamphetamine distributors, looking for the meth operation sources of the necessary precursors is part of that. Precursor sales may involve Hezbollah, a terrorist organization, which is in the illegal precursor business in the United States and Canada. Fusion Centers along with appropriate state and federal organizations would need to know of the investigation, and coordination becomes immediate. If the investigation is a gang-related auto theft/chop shop case, immediacy is not present, at least not usually. If the major investigation involves condominium buy and sells by "flippers" with loan inflation, cash-outs, and/or foreclosure/bankruptcy frauds, the department is in middle ground; big money is moving around, not usually terrorist driven, but any large sums moved fraudulently to or through overseas financial institutions connect to terrorist or supporting organizations sufficiently to get some attention.

Non-law enforcement inquiries into department records should be done by personal appearance, post mail, e-mail, or telephone and appropriately responded to by department policy. They should all be reviewed, checked, redacted where appropriate, and responded to in compliance with policy and law.

All public record file inquiries will usually be responded to automatically without department supervisory approval. However, notice of that inquiry is sent to the department supervisor of the unit that placed the indexed item in the file.

Inquiries from other law enforcement agencies will also be automatically responded to if received over the secure law enforcement communication network or after appropriate identities are established, for all matches to the inquiring communication center, preauthorized special units, and or/personnel of the inquiring agency. Notices of all such inquiries will be reported to the file's originating department unit or division.

This book's fictional department now has in place a central desk reporting system for major cases, with a specific case manager controlling the *case index,* which is married to the *department index.* It is poised to assume control of a major case in any form since it is flexible with up and down personnel capabilities to get larger or smaller and east-west capabilities to expand scope or shrink. It results in less waste of time chasing case documents and more effectiveness due to focus and attention to details.

Continuing down the path of listing additional sources of information and file structure would be overly repetitive; the same attention to detail and thought is required to accomplish that. (Think, think tank.)

I was going to draw a diagram of a department file index, but it takes a wall of hanging paper to do that. When reduced to this page size, it appears to be a fur ball.

You can do a *case index* in your head. That is because, other than the basics, the coordinator makes it up as the case moves along.

Upon reflection, that drawing of a department case index would replicate a spider web. Picture that: numerous intersecting points in symmetry such that, regardless of where the spider is, it feels the slightest breeze and alerts to the vibrations transmitted through the web. The slightest touch of a live being makes it react to the point of touch to explore. When suitable prey is observed, the spider seizes it and wraps it up.

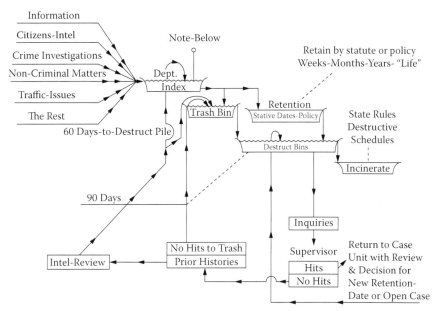

Index (simplified view)

Note: Inquiries with Hits in Trash or Retention Pools Receive Direct Replies to Inquirer

Figure 15.1 Index.

The Wind-Up Chatter 16

I wrote this book more to generate questions in your mind than to provide specific solutions to every option available. If it has accomplished that goal, good. You have at least started organizing your own thoughts by concentrating on internal file improvement issues. Adopting fixed solutions from a book would be merely cloaking the issues with a representative format. That is how business management works; some call it a formula plan to avoid the detailed work necessary to pass muster at the bank loan office; an intelligence unit may be interested in some of those. Police departments need to create the structure and details to fit all case control issues. Remember, the police live in a world of chaos, serious chaos, where no two events are alike in all conditions, options, techniques, or methodologies.

I also stuck a number of very simplified "forms" in the Appendices. Those could not be used in any department in the United States in the "as is" format. They are there to scribble on. Make a few copies and pass them around to subordinates or police friends. Have them reformat, add, delete, and change placement, size of lines or boxes, routine check-off spots, and any other matter they can think of. No two will look alike. It is a mini-think tank without preparation, and these are aids in starting the case control index and integration into an existing system. The thinking that officers will put into something they see as an improvement to existing conditions will surprise you. Just tell them the final product must fit into the total case and department data collection process without increasing the current paper load.

One of many things that a police case manager has in common with a Marine Corps platoon leader is that they answer the question "What's your plan of attack?" the same way: "I don't know yet; I'll figure it out when I get there, get to grips, and see what I'm dealing with."

The Marine Corps and police organizations' management has taught them how to do that, provided them with the ability to use whatever tools are available at that moment in time, under those specific conditions, to do it as effectively as is possible, to adjust as conditions change, and to do that with confidence and ability. That is called training, preparedness, and leadership. The police and the Marines have that in abundance. This book hopes to make what you do and decide to do easier by organizing thoughts and operations so you can be flexible, shift gears, and multitask with some hope of capturing all the work the case team did, presenting the result in a rational manner, and succeeding in avoiding serious pitfalls. Consider this book to be a guideline.

We cannot make a guess as to what will work; it must work. The thoughts now working in your head are directed toward making the department's effort work well, or at least better. If you are a young and relatively new police investigator, or academy student, you now have a very good idea of what you need to know, what goes into case control, and the learning tasks you have ahead of you in order to take your place in the management ranks of your department.

More Chatter

The media were treated rather harshly in this book; that is because they deserve the reputation they have earned. Having said that, there are some very good people in that business, especially the press; the TV news departments have shown a scarcity of reliability, admittedly with a few exceptions. The crime news "talk shows" are a disgrace. Entertainers' muckraking in someone else's tragedy is a fitting description. I suggest police managers rely on some form of the press-police agreement noted in Appendix C. The press is not to be trusted with any detail of the investigation beyond that agreement. If the press will not agree, impose it on the department. One of the leading reasons some police departments did "open up" to the press was a failed attempt to discourage speculation by providing some facts. As Doctor Phil says, "How's that working for you?" Another was to reduce public alarm or fear in certain cases. Again, not much success with that either.

For those of you with serious public record laws, try working with your political controllers to clarify when a criminal case is closed—particularly if you have "victim abusive" public record laws, like Florida. In truth, closing occurs only when it is completely over, after trial and all appeals are settled. In guilty pleas, it is after sentencing, with a caveat that any specific reservations of the right to appeal are no longer a factor. In cases where the criminal has not been identified and no further investigation is active, use the statute of limitations. When warrants for the accused are issued, the statute of limitations is extended as long as reasonable activities to locate the defendant continue; that case remains open until a warrant is recalled by the court or prosecution is abandoned. Or, as in New York City, the police say "fugettaboutit."

Courts have held that the crime itself is a public matter and that the press has permission to access that information. Many states have enacted public record laws that set the standards and guidelines as to what is public. I suggest that police photographs of the interior of a home and its contents, including bodies, are not "part of the crime;" they are part of the investigation. Nor are 911 calls to the police part of the crime; they are part of the investigation, starting with the timeline and the original informing statement, some of which are admissible evidence. Delineate each item in a case by application of that general formula. Protect your investigative keys. Protect the privacy of your client, the victim and family or business, as best you can. Courts, legislatures, press, and police have so muddled the issue that it will take a while to sort out to get it right; consider making the effort through your associations.

More Chatter

Future matters for current thought and intentions: I placed Appendix L, an outline of a twenty-year plan, in this book for a purpose. Every minute we breathe we advance into the future, or at least stay in the new present called "now." If you're not counting, the time in which twenty years passes is rapid and you find your department in the "now," only twenty years older. Police and sheriff's departments and their associations must look to the future with a continuous improvement plan with the actions necessary to move the plan forward. This is not a simple task; it requires deep thinking and cooperation among law enforcement agencies and the political controllers. If police agencies and the associations put forth a clear model for a state to follow, based on the interests of the public, it will gain the attention it deserves.

Many states drift along this path without a clear vision of who they are, where they fit, what they do, and frankly, how to do what they think they should be doing. Look at a growing city: it has a police force backed by a county sheriff's office, backed by a state police, or a state investigative agency and a highway patrol, or … . on and on. Look at it twenty years later: a city, county, and five suburban police departments, some with detectives, some without. You see how this is building. Look at any state and define the police system in place; it is called helter skelter, and it has no system unless you call it patchwork. The multiple designs and the multiple reasons for the nonsystem are history; we are looking at "now." The current cost to the public of this nonsystem is enormous; however, it is the inefficiencies within the service that hurt them the most.

Each sovereign state in our union is the sole source of all police power and authority. All "local" police power and authority come to them via a delegation from the state, by state law, state charter, or state constitution. All power and authority remain vested with the state since they have the means to control or change any such matter they deem appropriate through their state constitutional authority to create such police powers. **That same state authority, in convention, created the federal government through their creation and adoption of the U.S. Constitution.** We have established that the state is the boss, at least in law if not in "politics." "Aaarrgghhhh. Thar's the rub," says the pirate of old.

Politics is a necessary tool to find an orderly conversion of sheriff's departments into police departments and consolidate small police departments into county or regional departments. At the state level, consolidate highway patrols and state investigative agencies into state police departments with an eye and goal to coordinate, improve, and train the managers and officers of the growing local systems. Efficiency, effectiveness, costs, deployment, and leadership identification and ... whoa. I have to stop right at this point; I have been presenting the arguments in favor of improving police service when I came to the issue of leadership identification. That is a state responsibility that was not delegated, not worked upon, by the states in a meaningful and systematic way. The logistics of the "conversions" is a very simple matter. Identification of leadership is and remains the state's responsibility, which is not a simple matter; the states have failed. I have a few new, modest suggestions; well, ... not new* and, I guess, not modest.

The best way to identify leaders is to create them yourself. That identifies the goals, manner, and the predetermined method and needs. All that is left to be done is to do it right. The American Revolutionary Army barely survived the rebellion due to poor leadership. They were lucky to have a few exceptional ones, including George Washington. The poor leadership was repeated in the war of 1812–14. It was fought to a draw; again lucky for us. The Army recognized the issue and successfully urged Congress to create a place called West Point. Leadership identification has never been more than an isolated problem since. The fact that we still exist as a nation with the most serious military power on the planet is rather strong proof.

States need to structure their police system to meet written goals and objectives and include the manner in which they will achieve them. I suggest they start with:

1. Create a fully accredited state police college for all commissioned officers within every state, independent of each other. That would create a pool of qualified and certified eligible officer candidates for any state, county, city, town, village, and district or authority police department. Those jurisdictions must then select their leaders, at all commissioned positions, from that cadre or from a sister state equivalent. That list would include qualified candidates from within their own agencies, if in fact they exist. In addition, standardization of rank of police officers would be based on established criteria. Departments that have the equivalent accredited education programs in place would continue or cease in any manner they choose.†

---

* This issue was quietly raised for discussion within the Florida Department of Law Enforcement in 1978 and ended with a change of the state governor.
† See the New York City Police Department's John Jay School of Criminal Justice standards and accreditation.

Detectives, noncommissioned officers, or supervisors would be required to meet qualifications and be certified in the same manner for the position they hold. Once on the state list, local promotional systems may continue or be modified as agreed with management or union contracts. **The basic state requirement sets the eligible pool, not the promotion list.**

The college would be responsible for overseeing the training of entry-level officers, supervisors, and detectives, the instructors, and the course requirements and curriculum. Locals would not be prohibited, but in fact encouraged, to extend training to meet local needs, in addition to the basic state education. This manner of development permits the college education to take place over any extended period of time, or take place with appropriate "credits." The state would accept outside accredited college courses to the extent of compatibility with state goals and objectives.

Further details, circumstances, exceptions, prior credit rules, and other such matters can continue at another time and place. The concept is the issue for this book. From reading the case management system, you can see the ease with which two agencies can assist and communicate with each other. It fits into an interagency consolidation-mutual aid management system. The same would be true with a state college for law enforcement.

One must see through the immediate impact and recognize unintended consequences. For instance, if the state paid the entire cost, would that result in an equal school completion rate to satisfy locals who are moving up within their departments? Or, the opposite, if the locals had to pay the entire cost for their attendees, ranking officers from state police and larger city police departments may soon fill the seats of locals. Is that good or bad? The answer is that it depends on the capability status of each individual local department. Does that mean some system of recognizing which departments are basket cases and which are well developed? See, it is not easy, but it's still necessary. It is a process that, once decided upon, continues for years, ever improving the service in totality of the overall objective—safe streets and highways with criminals in jail.

2. Improving the state training and leadership issues makes it prudent and necessary for the state to control all the police standards and training at the state-approved level. This would include all such "criminal justice" courses taught at community colleges and universities if they wish course recognition in law enforcement departments. In addition to the state's basic criteria, the control and approval would include all local training activities, qualifications and certification of courses, credits, instructors, and curriculum, and creation of law

enforcement libraries. Law enforcement training that does not meet credit-level standards must be approved as to content to avoid contradictory courses. Anyone can teach or attend them, but they would be of no use to the student in or seeking a law enforcement career unless the course and instructor were state approved. That would get rid of the nonsense taught in many "criminal justice institutes."

3. States must review the state-level police structures to determine whether consolidation of highway patrols and state investigative agencies would be of real benefit to the public. The first-blush appearance is a resounding yes. States with small patrols and small investigative agencies should also do a review. Utah or Wyoming may wind up continuing as is. Florida needed a complete overhaul and restructuring forty years ago; it still does.

4. Elected sheriffs, and in some places elected chiefs of police, need to be phased out and replaced with leaders with law enforcement qualifications and certification credentials. Alternatively, require elected sheriffs to meet the state standards prior to taking office. Local police leaders should be under the control of the local taxing authority, a city or county manager. All these should be controlled by local elected officials operating under state legislated rules. The end goal is to make those jobs nonpolitical with standards and procedures for appointments and removals other than by elections. Can you imagine a popular election for chairman of the Joint Chiefs of Staff, or the director of the Federal Bureau of Investigation, or a superintendent of state police, or the chief of police in your city?

5. Improved entry-level police standards need to be upgraded on a continuing basis. Most of the larger and modern agencies now require a minimum of two years of accredited college education as a door opener. Some state investigative departments compromise their usual standard of four years of college and two years to four years of prior police investigative experience with a total of seven years of experience replacing the college requirements. They discovered that a BA degree in physical education or a master's degree in aerospace engineering was of little use; investigative experience trumped the degrees. The balance was achieved based on the "market pool." The New York State Police, as an example, require two years of college credits (sixty) and test every two years from an applicant base of 15,000 to 25,000 potential troopers. They have little trouble in gaining quality recruits, often from other police agencies; they recruit nationwide. The New York City Police recruit continuously and hire at every recruit class starting date, occasionally with unfilled vacancies. They have a small standing pool from which to select. They too recruit nationwide; they also operate their own fully accredited

college but still require two years of college credit as a condition of employment. (There are military service substitution formulas in both departments.)

Entry-level education requirements must be continuously reviewed and upgraded when possible; the internal level of education requirements must also continue to improve. If you start with a two-year college credit entry, by the time the officer is ready to assume commissioned status, a four-year rule should be required. Those credits can be, and in most places are, gained though internal accredited courses. If you do train and school internally, the department may focus the education to meet its current and future needed "majors." Internal special classes should require a focus—e.g., forensic chemistry, constitutional law, personality disorders and traits, methods of dealing with such matters. These would be followed by master's programs in policing and management, topped off with programs in the philosophy of policing, government, and law enforcement.

I think I am running out of steam.

I have written many suggestions and short one-line statements in this book without detailed reasoning as to why, assuming you identified them from your experience. If you have not, please consider discussing them with other officers; they will become readily apparent. If you are not an experienced law enforcement officer, consider discussing the issue with one. If you are unsuccessful in getting an answer to your questions, I can be contacted via e-mail through the publisher. I will respond as best I can.

Thank you for your time and patience with a laborious topic; I have tried to make it an "easy read," insofar as the subject matter permits.

The third beginning; this subject matter never ends.

Exercises

Like to try thinking a problem through? Sit down with a notebook and work on the exercises. Have a partner try the same exercise independently and then compare notes.

Exercise #1: Proactive Exercise

On August 10, 2009, during the early morning hours, the sixty-five-foot fishing vessel *Black Bart* was observed by a U.S. Coast Guard patrol vessel heading up the Muddy River in Pine Tree County, north Florida. The vessel was followed to a remote landing site where it tied up, lights came on, and a shore crew was visible. The Coast Guard moved in, and during the ensuing confusion only three hands were seized on the vessel. Three were seen escaping, and estimates ranging from five to eight men on shore were seen running and then driving away in four different trucks. One truck was left behind.

The three subjects taken into custody were:

1. Captain Nelson Bligh, 35, Tarpon Springs, Florida
2. First Mate Jorge Hernandez, address unknown, citizenship unknown
3. Seaman Able Jones, address unknown, citizenship unknown

The vessel was loaded with twenty tons of high-grade Colombian, street value $44 million (at $1,000 per lb).

The cash value paid for on-shore delivery (at $100 per lb) was a $4.4 million cash investment.

The vessel, never used for fishing, was a new, fully rigged, custom-built shrimper valued at $518,000. It was built at Smugglers Cove Shipyard, Bayou Le Batre, Louisiana.

All-new electronic equipment was on board, including the following:

- 1 Easy Find Loran: $8,500
- 1 Night Eyes Radar: $5,600
- 1 Lead Line Electron Depth Finder: $3,500
- 1 Ears 50 Channel Scan Radio: $4,000

- 3 Here's Where You Are handheld GPSs
- 4 Pump Your Heart Out 12-gauge shotguns, three M-16 Army assault weapons, and five Roy Rogers 9 mm semiautomatics, no serial numbers

There was one coastal chart onboard, with coordinates penciled in at a point forty-five miles off shore, marked with a light "X." Navigation pencil lines indicate the vessel left from Tampa Bay to the "X" and then traveled north to Pine Tree County. There were also three Caribbean charts, including for the Gulf of Mexico, Bahamas, and east to Aruba.

Jorge Hernandez had a slip of paper on him with the name "Henry" and a Tampa phone number, 555-5566 (a known mob lawyer).

Captain Bligh had a slip of paper on him with the name "Manny" and a Key West number, 555-8765 (a suspected smuggler with a fleet of trawlers).

The off-loading site consisted of approximately 100 acres of an old fishing camp, with a newly constructed eight-foot cedar fence around the perimeter and a prefabricated cabin with about eight bunks built into a dormitory wing. The camp was owned and incorporated by Paradise Cruisers, John Q. Smith, President, P.O. Box 616, Georgetown, Grand Cayman Island; registered agent "Henry" law office, Tampa, Florida.

Written on the wall over the phone were three telephone numbers:

1. Tampa 555-1234, listed to a dock owned by Captain Bligh and purchased with a loan from the head of a local stevedore union, Boss Joe Squeeze, a suspected racketeer
2. Key West 555-4321, listed to a radio station with a 500-foot tower and one powerful unauthorized radio transmitter on the premises
3. 555-2341, the phone number at the bunkhouse

The ship's papers showed a registration to Ajax Fishing Inc., 7th Street, Salinas, Kansas.

Your boss has decided to do a major-case intelligence workup in this matter. He asks that you provide a good intelligence briefing along with your recommendation on the resources estimated to investigate this as a major case. He also wants you to provide an initial investigative start schedule with critical-path suggestions. The people in custody have been jailed. Bond was set at $500,000 for Captain Bligh, with no bail for the unidentified crew members. None of the three men's fingerprints appear in any U.S. database. They are being prosecuted in the Florida local judicial circuit, all represented by "Henry."

Exercise #2: Task Sheet

Problem

Your chief has asked you, as the chief of detectives, to draft an agreement to establish a formal working relationship between the local prosecutor and your police department. The thrust of the agreement should focus on the managing and coordinating of major crimes and the prosecution of those cases, with appropriate information feedback to both agencies.

Task

Provide a written draft of the agreement listing the:

1. Benefits to be obtained
2. Case control agreements and responsibilities of each agency
3. Information exchange
4. Organizational placement and control
5. Feedback mechanics

Exercise #3: Task Sheet

Problem

Your department, a municipal police agency of seventy-five sworn officers, is attempting to establish a working relationship with a local county sheriff's department, also with seventy-five sworn personnel, regarding the managing and coordinating of major cases. Your chief has asked you to prepare, for a conference, a list of topics that should be covered in the interagency agreement.

The chief also has asked for your advice on what posture he should take.

Task

List the topics that should be agreed upon and your suggested department position. Attempt to take positions on jurisdiction, communication, resource sharing, and major-crime response tactics.

Exercise #4

On the next page is a typical American urban area with multiple police jurisdictions (see Figure 17.1).

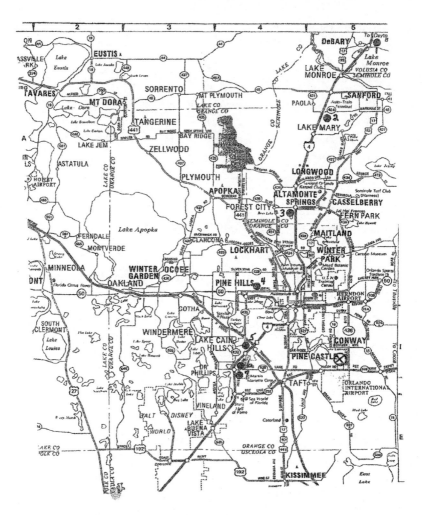

Figure 17.1 Map exercise.

The hypothetical problem: Living in the *circle* is the queen of a major local credit card theft and use ring. She is a classy lady who frequents lounges of major chain motels along tourist routes. Seven such locations are represented by the dots. At these motels, she steals credit cards while offering sexual favors. The queen then sells or "rents" the cards. Moreover, you suspect she contacts her former "clients," suggesting she needs money to buy back photos and negatives of the room visits, which "someone" obtained. These gentlemen live in various cities and towns in four different states and four foreign countries. The data received from eight victims indicate there are at least five "classy ladies," all answering to one name, "Queen," and two phone numbers for the service.

Design a case control system to investigate this sophisticated lady. Decide:

1. Who should control
2. The agreements, resources, and organization needed
3. The initial penetration methods or critical path
4. Estimates of time and anticipated results

Jurisdictions

The map in Figure 17.1 shows the jurisdictions. The key to the map is as follows:

Circle – Orange County
Dots:
    1 Volusia County
    2 Seminole County
    3 Altamonte Springs, Seminole County
    4 Orange County
    5 Orlando, Orange County
    6 Orlando, Orange County
    7 Orange County
    8 The states, New York, Kansas, Ohio & South Dakota
    9 The countries, Canada, Japan, Germany & Trinidad

Appendices III

Appendix A: Dispatcher's Guidelines

The name, address, time, and nature of call records should be kept at each communication center. In addition, a list of instructions should be readily available to each dispatcher. The list should contain standard instructions to be given to the caller.

For major-crime reporting, the list should contain at least the following:

1. Do not touch or move anything.
2. Do not permit anyone to enter the area.
3. Remember anyone who has been in the area.
4. Wait for the patrol or send someone to wait in the street to direct the first car to the scene.

Special instructions should also be readily available no matter how infrequent the type of major case. For example, kidnapping and abduction cases are rare, but the call receiver must be adequately trained to give at least the following instructions:

1. To the caller:
   a. Do not handle any note.
   b. Do not permit anyone, except a parent or legal guardian or husband/wife, to READ or become acquainted with the note contents.
   c. Do not inform any other person in the world.
   d. While waiting for a law enforcement person, make a list of all persons known to the caller who are aware of the kidnapping.
   e. Get full details of the kidnapping over the phone. If an investigator is immediately available, transfer the call to that person. At that point the dispatcher must contact the department-designated law enforcement supervisor listed in the dispatcher instructions and inform him or her of the call.
2. Within the department:
   a. Maintain secrecy; no radio broadcast should be made in this matter unless a life-threatening issue is clearly a problem at the location where the call originated.

b. The law enforcement supervisor, or a civilian dispatcher, must make a list of all, if any, people within the department who are aware of this matter. That list must be turned over to the supervisor of the case.

c. Above all, no press or media notification should be permitted. If any occur, inform all persons on the list they are under investigation.

(This is one of the few cases within a law enforcement organization where the threat and actual follow-up result in "nasty" internal investigations. A human life is at stake; anything less would be immoral. I'm talking a no-holds-barred investigation: waivers of all personal phone records demanded, an internal audit of all department phone calls (you have an order prohibiting disclosure; use it; this is why it is there), sworn statements, outside pressure on all media persons who received the information, including, if your prosecutor agrees, subpoenas (that gets a little tricky unless your state has a law that such conduct is a crime). The mere notice that such an investigation will take place usually ends the "squealer" problem. I don't know why it is called a leak; that's a plumbing problem. Union contracts should allow for investigations such as these in limited circumstances. If they do not, make sure they do next round.) This is just short of a rant, so it doesn't count.

d. Arrange for an immediate interview by an investigator at a discreet location.

e. Have a supervisor call the FBI for their information or action after confirmed.

f. No outward indication of police activity should be permitted. Patrol cars are notified of all information by secure communications only and take up response plan duties.

g. Initiate a discreet surveillance of the victim's home. With secrecy. If that is a problem, a supervisor makes that decision.

Once you get a supervisor's grip on exactly what situation exists, then the decisions as to all issues are open to the investigative team and supervisors. These decisions are never made at the dispatcher level. In Amber Alert scenarios, the initial call or call back is done by a supervisor/investigator, ASAP. If no supervisor is available, the senior street officer catches the case and all decisions and makes them immediately.

This is one example of special instructions for a specific event. You must think of all such special instructions required for your department, develop a procedure, and provide for implementation.

Appendix B: General Post Orders

The purpose of the order book is to provide guidelines and instructions to the officer on patrol. It will provide an orderly and systematic approach to policing an assigned area. It is intended to guide rather than restrict the issues set forth in this book. Initiative and innovation are encouraged. Orders such as these serve more than a single purpose; they also are part of the department discipline or control methods of on-duty personnel. Do not be distracted from the issues of this book by other department concerns. (Item **7 [b], sect. 4, and** items **8 and 9 [c]** are the pertinent orders for our purposes.)

1. Members on patrol post assignment shall be familiar with department rules, regulations, and policy manuals.
2. Officers assigned to patrol a post shall confine their patrol within post boundaries. They shall not leave their post except:
   a. When responding to an emergency or to assist another officer when common sense dictates such action.
   b. When approved by a competent authority.
   c. When the necessity of business requires the leaving of the assigned post, such as breath tests, hospital accident interviews, processing or arraigning defendants, pursuit of violators, etc.

   In all instances (no exception), the radio control point shall be advised of a patrol leaving its post and purpose thereof.
3. Officers reporting for duty shall immediately go on post.

   Officers on post shall return to their station at the end of tour using only as much time as is required for vehicle checks and administrative work. Reports, such as time and activity, arrest, investigative, accident, etc., shall be completed on post where feasible. Officers will not return to stations during their tour unless required for official purposes and approval is received from the officer in charge of the shift.
4. Meals: The officer in charge of the shift shall designate the meal period for each post. They shall be staggered. Any changes in mealtime shall be approved by the officer in charge of the shift.
   a. Meals shall be taken on post.
   b. Meals may be taken off post within two miles of the post boundary when decent facilities are not available on post.

    c. Meals may be taken at residences under the same conditions as listed in (a) and (b).

5. Communications

    a. Officers shall check in and out of service on the radio at the beginning and end of tours.

    b. Officers shall monitor the radio at ALL times and shall immediately answer all calls.

    c. Officers shall be alert for calls to adjoining posts for any emergency where assistance may be rendered. Advise the radio control point of your location and intended response.

    d. Officers will not leave the car radio unattended without advising the radio control point. When issuing traffic tickets, roadside interviews, etc., attempt to monitor radio calls.

    e. Officers in charge of a traffic road check, roadblock, or detail shall assign one member the responsibility of monitoring the radio. (Portables may be utilized.)

    f. Patrols shall be aware of poor radio reception areas and bring them to the attention of supervisory personnel.

    g. Dispatches, orders, and complaint assignments received over the radio shall be answered and obeyed. If questionable, they shall be taken up with your immediate supervisor, not with the dispatcher, after the assignment is completed.

6. Officers shall have knowledge of their assigned post, geographical features, demographic data, physical features, locations of banks, liquor stores, gun shops, jewelry stores, and similar criminal targets. Members shall be aware of trouble spots, natural problem areas, such as taverns and stadiums, etc. Know the location of emergency equipment. Officers on patrol shall identify themselves and get to know persons and citizens on their post whom we can serve. Officers shall acquaint themselves with the criminal elements on their post.

7. The post order book shall consist of an Accopress binder with a permanent fastener on the left side and clamp on right side.

    a. The left side shall contain permanent orders and shall include but not be limited to:

        1. Post description page

        2. General post orders

        3. Map of post

        4. Map of station posts

        5. Post data page (administrative control)

        6. General information sheet for townships (administrative)

        7. Any other permanent post order

        8. Fire districts, power and telephone company information, etc.

9. Geological survey maps of the post area. Zone and station commanders may add additional permanent orders to the post book. Copies of such orders must be sent to headquarters for inclusion in the post order book file. The post must be identified by number. The geological survey maps shall be protected and used only as intended—for searches, etc.

b. **The right side shall contain the following but not be limited to:**
   1. **Temporary orders**
   2. **Routine check sheet**
   3. **Buck slips, notes, complaints, and special residential check sheets pertaining to posts.**
   4. **Any other temporary material or specific order deemed necessary by zone or station commanders.**

Temporary orders may include, at the discretion of station supervisory personnel, such items as (a) directions of when and where patrols will function; (b) directions, either general or specific, as to when to check or perform functions at churches, schools, shopping plazas, residential areas, commercial or industrial parks, lovers' lanes, assignments such as RADAR operation, time and place designated for traffic accident reduction programs, and intersection surveillances; (c) items or assignments for patrols to gather criminal intelligence such as license numbers at known criminals' homes, gambling spots, trouble bars and drug user habitats. These matters shall be reported to shift supervision at the end of the shift, or if scanned or entered electronically, immediately reported into the index system in the approved format. Other temporary orders may include where special patrolling is necessary to prevent or combat drag racing, trespassing, noisy parties, vacation residence checks, etc. These matters shall be reported to shift supervision at the end of each shift.

These shall be deemed routine matters and are not necessary to separately report to headquarters. This is intended to guide the patrol as to where and when patrols should operate. Supervisors should use good judgment in their assignments.

8. **Shift supervisors are responsible for ensuring that all officers on post duty shall be familiar with emergency response policies, duties, responsibilities, methods of responding, and, in particular, the methods suggested for the specific on-duty shift, which depend on local circumstances. These include routes, car-to-car en route communications, fast-slow responses, locations, intents, suggested matters from patrols and communication centers, and scene approaches.**

9. Control and implementation
    a. The post order book shall be carried in the patrol car on post.
    b. Where more than one patrol is assigned to a single post, one shall be designated in charge and assigned the responsibility of the book and its orders by the officer in charge of the shift. The second car shall have appropriate post sheets for combination at the end of the shift.
    c. The routine check sheet is provided for convenience and started daily by the first shift. It is recommended that this sheet be used for business establishment checks and supervisory checks. When members deem it good police information—vehicle checks, license numbers, persons, etc.—it will be entered on this sheet with index items entered daily at the end of the third shift. This sheet will be retained in the post order book until sixty days have passed, then filed in the station file. Information deemed to be of immediate use for other patrols or detectives shall be copied to the on-duty supervisor for action, file/index retention, or distribution.
    d. Each station will set up a post file, one file for each post. All items, after they have served their purpose in the order book, shall be filed in the station post file under the proper post number for sixty days and then destroyed.
    e. Members shall initial and mark with the date/time all temporary items in book to indicate when checks were made (e.g., if a patrol order is issued requiring a residence check to be made, each time the residence is checked by a patrol the order slip should be dated, timed, and initialed).
    f. This order in no way eliminates any other department or division orders regarding reports, recording of information, or filing requirements.

Appendix C: Press Guidelines

The U.S. Constitution guarantees the right to a speedy and public trial by an impartial jury (Sixth Amendment) and freedom of the press (First Amendment). The traditions of American justice also prevail, and the police and press are reminded to keep them foremost in mind.

1. An accused person is presumed innocent until proven guilty.
2. No person's reputation should be injured by careless or indiscriminate accusations.
3. Accused persons are entitled to be tried and judged in an atmosphere free from sensationalism and passion and certainly without prejudice.

Guidelines

When an arrest is made, the police should release to the media all of the following information for publication (unless specifically prohibited by statute, as in juvenile cases).

1. The defendant's name, age, address, and similar background information.
2. The substance of the charge and statute.
3. The identity of the investigating agency and length of the case; and the circumstances immediately surrounding the arrest, including time and place of the arrest, any resistance, pursuit, or other circumstance, and possession of any weapons. Other items seized at the time of arrest will not be immediately disclosed until evidentiary or case investigation issues are resolved.

The release of other types of information may be detrimental to the investigation, the prosecution, the defense, and above all, the rights of the accused to be judged impartially.

Information concerning the following should not be released by the police, and only by the prosecutor after due and deliberate consideration:

1. Any confessions, statements, or alibi.
2. Statements or opinions as to the character or reputation of the accused or any other party in the case.
3. The results or performance of any tests.
4. Any refusals of the accused to take a test or cooperate with the police. Conversely, cooperation by a defendant in providing information or reenactment of the crime should be kept from the press.
5. Any statements concerning credibility or anticipated testimony of prospective witnesses.
6. Opinions concerning the evidence in the case, or identity, testimony, or credibility of any witness.
7. Prior criminal charges and convictions are a matter of public record in most states and may be released under the statutory rules. Non-public history records may have statutory restrictions as to release. However, the press should be warned that publications of such information may prejudice the trial and/or be damaging to the accused.
8. Photographs may be permitted, but the accused should never be posed or brought to a point for the sole purpose of taking photos for publicity. The press usually has ample opportunity to photograph an accused during transportation to court, jail, etc.
9. Photographs of suspects may be released where warrants have been or will shortly be issued. Police numbers (mug numbers) should be excluded.
10. Police should never make any statements as to their beliefs in the guilt, or any prejudicial statement, or any statement on matters excluded from the jury or out of the bounds of evidence. No forecasting of the trial outcome should be permitted.

The accusation made by the police as the result of an arrest speaks loud and clear for the police; any further releases are prejudicial, unprofessional, and a discredit to the police.

When a crime has been committed, the news media *may* be informed of:

1. **General facts pertaining to the crime.**
2. **Nonspecific findings of physical evidence or proceeds of the crime, service of search warrants, and the general results of the search. Information as to how these items were discovered or obtained must be withheld. Court inventory returns must be sealed when investigations continue or would be prejudicial to the defendant.**
3. **Photographs or composite sketches of the wanted person(s).**

If disclosure of information on wanted persons would be either harmful to the investigation or an endangerment to law enforcement officers, the information, of course, should not be released.

Any information regarding an open criminal investigation is not a public record. Disclosure of such information is prohibited, except as outlined herein.

Appendix D: Crime Scene Contamination Card

Crime Scene Contamination Card

Det. Name _____ Invest. _____

Case No. _____ Crime _____

Victim _____ Address _____

_____

Name of Officer Responsible for Security _____

Contaminated by Whom and How:

1. _____ Time In _____ Out _____

Fill in your requirements:

(The Orlando, Florida, Police Department effectively ended officers wandering around crime scenes by the simple change of title of the "Present at Crime Scene" record to the "Crime Scene Contamination Card.")

Appendix E: Duties of Neighborhood Interview Team(s)

Canvass the entire neighborhood in a systematic method. Miss no one. Go to the best locations first. Teams acting in parallel will be assigned specific areas.

Interviews

1. Determine if the person was a witness.
2. Do they have anything of value to offer?
3. Get statement(s) (positive information).
4. Transport or schedule witnesses to headquarters for formal detail statement(s).
5. Get basic information and disseminate.
6. Visually inspect persons and premises open to sight.
7. Determine who else was or should be present at the place of interview. Determine where they are and account for them.
8. Locate and interview missing subjects (this may be a new assignment—may go to lead team).
9. Ask each interviewed person what each of his senses revealed to him.
10. Identify all prior activity at the crime scene.
11. Take negative statements orally, note them, and take written negative statements at a later time.

Duties of Search Teams

The search team consists of an investigator plus sufficient uniform officers to search the crime scene and surrounding area(s) systematically. They should carry adequate light and redo the search at first daylight. Search immediately; redo at first opportunity if in inclement weather. Make sure it does not turn into a scavenger hunt. Carry an instant photo digital camera; the crime scene vehicle should be equipped with a paper reproduction capability. Photograph anything of evidentiary value and send the photo image to the supervisor immediately. Secure additional evidence finds for the crime scene unit to follow up on if they are significant items (use judgment). Check escape routes, dumping areas, garbage cans, fields, drainage, sewers, etc. Do it right. For example, do not just lift the lid of a garbage can; weapons are often stuffed down inside the refuse, and disguises are often hidden under refuse. Check roads, sewers, drainage, and fields for at least 1,000 feet on either side of the road. Use judgment and experience norms (murderers toss guns; robbers and drive-by shooters keep them).

Appendix F: Case Coordinator Duties

1. Start a chronological log of all pertinent occurrences, orders, and replies.
2. Hold frequent conferences and discuss the facts of the case to date. Cooperate with other agencies. Set the case policy (limited to within regulations) on payment to informants. Handle the news media in coordination with the public information officer and administrative organization of the case, including assignments of leads and reporting. Also, have each team discuss the facts; do not let "theorists" gain the floor to the exclusion of facts.
3. Plan and supervise the investigation under the direction of the officer in charge (case manager).
4. Assign and control leads (lead sheets) and require report-back deadlines. Adhere to these deadlines. Check all reports for completeness. Raise questions to the investigator as soon as possible and clear up any language or misunderstandings immediately. DO NOT ACCEPT POORLY WORDED REPORTS; HAVE THEM CORRECTED IMMEDIATELY. Remove anyone from the case who is not capable of clear reporting.
5. Keep all notations current on all major developments during the course of the investigation.
6. Consult with investigators on matters that are not of sufficient importance to be brought to the immediate attention of the member in charge.
7. Keep the member in charge informed of all pertinent information (work in the same area as the supervisor). When the supervisor leaves to roam about, keep in touch. Keep him or her up to date on case progress, both positive and negative.
8. Ensure that all investigators are aware of necessary facts of the case (and keep a record). Remind each investigator of the secrecy rules about information leaks to the press and outsiders.
9. After the crime scene is secure, assign (and require a report from) personnel to remain in position to surveil the scene for at least twenty-four to forty-eight hours (use judgment).
10. Use a uniform detail to protect private property and the privacy of victims from the press and curiosity seekers until this service

is no longer necessary. This officer is to be alert for information or suspicious happenings (check back with him or her). Direct the officer to establish rapport with the victim, seek any forgotten information or ideas, and pass information on to the detective control point immediately.

11. Require all investigators to submit their reports by the end of the day. Arrange for the typing of reports and case index. Reports that are clear and written in ink are a matter of department choice.

12. All leads and tips from the public, including leads from other police agencies, must be routed to the coordinator, regardless of the source of reception. Ensure that the entire investigative team is aware of this rule. Reduce all leads, tips, etc., to writing. They are to be assigned by the supervisor if HE OR SHE DECIDES they are pertinent. Have the supervisor and investigators read and initial all lead sheets.

13. Ensure that any investigators not qualified, producing inferior work, or leaking information are removed from the case. DO NOT WAIT.

14. Establish the case index as soon as possible. Prepare, report, and supervise the preparation of reports. Ensure that all reports are submitted promptly. Ensure that one overall report is written by the lead investigator/case agent.

15. Review all reports for leads, inaccuracies, or misleading language, and do not accept incomplete reports. Have them corrected or explained immediately.

16. Prepare and maintain inserts for the prosecutor's summary index.

17. Prepare index cards from each pertinent memo or report during all appropriate and important phases of the case. Examples of what you may wish to index are:
Names
Addresses
Businesses
Telephone numbers
License numbers
Dead bodies, via identification characteristics
Terrain searches (plus maps)
Hideouts, dumps, bars, businesses
Lab examinations
Evidence, statements (location)
Any other specific information called for by the peculiarities of the case
Personnel involved in the case

ALL THESE ITEMS SHOULD BE INDEXED WITH REFERENCE TO THE REPORT PAGE OR MEMO NUMBER.

Indexing is easier if your department's main index file is set up to absorb this information with relative ease.

Appendix G: Case Assignment Sheets

Case Assignment Sheet

Assignment No. _____ Officer Assigned _____

Date _____ Time _____

Case ID No. _____ Victim (Name) _____

Case Officer _____

Deadline _____

Assignment: Remarks – Instructions

Reported back (Due date) _____

By (Officer name) _____ Time _____

Complete _____

Incomplete _____

Oral Report by _____

Written Report by _____

Comments _____ Satisfactory _____

Supervisor's Initials _____ Coordinator's Initials _____

Incomplete. New lead assigned to: _____ Date _____

Time _____

Lead No. _____

Initials _____

Lead Sheet (Paper or Electronic Submission)

Case No. _____ (or folder/file) Date _____

Time _____

To: (Detective/Agency Directed/etc.) Via: Hand Delivery/Fax/Phone/UPS, etc.
Address: _____

Type of Action: Interview/information/search detail/records/etc.
Subject: Interview name/search place/neighborhood/etc.

Name _____ Age/DOB _____

Address _____ Race _____

City _____ Home Phone_____

State _____ Business Phone _____

Reply to: By date _____

Investigator (Case or case manager) _____

Employee No. _____

Date _____ Time _____ Photo _____

Case No. _____ Latents _____

Remarks/Instructions: Date, Time, and Location are required for each paragraph or event. _____

Initials: _____

Remarks and Instructions (cont'd.)

1. Date _____ Time _____ Location _____

Each event, act, or interview paragraph starts with Date, Time, and Location. Your written report should follow this same format, with each paragraph sequentially numbered from start to finish with the same headline: Date, Time, and Location.

Require illegible writers to type a follow-up with the written report attached.

Lead Sheet

Name_____   Age/DOB _____

Address _____ Race _____

City _____ Home Phone _____

State_____ Zip _____ Business Phone (cell)_____

Investigator _____ Employee No. _____

Date _____ Time _____ Location _____

Case No. _____ Photo _____ Latents _____ DNA _____

Instructions _____

_____

_____

Remarks _____

_____

_____

_____

_____

_____

_____

Initials _____ Date _____ Time _____

Lead Chart

Case No. _____ Case Name _____

No.	Officer Name	Lead ID	Date	Time	New Lead	Date Comp.

Initials _____ checked by _____ Date _____ Officer ID _____

Appendix H: Authority

Chapter 934, F.S., establishes criteria and procedures for obtaining approval for nonconsensual interception of wire or oral communications.

(2) DEFINITIONS:
  (a) Wire Communication is defined as any communication transmitted through the use of wire, cable, or other like facility.
  (b) Oral Communication is defined as any utterance made by a person who exhibits an expectation that such communication is not subject to interception under circumstances justifying such expectation.
  (c) Intercept is defined as the aural acquisition of the contents of any wire or oral communication through the use of any electronic, mechanical, or other device.
  (d) Electronic, Mechanical, or Other Device is defined as any device or apparatus that can be used to intercept wire or oral communications other than telephones, hearing aids, or similar devices being used to correct subnormal hearing to not better than normal.
  (e) Order is defined as an order from a judge of competent jurisdiction authorizing a wire or oral interception.
  (f) Judge of Competent Jurisdiction is defined as any Justice of the Supreme Court (jurisdiction statewide), Judge of a District Court of Appeal (jurisdiction within his district), or Circuit Judge (jurisdiction within his circuit).
  (g) Offense is defined as murder, kidnapping, gambling, robbery, burglary, theft, dealing in stolen property, prostitution, criminal usury, bribery, extortion, dealing in narcotic drugs or dangerous drugs, violation of the Anti-Fencing Act, or any conspiracy to violate any of the above-specified offenses, or other specified offenses as may be added from time to time by statute.
(3) BACKGROUND/SCOPE/PURPOSE: The purpose of this directive is to establish both policy and procedure for implementation of Chapter 934, F.S., concerning nonconsensual wiretapping and electronic surveillance through judicial order.

(4) POLICY

   (a)   When Order is Needed: An order will be obtained in all cases where interception of any wire or oral communication by means of electronic, mechanical, or other device is necessary with the exception of those cases that come under the purview of Section 934.03(2)(I), F.S., which reads: "It is lawful for a law enforcement officer or a person acting under the direction of a law enforcement officer to intercept a wire or oral communication when such person is a party to the communication or one of the parties to the communication has given prior consent to such interception and the purpose of such interception is to obtain evidence of a criminal act."

   (b)   Authorization: No interception where an Order is needed will be undertaken or participated in by any agent or employee of this Department absent direct authorization by Field Counsel and subsequent approval by the Executive Director or his designee.

Additionally, by statute, an application may not be made for an intercept order without prior approval of the application by the Governor, the Attorney General, or a State Attorney.

(Note: Jurisdiction of the Governor, Attorney General, or any Justice of the Florida Supreme Court is statewide. Jurisdiction of State Attorneys and Circuit Judges is within their circuit. However, any State Attorney may approve an application to be made to any judge of competent jurisdiction even if that judge is outside the State Attorney's circuit.)

   (c)   Minimization: By law, a court ordered interception must be conducted in such a way as to minimize the interception of communications not otherwise subject to interception. The order authorizing interception also specifically instructs the agent(s) to minimize. Minimization is the cessation of interception. This means stopping both listening to the monitor and recording the conversation.

Interception (monitoring and recording) is only permitted by law and by the order for those certain conversations concerning the crime and crimes set forth in the order and conspiracy to commit same. However, calls concerning crimes other than those listed in the order can be intercepted if they involve those offenses listed in Chapter 934, F.S.

Remember: There is no legal difference between listening, monitoring, and recording. Whether a conversation has merely been heard or recorded makes no difference; it has been intercepted.

   (d)   Disclosure of Interception: No agent or employee shall, except as provided by law, disclose or disseminate any information concerning the contents of any communication intercepted or evidence derived thereof. Additionally, no agent or employee shall reveal or acknowledge to any other person not having a "need to know" the fact that a particular interception has taken, is taking, or will take place.

(e) Cooperation with Other Agencies: The Department will continue, as in the past, to cooperate with other valid law enforcement agencies in pursuit of a common purpose of apprehending law violators. The Department will provide electronic intercept equipment to other valid law enforcement agencies upon requests for assistance or joint operations. The request for assistance or joint operations must include a copy of a valid court order authorizing the interception and directing the Department to provide assistance. The Department will install, control, and maintain the equipment for the duration of the court order.

(f) Manufacture or Possession of Electronic Devices: Manufacture or possession of any electronic, mechanical, or other device, as defined in (2)(d), by any agent or employee of the Department without the express authority of the Executive Director or the Director of the Division of Criminal Investigation is absolutely prohibited.

(5) PROCEDURE:

(a) Request for Authorization: Agents requiring a wire or oral intercept will prepare a rough draft of the Application for Order (Request for Authorization to Apply for Interception of (Wire), (Oral) Communication Form) and submit that "rough draft" for approval through the chain-of-command in the Division of Criminal Investigation. Then, if properly satisfied, the Director of the Division of Criminal Investigation shall forward the Application for Order to Field Counsel for review for legal sufficiency. After legal sufficiency is established, Field Counsel will advise the Executive Director and obtain approval to perfect the Application and secure the Order.

In applications where a local State Attorney and local judge are used and time is of the essence, it will not be necessary for Field Counsel to review the authorization to apply for same, the application for same, or the court order. However, it will be necessary for the affiant to comply with the request through his supervisor, Division Director, and the Executive Director for approval. This approval can be obtained verbally from those persons and subsequently documented, and submitted to the Executive Director through Field Counsel. At the time of such documentation on the Request for Authorization form which reflects approval by those various persons, the space for Field Counsel approval should state that the Application was prepared and authorized by State Attorney X; that the Order was issued by Judge Y; and the respective judicial circuits for both should be shown. In all events, and as soon as possible, a copy of all the documents and Attachment A should be prepared and sent to Field Counsel where it will be maintained in the Field Counsel file.

In any case where an Application for an intercept is to be authorized by the Attorney General and issued by the Supreme Court of Florida, then, in that event, this Department Directive will be fully complied with and Field Counsel will make the necessary review prior to arranging a meeting with the Attorney General and the Supreme Court. Any and all initial contacts with either the Supreme Court or the Attorney General will originate from Field Counsel.

This does not preclude subsequent contact between the case agent and a Justice or the Attorney General in areas such as inventory or progress reports when specifically requested of the case agent by the Justice or Attorney General. The case agent will, as soon as practical, advise Field Counsel of the time and place of any such appointment.

The federal electronic surveillance statute, Title III of the 1968 Omnibus Crime Control Act, necessarily permits surreptitious entry of a building (business or residence) to install interception devices, whether for wire or oral intercepts, that otherwise meet Title III requirements. By analogy, since Florida's Chapter 934 is patterned after Title III, the same criteria may be said to apply in Florida courts as in Federal courts until different Florida criteria are promulgated by judicial interpretation.

Whenever a surreptitious entry is necessary to install or remove a device, the judge issuing the original Order must specifically authorize each entry based on the following criteria taken from *In re Application of U.S. 22 CrL2025,* entry including specific details as to how the entry and exit are to take place;

1. The judge must specifically find that the use of the device and effective means are available for the State to conduct its investigation; and
2. The judge must specifically authorize such an entry.

As should be apparent, precise drafting of the Application and Order, as well as continuing judicial supervision, is a prerequisite for a valid entry and interception. Therefore, Field Counsel must be contacted at the earliest practical moment to begin assisting in preparing the necessary documents.

(b) Execution of Order: The Order will be executed as soon as practical after its issuance, and terms and conditions set forth therein by the issuing judge will be strictly complied with by the case agent. Any appreciable lapse in executing an order must be reported as soon as possible to the agent's supervisor.

(c) Reports: The case agent shall cause a full report to be made to the Field Investigations Bureau Chief and Field Counsel, in "Investigative Report" form, via chain-of-command, of the results obtained from the interception as and when necessary; but, in any event, shall make at least one such report via teletype or telephone every twenty-four-hour period during which the intercept device is activated.

(d) Termination of Interception: Unless extended by the Court upon proper application, the case agent will be held responsible for termination of the interception immediately upon attainment of the objective stated in the Order, whichever is earlier. The statute is very specific on this point inasmuch as it is not designed nor intended for the gathering of general intelligence information.

(e) Recording of Interception: All court ordered interceptions shall be recorded on suitable equipment with the utmost care being taken to insure that the recording device is in proper working order at all times during the interception.

At appropriate intervals or, in any event, no later than termination of the interception, it shall be the duty of the case agent to cause to be made a tape copy of the original recording for use of the Department.

The original recording shall be sealed in an evidence bag and retained in the custody of the executing agent(s), along with full documentation of chain of custody, until termination of the interception.

Upon termination of the interception, the original recordings must be forthwith submitted to the judge who issued the intercept order in order that he may seal them and issue an appropriate order governing their place and manner of custody. In the event the judge docs not have available a proper place where the security and integrity of the original recordings can be maintained, the case agent should suggest that an order be entered directing custody by the Department. The seal is mandatory and shall be done in a tamper-proof manner.

In the event that the recording or listening device suffers an unforeseen failure, replacement will be effected as soon as possible and the facts concerning the failure shall be fully documented in writing. Any communication overheard while the recording device is inoperative shall be reduced to writing as nearly verbatim of the communication as is possible, signed, dated, and identified, and thereafter treated in the same manner as an original recording.

(f) Evidence of Other Crimes: In the event evidence relating to offenses other than those specified in the Order is heard, the communication may be disclosed to other state and federal law enforcement officers and used to the extent such use is appropriate to the proper performance of the official duties of the officer receiving or making the disclosure and may be used as evidence, provided application is made as soon as practicable to a court of competent jurisdiction for such authorization. Approval will be granted on showing that the communication related to an offense for which an order could have been secured and that the communication was otherwise intercepted in accordance with law.

(g) Transcript of Intercepted Communications: It shall be the responsibility of the case agent to have prepared a summary transcript of all communications during the course of the interception, preferably on a daily basis, unless a verbatim transcript is required. Copies of the transcript will be forwarded to Headquarters on a daily basis immediately upon completion.

(h) Notice to Violator and Other Parties: The statute provides that within a reasonable time, but not later than ninety (90) days after termination of an interception, the issuing judge shall cause to be served on the person to intercepted communications as the judge may determine proper an inventory which shall include notice of the fact and date of the entry of an Order and whether or not communications were intercepted. If the application for the Order is denied, a notice of the fact that an application was made and denied must be sent to the person named in the application. It is also to be noted that the judge may, upon showing of good cause, order service of the inventory postponed.

It shall be the responsibility of the case agent, in conjunction with Field Counsel, to assist the judge in the preparation of the inventory.

It is noted that the statute requires that applications made and order granted shall be sealed by the judge, with custody as directed by the judge. The applicant should, therefore, have the judge sign an original and one copy of each, the copy to be maintained by the agent and the original sealed by the Court. Again, if a proper place for safekeeping is not available to the judge, the agent may properly suggest custody by the Department after ascertaining that the sealing is done in a tamper-proof manner such as using sealing wax or writing his name across the gummed edges of the envelope.

If there are ten persons that have been intercepted, there should be ten separate Notices of Inventory prepared, one for each individual. There are exceptions that can be made to this procedure. The occasions when exceptions can be made should be discussed verbally with Field Counsel by the case agent.

The case agent, upon completion of an intercept, must complete the form "Report of Police and Court Action Resulting From Intercepted Communication." All appropriate spaces must be completed, the form typed, and forwarded to Field Counsel.

Appendix I: Patrol Post Report (or Field Interview Report)

This patrol post sheet is used for all contacts, notes, and observations required or initiated by the patrol. Use it to report, file, and index to uniform supervision where it is checked and routed, by copy to intelligence, detectives, or specific cases where index matches are found. It can be used for stops, street contacts, specific place addresses, and noted vehicles parked or moving without stop. Random or routing prowl vehicle checks are listed on another form. (Build it.)

Post 4: Contacts

Date _____ Time _____ Place _____ Officer No. _____

See if you can complete this form on one page.

Patrol Post Vehicle Check Sheet

Post 4

Date _____ Time _____ Location _____ Tag _____ State _____

_____

Notes:

_____

Date _____ Time _____ Location _____ Tag _____ State _____

_____

Notes:

_____

Or more. Use this sheet for random road and spot checks; index at end of shift. If the system has the capacity to call in license number for wants and DMV data, integrate the reply and distribution to appropriate commands. Index directly to the trash bin for sixty-day holds and destroy if not past or future hits.

Appendix J: A Think Tank Method That Works for Law Enforcement Organizations

Preparation

One to two weeks prior to the "think tank" meeting, send to the selected participants sufficient information about what is expected of them and what they may encounter. Let them study it; suggest they prepare by making notes, conferencing with coworkers, or just thinking about the matter. Some may research options or other sources of information; have them bring questions, etc. Encourage their preparation effort by letting them know the "tank" will be open, informal, confidential, and focused on the issue (not a gripe meeting). State the general purpose of the meeting, such as to redevelop (or design) or improve our department's major-case control system, regular case investigations, and crime complaint services, which are usually "lightly reported," and integrate that with the department's record section, communications, and statistics information. All while catching the bad guys.

The Tools

Tools are the success or failure of a think tank. Here are some suggestions:

- Room to put all ideas up on flip charts, which will be consolidated into coherence by the crew.
- Seven to ten easels at least 3' × 5' so they can accommodate flip charts.
- Oversupply of crayons or markers.
- Clips on which to hang the flip charts.
- Masking tape
- Things to hang the flip chart sheets on as they pile up.
- Eraser and chalk if you have blackboards available (I prefer charts with lots of chart paper)
- Notepads and notebooks
- Many marker pens in many colors

- Butcher paper
- Comfortable lounge chairs
- Space to walk around in
- A separate room for those who need a few minutes' timeout to talk or think
- Access to the outdoors to breathe or smoke, if there any smokers left
- Pencils
- Dictation machines
- And more

The Setting

The setting should be casual, quiet, and informal. Set aside at least a full day for a project of the scope in this book. Two days would be better. And it would be better still if you could be at a quiet setting overnight, with a bar and lounge where you could continue in groups or pairs any discussions, either around the bar, pool, or elsewhere outside. Stay away from golf resorts, places like Las Vegas, etc. This is a work session—there's no time for entertainment; the idea is to trigger ideas. A place is needed where interruptions will not interfere with the session. Review a scaled room plan with needed facilities, or visit the place first. No sense going to the trouble and winding up in a dump.

The Meeting Room

The meeting room should contain comfortable seats, no tables, with the chairs set in a circular pattern if possible, with space between them. There should be sufficient room for attendees to split off into small groups for breakout discussions. Refreshments should be available in the room, and they should be handy, without waiters or other people coming and going. There should be plenty of hot coffee and tea available, along with beverages of sufficient variety to keep the ice tub full. Make sure restrooms are nearby. One "No Smoking" sign should be posted. All outside communication must be turned off.

Structure

The following structure is suggested:

- Leader: You might consider an experienced skilled outsider instead of a department commander. That opens things up quickly.

- Eight to fifteen, tops sixteen, participants: a crew with expertise in all areas of the point of discussion
  - Leader: top-notch mid-level commander, if you cannot obtain a facilitator
  - Detective supervisor or two
  - Uniform supervisor or two
  - Administrative supervisor or two
  - Communications supervisor or two
  - Detective or two (in the three- to five-years of *detective* experience bracket)
  - Uniform patrol officer or two (in the five- to seven-years of experience bracket)
  - Department computer administrator or two
  - NO LAWYERS
  - NO TOP-LEVEL BRASS
  - NO DEPARTMENT POLITICAL CONTROLLERS
  - NO UNION LEADERS

The Meeting

The meeting should be opened by the leader or outside facilitator, who will briefly discuss the premeeting materials sent out to refine the issue and stress the following:

Both the contents of the meeting and the people participating in it are confidential. What happens in Vegas stays in Vegas. Inform everyone that the department is seeking productive criticism and feedback, with a broad perspective of the issue. Encourage a wide range of thinking. Focus on problem solving. Seek ideas for improvements and new innovations, identifying flaws. Stress that there is no such thing as a "stupid remark" or suggestion. Tolerance is the group rule. Remember that at one time many people said, "It will never fly, or even get off the ground, Wilbur."

Insist on respect for one another, regardless of rank, experience, or place in the organization. This will be a free flow of information from all perspectives. Each participant should be introduced or, if you wish, have them introduce themselves if any or all are unknown to each other. Have all participants make a short statement as to what they think the meeting is about, what they expect it to produce, and any impact they expect it to have on the department or their particular section within the organization.

Stress the purpose of the issue, the usefulness of the project, and preliminary solutions or ideas. We are after the practicality of the ideas, the identifiable side effects, and the predictions of unintended consequences.

The Rest Is Easy

You state the problem.

The group then identifies the problem with specificity, then clarity, then in as much detail as possible. Don't identify the solutions yet, just the details, which will reveal obstacles or matters that must be worked out. The easels should be overflowing by this time with the information needed by the case manager, its structure, and directions on how to get the information to him—i.e., the feed.

The group then discusses the problems, without any judgments as to anything. That is very important at this stage. Judgments stop information flow. Take note of ideas. This is where you may run out of various boards and paper as you put them up, so consolidate them and organize them into logical order or as parts of the whole problem. After a while take a break and allow one to twenty minutes for everyone to have a quiet introspection on the issue and to let them organize their thoughts.

For a problem of the scope in this book, you will wind up with a section of the problem on each of the easels with sheets of excess ideas hanging from the walls by masking tape.

Now place the various ideas in a logical order for discussion.

Solve the problem with as much specificity as possible and keep reducing it into further detail, which is always the crux of the problem. You will find that the detail raises more questions than answers, and these need to be resolved and fitted into the proper easel in some order or solution.

The Rest Is Easier ... Solve the Problem

Identify the path to implementation and completion.

Once that is achieved, get the group to break into small committees of one or two, and put all the ideas and elements of the path in order. Designate a method of putting the result into some kind of document, broken into sections. Clean it up, get rid of the duplications, identify the associated problems or associations with other sections, and place pointers to that section for inclusion and integration.

Once that is complete, you have a report. And once that is cleaned up, you will find additional problems that must be worked on after due reflection and discussion. Mark up the report, attacking it with the goal of solution rather that negativity.

Once you finish what is essentially a rewrite, you emerge with a *beginning* to the solution. The report is signed by all attendees as read, and notes are added containing objections and/or comments, if any, which are initialed.

You now have a working document, a base from which to start your major-case managing and coordinating system overhaul.

If your agency is of such size that you need outside experience or assistance, you will find that the think tank exercise will greatly reduce your cost and time, and most of all will increase the quality of the final product beyond the usual low expectations of "contract" help.

Appendix K: Follow-Up Think Tank

After the first tank session, the report generated is reviewed at command level and then discussed with any appropriate attendees for follow up. Once the entire command staff has reviewed the report and submitted their written comments and questions, an in-house conference is called with the selected leaders of the first think tank session: the leader; the detective, communications, uniform, and administration supervisors; and the tank computer person. If anyone else emerged during the first session who was particularly knowledgeable and helpful, invite him or her.

After this meeting and discussion, the leader of the first session will consolidate the reports and discussion notes into issues, problems with each issue, goals, and some directions and limitations due to outside-of-department realities.

A second think tank session is then scheduled. The department command will select one command-level person to attend; the five, possibly six, and maybe seven of the aforementioned original tank members will attend. They will present their findings for expanded discussion and assist the newcomers in understanding how they arrived at the conclusions presented as well as joining the discussion. By now the selection of the first place for the tank session has settled in; most likely you will try another place due to the experiences at the first place. That is, use that experience to improve things. You may even cut down the tools and supplies and come up with some additional efficiencies.

In addition, include selected technicians from communications, a top-notch programmer, one computer system designer (two if you have them; it is fun to watch them argue, even if the language is unintelligible), the computer section director, one selected higher-level supervisor from detective, uniform, and administration, and a forms expert. By this time most of the problem has been identified, the trouble spots noted, and a rough idea of the goal that is achievable is emerging.

The second tank session will further clarify the problem detail, address the rough spots, and identify the items and plans needed to achieve the now-clearing goal. Prepare a refined summation of the first tank with the added command input. Resources will be identified and a practical path to achieving the improvements will emerge. The technicians will identify the tools, equipment, and their capabilities. The supervisors will identify the process and provide an outline of the case control. The computer system designers will provide the critical path needed to meet department goals, access paths, and security methods, with the ability to communicate within the department while connecting to the overall law enforcement communication system. Methodologies have arrived.

The forms guy will spit out the format and consolidation of information for data input married with the case investigation reporting and dispatcher to statistics, to street input, and to control forms.

Out of that, a plan and report are completed and sent to the various commands within the department for review, observations, objections, and comments. Then resources are identified for implementation, budgets are prepared, a method of implementation is prepared, and a schedule is presented to the department command and necessary civilian controllers.

If the department is a small, twenty-member organization, the chief could sit in the back room over a weekend and do the whole thing with a writing pad and pencil, or come Monday put the "Call the State Police" sign back up.

Appendix L: Twenty-Year Plans

Police and sheriff agencies ought to think of their future. Population changes, growth patterns, and legislative activities require forward thinking to meet the challenge of change, before it becomes a challenge of correction. All those things have an impact on operational duties and abilities. Assignment of personnel, changes in crime patterns, and additional or repealed laws all affect the agencies' posture. It is better to present (or at least have prepared) a plan to your civilian political controller than to respond to one created by the political authority without having a document of your own in place to assist and point out important situational matters for their consideration.

Lt. General Nathan Bedford Forrest III (CSA) was famous for his explanation for why he won so many battles: "Git thar first'us with the most'us." A lot of wisdom was displayed in that simple statement—the forerunner of the U.S. Army mobile attack tactics.*

Assign a member of your staff to write a plan. Not a committee; that will not produce anything but an argument. This should be the thinking of one person. Select a good supervising officer of middle rank who has several years of solid experience in uniform, investigative, and administration duties. Do not give this officer too much direction; just tell him or her to look around, observe the history, and think of the future. Have the officer tell you where the department will be in twenty years, what it will be doing, and what it will need to get there. You decide whether to present it or not, to staff for discussion and argument.

One way to explain such a plan is to show you the substance of one of a variety of options.

Example of a Twenty-Year Projection

The state police are the major law enforcement unit of the state, providing the governor with a well-trained, operationally sound force available for any disaster, major disturbance, incident, or event that requires rapid deployment. The force could place 100 officers at any given spot within one hour,

---

* Retold to me on several occasions by a personal friend, Paul Dinkler, a distant descendant of the "general." The family prefers that the general be remembered as a riverboat captain and gambler.

500 within three hours, and 1,000 within six hours, and could convert to a twelve-hour shift, statewide or regional, dependent on the commitment, for the duration to maintain regular service levels everywhere.

In addition, they will enforce all laws as directed by the legislature—criminal, traffic, etc.—and provide public security, peace, and order by preserving life and property throughout the state. List all the major categories, then add or show methods of reducing or eliminating subprograms or initiating new ones—essentially, your intents and capabilities. Then add the special issues you handle, such as:

- Conducting all government corruption investigations as directed by the governor
- Investigating statewide criminal activities
- Providing major-case support to county and local police departments, when requested
- Providing riot suppression in all cities (except New York City unless requested), state prisons, and penitentiaries
- Protecting the state capitol during major events or demonstrations
- Policing state facilities during strikes or other unrest

While the preceding list is not complete and does not identify the subcomponents of the assignments, it encompasses the focus of the organization.

Then, in addition to the aforementioned, look into your future. A modern state police agency may be considering the following:

- Development and assistance to local police forces is a major responsibility. This will be achieved by a philosophy of training via the state police academy.
- Assuring local agencies training assistance in all matters requested, including regional or troop libraries with law enforcement-related materials, books, lecture outlines, papers, and manuals. This assistance would include accredited seminars to count toward a college degree and take place in various areas of the state. The state should bear the economic burden of this program. Avoid commissions, state consortia, or groups of agencies unless advisory only.
- Develop a standard of post staffing that includes a slow and assured state police withdrawal from cities, towns, or villages as they achieve capacity and capability to the degree that they become effective and efficient in handling matters on their own. Then continue to respond to requests from the local law enforcement agencies.
- Expand the toll road coverage to include all connecting state four-lane limited-access highways, including all city connectors. Eventually consolidate all into dedicated posts controlled by a troop.

- Continue to develop the state police academy to include additional education courses, English, Spanish and other foreign language courses, along with other identified special needs. Expand (or start) the police management course for commissioned officers and include the local police. Push for legislative requirements that every police officer, including locals, successfully complete said course prior to any promotion process or appointment to higher rank with management responsibilities within the state. This will eventually evolve into a fully accredited university of (name your state) state police. Accreditation for 120 hours would include the basic school, the education courses, management and special classes, and additional special trades and professions needed for improved and excellent service from all police agencies. (If the New York City Police Department can do that through the John Jay School of Criminal Justice with great success, all states can.) Advanced management programs and special subjects to meet special needs would fill the degree requirements. The list is endless. Credit courses from other universities would be counted where applicable to the state program.
- Support and set standards for consolidation of metro areas into county police departments or regional metro police departments in association with the state police role in such areas. Where those are created, the sheriffs would maintain jails, court process services, and courtroom support services.
- Increase the number of special skills of the state bureau of criminal investigation (BCI). Increase the ability of the BCI to conduct targeted investigations against organized criminal groups, gangs, career criminals, and special-target investigations. Increase and organize the BCI intelligence capacity to identify and track criminals and their activities (today, add terrorists).
- Enter into a discussion with experts, legislature leadership, and the governor's office to determine the best approach to deal with the looming increase of illegal and uncontrolled drug use among our young population. Starting suggestions to consider are: decriminalize the minor infractions and control them under the alcohol control laws; determine if clinic or medical help would be effective under control of the Department of Health or Correction; or increase penalties to more severe proportions for dealers. The problem is huge and must be addressed.
- Adopt the post standards that set patrol post size based on emergency response times (arbitrarily set at eight to ten minutes maximum to create a starting point in which to reach a goal fitted to the area requirements). Then balance the response time with time expended for nonpatrol matters, with a flex point of 10 percent but

never less than 45 percent time on patrol, with a goal to achieving 55 percent time on patrol. Staff the post with a goal of twenty-four-hour policing, then start reducing response time when able. (Patrol time includes a myriad of activities, other than special assignments for particular events or matters, such as: traffic control, business and residential checks, public contacts/relations, stops and interviews, school checks, area drive-through, road checks).

- Create a civilian expert advisory board with accomplished persons in selected fields of study to aid and assist state police management on issues within their areas of expertise.
- Update and continue to develop the hazardous-materials unit, which specializes in control of carriers, inspections, notice of transport of certain toxic materials, and response to any highway or public area hazardous-material accident—all coordinated with fire and rescue units; and special attention to security and routing for shipments of nuclear materials and weapons, by highway or rail.
- Upgrade qualifications for noncommissioned and commissioned officers through the state police academy. Create entry-level education requirements for all new hires. Suggest a start at a two-year accredited degree for troopers and appropriate degree or education standards for civilian personnel.
- Develop computer programs to replace the current manual major-case control, intelligence information collection, and the supporting record system with a master index open to identified inquiries. Coordinate the current efforts within the state police.
- Develop computer-aided dispatch to all state police vehicles. Suggest to the legislature the creation of regional 911 centers staffed by qualified civilians under the supervision and control of participating agencies (police, fire, medical) with overall responsibility vested with the state. Create immediate communication ability with *all* local agencies. Consider consolidating communications with locals.

If some of these things seem a bit dated, since many are norms today, you are right. The preceding plan was written in 1970 in a bit more detail (a ten-page document) with a few additions or deletions that were specific issues particular to the state police, along with suggestions of things needed to "get there."

In 1970 the New York State Police (NYSP) developed such a plan. The state was growing at a relatively slow but steady pace; the cities were either expanding or new suburban communities were developing. The state had city police departments, county sheriff offices (elected), along with some village and township police departments of various sizes, from the very small (5–250) to medium (250–1,000). The state police had slightly over 4,000 uniform and investigator positions, supported by about 900 civilian employees.

The NYSP had jurisdiction within every square foot of the state; it operated in all cities and counties in varying degrees with its investigative force. The uniform force generally operated outside of the cities, with some exceptions, and overlapped jurisdiction with all counties and some village and townships. The NYSP lightly attended to villages and townships that ran successful patrols. Investigative assistance was available to all. Laboratories were available to all. Aircraft services were available to all. Uniform backup was available to all.

(This resulted in a recommendation that the state police seek a level of 5,000 officers, uniform and investigative, along with a civilian staff of about 1,500 people. It also resulted in an estimate that, as locals grew, the state police force would cap out at about that same level [5,000 to 6,000] by the 1990s. After that, there would be a slow decline in uniform services depending on local advancement and barring unforeseen events or circumstances.)

These ideas can be adapted to cities and counties with ease; just stick to the theme. Identify who and what you do, where it should be, and how to "git thar first'us." This time with the "best'us."

The third beginning; this subject matter never ends.

It has been a pleasure working with you.

Index

A

Access rules, 236
Administration
    case file index, 230–231, 233–234, 235,
        236
    case tracking system, 15
    CDR, 173
    decisions and detective command, 96
    information for case file, 38, 112, 116,
        119, 121, 131, 184, 189
    inspection of internal systems, 18
    police report about prosecutors, 48
    problems, tendencies and delay causes,
        13–14, 148, 201
    procedures, 41, 160
    retention of information, 213
    think tank, 295
Agencies that work with, for or next to each
        other. *see also* Other agencies
    assistance agreements, 32
    crime broadcast procedures, 31
    jurisdiction and responsibility for major
        cases, 31
    press agreements, 32
    reporting of information, 31
    response to crime scene criteria, 31
    roadblock plans, 31
Agent. *see* Lead case investigator (agent)
Aggressive accounting, 157
Analysts
    case index, 185
    CDR, 180
    civilian, 159
    crime, 150
    intelligence phase of proactive cases,
        171–172
    investigative phase of proactive cases,
        186–187
    line/support persons, 5, 121
    preparatory phase of proactive cases,
        159–160
    qualifications, 160
    reporting structure, 170

Appeal phase. *see* Arrest, trial and appeal
        phase of proactive cases
Area patrols, 62
Area search, 60–61, 90
Arrest, trial and appeal phase of proactive
        cases, 8, 193–200
    arrest, 197, 206–207
    department command, 193
    detective command, 193–195
    investigators, 197
    pick-off method, 206–207
    prosecutors prepare for court, 198–200
    supervisor, 196
Arrest, trial and appeal phase of reactive
        cases, 8, 125–132
    defense counsel, 132–134
    investigators, 128–129
    laboratory, 130
    PIO, 127, 130
    prosecutor, 130–131
    supervisors, 128–129
Assigned lead case investigator (agent), 99
Assignments for work, 209
Assisting agencies. *see also* Other agencies
    guidelines during CSP, 74
Authority, 279–286
Autopsy
    agreements, 45
    arranged for by ME, 79
    attended by crime scene unit, 115–117
    attended by ME, 119
    photographs, 77
    President John F. Kennedy, 120
    timely, 46, 77

B

Battle of the Bulge resource management,
    138–139
Bethesda Naval Hospital autopsy, 120
Bishop, Jim, 55
Bugliosi, Vincent, 55

C

Camera
    car equipment, 146
    digital, 21, 269
    locations, 226, 237
    red light, 237
    surveillance, 122
Canvass instructions, 93–94
Capturing timeline, 85–86
Car equipment, 30
    camera, 146
    check sheet, 288
    computer, 28, 72, 225
    inspection, 146
Cascade destruction system, 214–215
Case
    administration, control, and
        organization, 32, 102, 103, 107,
        271
    assignment sheets, 275–278
    critical paths, 167
    disposition systems, 136
    information flow, 24
    management system, 110
    milestones, 7
    objectives, 166
    report back procedure, 93
    reporting identify central point, 100
    report system, 106
    retrieval options, 24
    solving exercises, 249–254
    summary, 198
    tracking, 24
    tracking system, 15–16, 136
Case coordinator
    actions during investigative phase of
        reactive cases, 110–111
    arrest and trial phase of proactive case,
        193, 194
    assignment flexibility, 106
    case investigation team of proactive
        cases, 181, 182
    case investigation team of reactive cases,
        89
    duties, 107, 187, 233, 271–274
    and evidence, 90, 92, 183
    and investigators for reactive cases, 93
    justification and helping eliminate
        oversights, 106, 107, 109, 112, 114,
        115
    and laboratory findings, 46, 119

    organizational chart, 95
    and pathologists, 118
    and prosecutor, 120, 127, 131, 132
    reasoning, 55
    reporting structure for proactive cases,
        170
    reporting structure for reactive cases, 68
    responsible for crime scene unit
        coordination, 116–117
    and support services, 121
    and technical equipment, 122
Case index or case file index, 211, 228–235,
    237, 238, 272
    administrative, 231
    arrest and trial phase of proactive cases,
        194
    CDR point, 180
    data, 229
    flags, 219
    formatted index, 235
    individual, 71
    intelligence phase of proactive cases, 172
    investigative, 231
    investigative phase of proactive cases,
        184, 185, 186
    investigative phase of reactive cases, 110,
        111, 122
    resource management of proactive cases,
        207
    response phase of reactive cases, 63
    specific, 22
Case investigation. *see* Major case
        investigation
Case manager
    case organization structure, 85
    prosecutors and criminal informants,
        189
    requires control system, 85
Case supervisor
    arrest and trial phase of proactive case,
        196–197, 198
    arrest and trial phase of reactive case,
        125
    case report back procedure, 93, 94
    central point, 100
    and defense counsel, 132
    department system of information
        control, 72–73
    and evidence, 91, 92
    flexibility, 21
    functions, 99

intelligence phase of proactive cases,
     175, 201–202
investigative phase of proactive cases,
     183–185, 187
investigative phase of reactive cases, 7
and laboratory findings, 119, 130
major case folder control, 58
post arrest case completion, 129
and prosecutor for proactive cases, 198
and prosecutor for reactive cases, 80,
     120, 127, 130, 132
reporting structure for proactive cases,
     170
reporting structure for reactive cases, 68
responsible for crime scene unit
     coordination, 116–117
responsible investigative phase of
     proactive case, 183
and support services, 121
CDD. see Central desk destruction (CDD)
     point
CDR. see Central desk reporting (CDR)
Central desk destruction (CDD) point
     file, 235
Central desk reporting (CDR), 100, 107, 110,
     115, 166, 227
controlled vs. uncontrolled, 169
intelligence phase of proactive cases,
     169, 173
investigative phase of proactive cases,
     180
point, 211
Chain of command, 13
Chief judge relationships, 44
Citizens
index, 224
police information sources, 224
releasing police records into public
     domain, 222
Civilian staffed crime scene units (CSU),
     20–23
Closed criminal case file data, 212–213
Closing procedures, 242
index, 235
timing, 235
Command staff
defined, 4
judgment, 3
meddling, 70
officer responsibility, 64
response to major cases, 63
responsibility, 11

successful, 11
Communications. see also Dispatcher (line/
     support)
coded, 225–226
control room, 24, 257
guidelines, 71–73, 260
intercept rules, 52–53, 281, 284
network, 236, 237
oral defined, 279, 281
personnel, 6, 62
reporting structure for reactive cases, 68
secure, 102
skills, 39
specialists, analyst, or companies, 6, 35,
     156
systems, 18, 25, 40, 212, 226, 234. 296
wire defined, 279, 281
Computer
car equipment, 28, 72, 225
crimes, 28, 143
data collection, 15, 58
dispatching, 28, 300
driven reporting systems, 92
index flag system, 97, 223, 232
vs. manual operations, 90, 215
system specialists, 15, 236, 295–296, 300
Congressional Research Report (CRS), 52,
     217
Conspiracy charges, 178–179
Contamination card, 92
crime scene, 267–268
Contingency plans, 33
Contracts, 287
Controlled multi-team coordination, 122
investigative phase of proactive case, 190
Cooperating agencies, 206. see also Other
     agencies
Coordinator. see also Case coordinator;
     Case supervisor; Lead case
     investigator (agent); Supervisors
     (supervisory)
case index file for proactive cases, 228,
     229, 231, 232
case trial preparation for reactive cases,
     129
computer index flag system for reactive
     cases, 97
controlled multiteam coordination for
     proactive cases, 190
controlled multiteam coordination for
     reactive cases, 122

coordinating all leads and investigative
    phase of proactive case, 184
crime scene unit's file for reactive cases,
    97
and evidence control point for reactive
    cases, 91
information dissemination, 184
intelligence phase of reactive cases, 175
investigative phase of proactive cases,
    181–185
investigative phase of reactive cases,
    98–115
reporting structure for proactive cases,
    170
reporting structure for reactive cases, 68
scene team for reactive cases, 89
Cost chart, 180
Courtesy, 66
Cover your ass programs, 11
Crime analysis, 150
Crime scene, 90
    collector, 21
    contamination card, 267–268
    Contamination Report, 22
    officer's duties, 117
    photography rules, 20–21
    reactive case investigations, 69–84
    team investigative phase of reactive
        cases, 89–95
    technicians, 76
Crime scene phase of reactive cases, 69–84
    begins, 69
    crime scene unit, 75–77
    department command, 69–70
    detective command, 74
    dispatcher, 70–72
    laboratory, 78
    medical examiner, 79
    needs and problem issues, 22
    PIO, 81–84
    prosecutor, 80
    uniform patrols, 73
Crime scene units
    crime scene phase of reactive cases,
        75–77
    detailed training and experience, 41
    equipped and prepared during reactive
        cases, 78
    guidelines for crime scene phase, 76
    identified, 5
    inspection routines, 41

investigative phase of reactive cases,
    115–118
line/support, 5
preparatory phase of reactive cases,
    41–42
specific plans, 42
support service to investigators, 42
tools and equipment, 42
training updates, 42
work plans, 34
Crime suppression program (CSP), 11
    procedural requirement, 72
Criminal informants, 148
    case manager and prosecutor, 189
Critical-path investigation method, 180
Critical task, 138
Critique phase. see also Intelligence phase of
        proactive cases
    proactive cases, 201–204
CRS. see Congressional Research Report
    (CRS)
CSP. see Crime suppression program (CSP)
CSU. see Civilian staffed crime scene units
    (CSU)

D

Dallas Police Department, 59, 61, 105–106
    120, 121
Data collection forms, 58
Day Kennedy Was Shot (Bishop), 55
Defendants
    arrest, trial and appeal phase of
        proactive cases, 193, 198–199
    booking, 8
    discovery and nondiscovery, 220
    information needed, 263
    press vs. courtroom, 49
    right to fair trial, 125
    tracking through criminal justice
        process, 203
Defender's office, 5, 132–134
Department(s)
    agreements with prosecutors, 47
    organization structure, 17
    racists, 67
    report system, 106
    resource management, 135–140
    web site, 222
Department command (command)
    arrest, trial and appeal phase of
        proactive cases, 193

arrest, trial and appeal phase of reactive
        cases, 125–127
crime scene phase of reactive cases,
        69–70
identified, 5
intelligence phase of proactive cases, 165
interagency agreements, 150
investigative phase of proactive cases,
        177
investigative phase of reactive cases, 86
preparatory phase of proactive cases,
        144–153
resource management of reactive cases,
        135–136
responsibility, 12, 23–24, 150
Department index. *see* Index or department
        index
Detective command (command staff). *see
        also* Supervisors (supervisory)
    administrative decisions, 96
    arrest, trial and appeal phase of
            proactive cases, 193–195
    arrest, trial and appeal phase of reactive
            cases, 126–127
    arrest and timing method, 195
    business people contacts, 35
    case control, 96
    case review, 202
    charting investigative course, 96
    crime scene phase of reactive cases,
            74–75
    developing unit, 35
    duties, 63
    identified, 5
    intelligence phase of proactive cases,
            165–170
    investigative phase of proactive cases,
            177–181
    investigative phase of reactive cases,
            96–97
    judge communication, 44
    liaison duties, 97
    medical profession contacts, 35
    organizational chart, 95
    PIO communication, 65, 81
    preparatory phase of proactive cases,
            154–158
    preparatory phase of reactive cases,
            33–37, 158
    prosecutor communication, 198
    response phase of reactive cases, 63–64
    responsibility, 75, 96

review, 166–170
social services contacts, 35
supporting investigation with resources,
        75
trades people contacts, 35
training unit, 35
Detective supervisor
    crime scene phase of reactive cases,
            69–70
    dispatcher communication for reactive
            cases, 72
    investigative phase of reactive cases, 98
    ME communication for reactive cases,
            79
    prosecutor communication for reactive
            cases, 81
    reports, 75, 76
    resource management, 95
    response phase of reactive cases, 63
    think tank method involvement, 291
    working case investigation team, 89
Discovery rules, 219, 220
Dispatcher (line/support)
    case file index, 231
    crime scene phase of reactive cases,
            70–72
    desk file, 234
    guidelines, 3, 257–258
    identified, 5
    investigative phase of reactive cases,
            86–87
    preparatory phase of reactive cases,
            24–26
    procedures, 25, 28
    public law issues, 218
    response phase of reactive cases, 7,
            56–58, 59
Due diligence, 157

E

Eavesdropping
    coordinating and managing for
            proactive case, 188
    intelligence phase of proactive cases, 167
    legal aspects, 149
    preparatory phase of proactive cases, 145
    warrants, 81
Electronic measures or devices, 146
    defined, 279
    index, 227
    police information sources, 227

surveillance statute, 282
E-mail, 48, 52, 80, 236
    crime, 222
    internal, 116
    public record, 220
    searches, 227
Encrypted radio operations, 71
Equipment inspection and readiness, 34
Establish jurisdictional guidelines, 19
Evidence, 6, 220
    arrest and trial phase of proactive cases,
        193–194
    collection, 9, 39, 43, 44, 76, 77, 197, 233
    contamination sheets, 197
    control point, 91
    crime scene phase of reactive cases,
        76–77
    discovery rules, 208
    exculpatory, 17, 148, 198, 219, 220
    handling, 7, 22, 34, 43, 80
    impeachment, 220
    inadmissible, 220
    inventory, 20–21, 129
    preparatory phase of reactive cases,
        41–43
    reactive case development cycle, 9
    review, 183, 188, 193
    sheets, 92
    stored, 235, 283
Exculpatory statements, 103
Execution of Order, 283
Exercises, 251–253
    task sheet, 251

F

Facade building, 11
FARC. *see* Revolutionary Armed Forces of
        Colombia (FARC)
FDLE. *see* Florida Department of Law
        Enforcement (FDLE)
Federal electronic surveillance statute, 282
Field folders, 17
File
    addresses, 232
    categories, 229
    CDD point, 235
    contains, 229–234
    dispatcher desk, 234
    locations, 232
    property, 232
    public records laws, 230

report page, 230
Financial fraud, 157
First-line supervisor, 4, 5. *see also*
        Supervisors (supervisory)
    intelligence phase of proactive cases,
        171, 173–174
FISA. *see* Foreign Intelligence Security Act
        (FISA)
Fixed form control procedure, 22
Flag systems, 18, 110, 160
    case manager controlled, 58
    features, 235
    function, 114
    index, 97, 131, 185, 198, 213, 235–240
    intelligence phase of proactive phase,
        174–175
    manual *vs.* automated, 115
    saves every inquiry and source, 236
Florida, 3, 19, 22, 31, 41, 156, 249–250
    public record laws, 242
    sheriff's office, 40
    state controlled multi-agency major case
        investigation, 191
    Supreme Court, 280, 282
Florida Department of Law Enforcement
        (FDLE), 108–110, 244
Flushing tool, 128
Follow-up searches, 90
Follow-up think tank, 295–296
Foreign Intelligence Security Act (FISA),
        52, 227
*Forensic Accounting and Fraud
        Investigations* (Silverstone), 157
Formatted index, 235
Freedom of information laws, 49
Frisk and grab, 66
Fusion Centers, 52, 212, 237
    intelligence phase of proactive cases, 166
*Fusion Centers: Issues and Options for
        Congress,* 52, 217

G

General post orders, 259–262
Geographical area
    intelligence phase of proactive cases, 165
    investigative phase of proactive cases,
        180, 185, 187
Geographical separation
    intelligence phase of proactive cases, 169
    investigative phase of proactive cases,
        185

H

Harvard University Homicide Seminar, 40
Helter Skelter: The True Story of the Manson Murders (Bugliosi), 55, 131
Henry Williams Homicide Seminar, 40
Human resource, 12, 27, 135
  case reporting, 13, 14, 136

I

IACP patrol operations, 62
Impeachment evidence, 220
Inadmissible evidence, 220
Inadvertent meddling *vs.* intended interference, 70
In-case index, 229
Index or department index, 18, 211–236, 238, 273
  administrators, 213
  budget controllers, 213
  case index for proactive cases, 228–235
  citizens, 224
  civil libertarians, 213
  closing procedures, 235
  department(s), 18, 238
  electronic measures, 227
  evidence, 217
  flags, 213, 214, 235–240
  information flow, 239
  intelligence operations, 226
  investigations, 225
  legislative staff, 213
  location and control, 223, 228
  officer observations and probes, 224
  other agencies, 226–227
  police, 213
  police information sources, 224–227
  politicians, 213
  proactive cases, 203, 211–240
  public records law issues, 218–223
  random data, 225
  search, 220
Index system, 186, 217, 223, 261
  features, 235
  intelligence phase of proactive cases, 168
  saves every inquiry and source, 236
Indict phase. *see also* Arrest, trial and appeal phase
  proactive cases, 8
Individual chip, 21
Individual crime scene collector, 21

Informant control, 148–149
Information
  analysis, 122, 227
  call in on so-called hot leads, 94
  collection, 214, 227
  dissemination guidelines, 49
  flag, 18
  flow, 239
  forward, 18
  handling, 18, 49
  indexed within department's files, 234, 239
  integration, 53
  laws, 49
  major-case calls are logged, 72
  positive *vs.* negative, 152151
  raw, 18
  received from out of state or federal agency, 222
  release guidelines, 50, 128
  report, 22, 93
  retention, 227
  stored, 18
  system capability, 18
  on wanted persons, 265
  written policy on releases, 50
Inspection
  continuous, 210
  equipment, 34
  institute, 210
  internal systems, 18
  process, 19
  resource management of proactive cases, 210
Intelligence
  case, 171
  officer, 145
  purpose of reviews, 201–203
  responsibility, 174
  section responsibility, 175
  system uniformity, 16
Intelligence lead
  handling, 18
  resource management of proactive case tracking, 208
Intelligence phase of proactive cases, 8, 165–176
  critique, 201–204
  department command, 165
  department intelligence section flag system, 174–176
  detective command review, 166–170

first-line supervisors, 173
intelligence responsibility, 174
investigator/analysts/surveillance,
        171–172
prosecutor, 174
responsibility, 175
Intelligence policy
    adjunct, 153
    description, 152–153
Intelligence workup
    intelligence phase of proactive cases,
        171, 172
    time involved, 172
Interagency matters, 19
Intercept, 279
Internal jurisdictional, 19
Internal leak, 196
Internal preparation, 20
Internal systems inspection, 18
Interviews
    resource management of proactive case
        two-person teams, 208
    teams, 103
    witness, 95
Investigation(s)
    activities systematically reported, 95
    background matters, 95
    case expenditures, 158
    case file index, 231
    exercises, 249–254
    index, 225
    long-term high-crime investigations, 151
    murder
        tracking system, 17
    priorities, 12–13
    reports, 112, 154
    resources, 97
    uncontrolled multi-team, 123
Investigative phase of proactive cases, 8–10,
        144, 177–192
    department command, 177
    detective command-monitor progress,
        177–180
    investigators/analysts, 186–187
    prosecutor, 188–192
    supervisor/coordinator, 181–185
Investigative phase of reactive cases, 7,
        85–124, 144
    coordinator, 98–115
    crime laboratory, 119
    crime scene unit, 115–118
    department command, 86

detective command, 96–97
detective supervisor, 98
dispatcher, 86
investigators, 89–95
medical examiner, 119
PIO, 121
prosecutor, 120
scene team, 89–95
support services, 121–124
uniform patrols, 87–88
Investigative unit commanders
    case expenditures, 158
    intelligence phase of proactive cases, 166
Investigators
    arrest, trial and appeal phase of
        proactive cases, 197
    arrest, trial and appeal phase of reactive
        cases, 128–129
    and case supervisor, 183
    claim and process all evidence, 117
    duties performed, 91
    first assignment, 39
    identified, 5
    intelligence phase of proactive cases,
        171–172
    investigative phase of proactive cases,
        183, 186–187
    investigative phase of reactive cases,
        89–95
    preparatory phase of proactive cases, 158
    preparatory phase of reactive cases,
        38–40
    recording information, 186
    response phase of reactive cases, 65

J

Judge
    communication intercept rule, 52
    competent jurisdiction defined, 279, 280
    develop working relationships, 44
    issuing, 283, 284
    order issued, 282
Jurisdiction
    defined, 279
    guidelines established, 19
    multiple police, 251–253
    policies and procedures, 19
    public records law study, 223

K

Kennedy, John F., 55, 56
Kennedy assassination, 55, 56, 59, 61
   autopsy, 120
   investigation phase of reactive case,
      105–106, 121
   PIO, 121

L

LaBianca murder investigation, 55
   arrest, trial and appeal phase of reactive
      cases, 131
   example of coordination/supervision
      failure, 101
   investigation phase of reactive case,
      107–108, 113
Laboratory (support)
   arrest, trial and appeal phase of reactive
      cases, 130
   crime scene phase of reactive cases, 78
   findings and ME, 46
   identified, 5
   investigative phase of reactive cases, 119
   preparatory phase of reactive cases,
      43–44
   requirements, 22
LAPD. see Los Angeles Police Department
      (LAPD)
LASO. see Los Angeles County Sheriff's
      officers (LASO)
Law enforcement agencies agreements, 30
Lead case investigator (agent), 99. see also
      Supervisors (supervisory)
   case reporting, 100
   establishes crime scene boundaries, 101
Lead chart, 278
Leaders error, 11
Lead interview teams, 105
Lead sheet, 276–277
Light-duty list, 159
Line/support defined, 5
Listening device, 122
   failure, 283
Long-term high-crime investigations, 151
Los Angeles County Sheriff's officers
      (LASO), 107–108, 113
Los Angeles Police Department (LAPD), 18,
      55–56, 103
   arrest, trial and appeal phase of reactive
      cases, 128, 131

coordination failure examples, 99–101
investigation phase of reactive cases,
      107–108, 112–113, 114–115
POI, 82
response phase of reactive cases, 57
supervision failure example, 101
uniform patrols, 73

M

Main department index. see Index or
      department index
Major case investigation
   control both reactive and proactive, 210
   critical tasks of reactive cases, 137
   defined, 3
   first twenty-four hours of reactive cases,
      137
   first twenty four to forty eight hours of
      reactive cases, 139
   implement procedures, 33
   inclusions, 3
   intricacies of proactive cases, 177
   investigation phase of reactive cases, 91
   management by objective approach for
      proactive cases, 151
   management system, 237
   management tracking system, 16
   noncritical tasks of reactive cases, 137
   preparatory rules, 107
   prepare investigation, 33
   rapid changes of case priorities, 90
   reporting, 257
   response, 60
   responsibility for supervision, 33
   team effort, 186
   types, 4
Management by objectives (MBO), 11
Management systems, 13–19
Manpower allocation systems, 13–19
Manpower case-reporting systems, 136
Manson murders, 18, 55–56
   arrest, trial and appeal phase of reactive
      cases, 128, 129, 131
   example of coordination failures, 99–100
   investigation phase of reactive cases,
      107–108, 112–113
   POI, 82
   response phase of reactive cases, 57
Manual index file system, 215
   location and control, 223
Marine Corps management taught, 241

Master file, 17, 129, 213, 214, 219, 231. *see also* Index or department index
Master index. *see also* Index or department index
department(s), 211, 212
MBO. *see* Management by objectives (MBO)
ME. *see* Medical examiner (ME)
Meals, 259–260
Mechanical device defined, 279
Media, 37
    communications personnel silence, 73
    guidelines, 263–266
    handling, 48
    information given, 45
    informed of, 264
    notification procedures, 50
    point of contact, 50
    reputation, 242
    speculation and rumor examples, 82
    statements from commanders, 69
Medical examiner (ME), 34
    agreement with police, 45–47
    crime scene phase of reactive cases, 79
    identified, 5
    investigative phase of reactive cases, 119
    laboratory findings, 46
    notice to victim's relatives, 46
    preliminary findings, 46
    preparatory phase of reactive cases, 45–46
    property control, 46
    responsibilities, 47
    role during CSP, 79
    timely reports, 46
Missing child, 108–110
Missing property, 106
Money laundering, 156–157
Monroe County Sheriff's Department, Rochester, New York, 146
Motives, 149
    confirmed, 6
    nefarious, 48
Multiple police jurisdictions, 251–253
Multitasking, 168
Murder investigation, 114. *see also* Investigation(s); specific name of case
    tracking system, 17
    triple, 50

N

National Crime Information Center (NCIC), 16
Nationwide uniformity or intercapability, 16
Navy pathologists autopsy, 120
NCIC. *see* National Crime Information Center (NCIC)
Neighborhood interviews, 34, 89
    development cycle of reactive cases, 9
    investigation phase of reactive cases, 104, 105
    teams duties, 269–270
Neighborhood search, 7, 30, 89, 94, 231
News. *see* Media
New York State Police (NYSP), 300–301
Nondiscovery states, 220
NYSP. *see* New York State Police (NYSP)

O

Offense defined, 279
Officer in charge of shift responsibility, 30
Officers, 259–260
Official file, 17, 129, 213, 214, 219, 231. *see also* Index or department index
Off-net communications, 72
Omnibus Crime Control Act, 282
Oral communication defined, 279
Oral reports, 102
Order book, 259
Order defined, 279
Organizational groups defined, 4
Oswald, Lee Harvey, 56, 59, 61, 105–106
Other agencies
    assistance agreements, 32
    crime broadcast procedures, 31
    guidelines during crime scene phase of reactive cases, 74
    identified, 5
    index, 226–227
    police information sources, 226–227
    preparatory phase of proactive cases, 160–161
    preparatory phase of reactive cases, 30–32
    roadblock plans, 31
    working and coordination conditions, 34

P

Paper method desk management, 91
Parkland Hospital in Dallas autopsy, 120
Parole departments
    intelligence phase of proactive cases, 169
    rules, 176
Partner up, 209
Pathologist, 5, 40
    communication with ME, 79
    forensic, 45
    procedure during investigation phase of
        reactive cases, 113, 117–118, 120
Patriot Act, 52, 217
Patrol
    car equipment, 30
    post index terms, 211
    post report/field interview report,
        287–288
    post vehicle check sheet, 288
    response plans, 59–60
    responsibilities, 29
People wasters, 207–209
Performance evaluation, 136
Personal chips, 21
Personnel work assignments, 209
PIO. see Public information officer (PIO)
    (support)
Plea ruling, 219
Plots confirmed, 6
Police
    agreement with medical examiner,
        45–47
    case files records retention, 216
    critique, 48
    effectiveness and positive results, 19
    initiated investigations, 145
    jurisdictions, 251–253
    notifying relatives, 79
    organization management taught, 241
    power and authority, 243
    records, 223
    requests for public records, 221
    responsibility, 46
    and sheriff agencies plans, 297–301
    to-prosecutor final case report, 193
    units not assigned to crime scene, 60
Police information sources, 224–227
    citizens, 224
    electronic measures, 227
    index, 224–227
    intelligence operations, 226

    investigations, 225
    officer observations and probes, 224
    other agencies, 226–227
Politics as tool, 243–244
Polygraphs and equipment, 23
Post order book
    consists of, 260–261
    location, 262
Preparatory phase of proactive cases, 8,
        143–164
    analysts, 159
    department command, 144–153
    detective command, 154–157
    other agencies, 160–161
    PIO, 162
    prosecutor teams, 162
    supervisors/investigators, 158
Preparatory phase of reactive cases, 7, 11–54
    crime scene unit, 41–42
    detective command, 33–37
    dispatcher, 24–26
    functional unit duties, 24–54
    investigators, 38–40
    laboratory, 43–44
    medical examiner's office (ME), 45–46
    organization responsibilities, 11–23
    other agencies, 30–32
    press officer (public information officer),
        48–50
    prosecutor's office, 47
    uniform patrols, 27–29
Press. see also Media
    communications personnel silence, 73
    guidelines, 263–266
    speculation and rumor examples, 82
    statements from commanders, 69
Press officer. see Public information officer
    (PIO) (support)
Privacy, 82, 87
    invasions, 213, 221
    rights, 48, 217, 218, 223, 271
Proactive case investigations, 8, 143–240
    arrest and trial, 193–200
    arrest/indict phase, 8
    critique, 201–204
    defined, 4
    definition, 141
    development cycle, 163
    examples, 143
    exercises, 249–250
    index, 211–240
    intelligence, 201–204

intelligence phase, 8, 165–176
interagency agreements, 161–162
investigation, 177–192
investigation phases, 144
investigative phase, 8
major-case work, 160
management and control methods, 4
personnel commitments, 150
preparatory phase, 8, 143–164
reporting structure, 170
requiring research and analytical skills, 160
resource management, 205–210
second intelligence phase, 8
tracking system inclusion, 16
trial/appeal phase, 8
wind-up chatter, 241–248
Probation departments, 169
Prosecutor
    agreements, 34
    agreements with police departments, 47
    arrest, trial and appeal phase of proactive cases, 198–200
    arrest, trial and appeal phase of reactive cases, 126
    coordinate witness schedule, 132
    crime scene phase of reactive cases, 80
    crime scene technicians discussion, 81
    detective supervisor discussion, 81
    example of coordination failures, 99–100
    identified, 5
    informing of impeachment evidence, 220
    investigative phase of proactive cases, 188–192
    investigative phase of reactive cases, 120
    long-term high-crime investigations, 151
    preparatory phase of proactive cases, 162
    preparatory phase of reactive cases, 47
    prepare for court, 198–200
    teams, 162
Public information officer (PIO) (support)
    arrest, trial and appeal phase of proactive case, 196
    arrest, trial and appeal phase of reactive cases, 127, 130
    crime scene duties, 81
    crime scene phase of reactive cases, 81–84
    handles all information releases to media, 65
    identified, 5

investigative phase of reactive cases, 121
    only information that may be released, 51
    preparatory phase of proactive cases, 162
    preparatory phase of reactive cases, 48–50
    response phase of reactive cases, 65–68
Public records, 26–27, 49
    index, 218–223
    jurisdictions, 223
    laws, 218–223, 242
    laws file, 230
    laws study, 223
    police requests, 221
    rules, 217

Q

Query flags, 214

R

Racists in police departments, 67
Raid personnel, 196
Random data, 225
Raw information, 18
Reactive case investigations, 3–142, 7–8
    arrest, trial and appeal, 125–132
    arrest phase, 8
    crime scene, 69–84
    crime scene phase, 7
    definitions, 3–6
    development cycle, 9
    investigative phase, 7–10, 85–124, 144
    management and control methods, 4
    preparatory phase, 7, 11–54
    resource management, 135–142
    response, 55–68
    response phase, 7
    tracking system, 17
    trial/appeal phase, 8
Recording
    device failure, 283
    interception, 283
Records retention, 216
Report structure
    arrest, trial and appeal phase of proactive case, 194
    reactive cases, 68
Resource
    Battle of the Bulge, 138–139
    controls, 205–206

expenditures reporting, 14
historic methods of effective and
efficient use, 138
management, 138–139
resource management of proactive cases,
205–206
used, 4
Resource management of proactive cases,
205–210
people wasters, 207–209
pick-off method of arresting, 206–207
resource control, 205–206
Resource management of reactive cases,
135–142
department command, 135–136
principal entities, 137–142
Response phase of reactive cases, 7, 55–68
detective command and supervisor,
63–64
dispatcher, 56–57
IACP patrol operations, 62
investigators, 65
PIO, 65–68
uniform patrols, 58–62
units duties, 55–68
Retention
information, 227
period, 215
records, 216
Revolutionary Armed Forces of Colombia
(FARC), 52

S

Searches
area, 60–61, 90
e-mail, 227
follow-up, 90
index or department index, 220
legal aspects, 149
neighborhood, 7, 30, 89, 94, 231
teams duties, 269–270
Second intelligence phase of proactive
cases, 8
Seizure, 81, 121, 145, 165
legal aspects, 149, 189
procedures, 49
Sheriffs, 4, 5 108–110, 236
agencies plans, 297–301
elected, 246, 300
forms, 18
major case response, 63

Shift supervisors, 25, 27, 28
response phase, 7
responsibility, 29, 261
Show and tell programs, 11
Silverstone, Howard, 157
Smuggling charges, 178–179
Spin-off case, 179
Stacked management task procedure, 227
State controlled multi-agency major case
investigation, 191
Statistical data collection format, 13
Stop and check activities, 66
Street officers, 146, 258
implementing response, 27, 32, 225
investigation phase of reactive cases, 103
Street supervisor, 26, 28, 31
preplan implementation, 59
responsibility, 30, 32
Supervisors (supervisory)
arrest, trial and appeal phase of
proactive cases, 196
arrest, trial and appeal phase of reactive
cases, 128–129
in charge of all resources, 206
control case investigative phase of
proactive case, 182–183
coordinating all leads and investigative
phase of proactive case, 184
defined, 4
duties, 63
establishes crime scene boundaries, 101
flag only, 215
identified, 5
intelligence phase of proactive cases, 173
investigative phase of proactive cases,
181–185
investigative phase of reactive cases, 98,
110–111
preparatory phase of proactive cases, 158
response phase of reactive cases, 63–64
Support agencies, 74
Support groups, 20
Support services. see also Laboratory
(support); Public information
officer (PIO) (support)
identified, 6
investigative phase of reactive cases,
121–124
Surreptitious entry, 282
Surveillance
camera, 122
controlling, 145, 146

defined, 145
electronic measures or devices, 282
intelligence phase of proactive cases,
        171–172
logs, 146
reports and logs, 187
statute, 282
teams resource management of proactive
        cases, 207

T

Tape transcription, 208
Tate murder investigation, 103
    arrest and trial phase of reactive case,
        128, 129
    crime scene phase of reactive case, 73
    example of coordination/supervision
        failure, 101
    investigation phase of reactive case, 99,
        107–108, 110, 112–113, 114–115
    POI, 82
    response phase of reactive case, 55
Technical units, 23
Termination of Interception, 283
Think tank, 22
    meeting, 291
    meeting room, 290
    method for law enforcement
        organizations, 289–294
    setting, 290
    structure, 290–291
    tools, 289–290
Three-year-old missing child, 108–110
Time and activity
    data collection, 14
    reporting instrument, 15
Timing and closing procedures, 235
Tracking system
    case information flow, 24
    murder investigation, 17
    proactive case investigations, 16
    reactive case investigations, 17
    retrieval options, 24
Trash bin cascade, 215
Trial phase. *see also* Arrest, trial and appeal
        phase
    proactive cases, 8
    reactive cases, 8
Trial ruling, 219
Twenty-year plans, 297–302

U

Uncontrolled multi-team investigation, 123
Uniform forces, 188
Uniform patrols (line)
    crime scene phase of reactive cases, 72,
        73
    developmental cycle for reactive cases, 9
    identified, 5
    investigative phase of reactive cases,
        87–88, 94, 95
    operational duties, 29
    plans include, 27–29
    preparatory phase of reactive cases,
        27–29
    reporting structure for reactive cases, 68
    response phase of reactive cases, 58–62
    think tank, 291
    written notes of all assignments and
        instructions, 61
Uniform supervisor, 30. *see also* Supervisors
        (supervisory)
    and index, 211
    response phase actions, 60
    responsible for seeing that all
        information is obtained, 61
    think tank, 291
Unit commanders
    case expenditures, 158
    inspection system, 155
    intelligence phase of reactive cases, 166,
        167
    resource commitments, 179
Unit critical assessment, 23

V

Victim
    background, 95, 110, 137
    identification, 6, 84
    prosecutor communication, 132
    rape, 221
    relatives notification, 46, 106, 126
    transporting, 118
Video walk-through, 21
Vision, 243

W

Wire communication defined, 279
Wire intercepts, 207
Witness

accounts, 102
arrest and trial phase of proactive cases,
        194
development cycle of reactive cases, 9
interviews, 39, 43, 60, 95, 137
preparatory phase of reactive cases, 27

protection, 127
review, 193
scheduling, 269
statements, 89, 129, 154, 217
Work assignments, 209
Working case investigation team, 89